Jewish Messianic Thoughts in an Age of Despair

Belief in the coming of a Messiah poses a genuine dilemma. From a Jewish perspective, the historical record is overwhelmingly against it. If, despite all the tragedies that have befallen the Jewish people, no legitimate Messiah has come forward, has the belief not been shown to be groundless? Yet for all the problems associated with messianism, the historical record also shows that it is an idea with enormous staying power. The prayer book mentions it on page after page. The great Jewish philosophers all wrote about it. Secular thinkers in the twentieth century returned to it and reformulated it. And victims of the Holocaust invoked it in the last few minutes of their life. This book examines the staying power of messianism and formulates it in a way that retains its redemptive force without succumbing to mythology.

Kenneth Seeskin received his BA from Northwestern in 1968 and his PhD from Yale in 1972. He joined the faculty of Northwestern in 1972 and has taught there ever since. He is the author of seven books and numerous articles; editor of *The Cambridge Companion to Maimonides*; and coeditor of *The Cambridge Guide to Jewish History, Culture, and Religion*. In 2001, he won the Koret Jewish Book Award for *Searching for a Distant God*, and in 2011, the National Jewish Book Award for *The Cambridge Guide to Jewish History, Culture, and Religion*. In 2009, Seeskin was named Philip M. and Ethel Klutznick Professor of Jewish Civilization.

Jewish Messianic Thoughts in an Age of Despair

KENNETH SEESKIN
Northwestern University

CAMBRIDGE
UNIVERSITY PRESS

CAMBRIDGE UNIVERSITY PRESS
Cambridge, New York, Melbourne, Madrid, Cape Town,
Singapore, São Paulo, Delhi, Tokyo, Mexico City

Cambridge University Press
32 Avenue of the Americas, New York, NY 10013-2473, USA

www.cambridge.org
Information on this title: www.cambridge.org/9781107017924

First published 2012

Printed in the United States of America

A catalog record for this publication is available from the British Library.

Library of Congress Cataloging in Publication data
Seeskin, Kenneth, 1947–
    Jewish messianic thoughts in an age of despair / Kenneth Seeskin.
        p.   cm.
    Includes bibliographical references and index.
    ISBN 978-1-107-01792-4
    1. Messiah – Judaism.   2. Redemption – Judaism.   3. Despair –
Religious aspects – Judaism.   I. Title.
    BM615.S395   2012
    296.3'36–dc23   2011030485

ISBN 978-1-107-01792-4 Hardback

To the memory of Gail Paula Seeskin

Contents

Abbreviations

For full information, see Bibliography.

C1	Kant, *Critique of Pure Reason*
C2	Kant, *Critique of Practical Reason*
C3	Kant, *Critique of the Power of Judgment*
CH	Walter Benjamin, "On the Concept of History"
DF	Emmanuel Levinas, *Difficult Freedom*
EM	Hermann Cohen, *Ethics of Maimonides*
G	Kant, *Groundwork of the Metaphysics of Morals*
GP	Maimonides, *Guide of the Perplexed*
MIJ	Gershom Scholem, *The Messianic Idea in Judaism*
MT	Maimonides, *Mishneh Torah*
MW	Emil Fackenheim, *To Mend the World*
PI	Steven S. Schwarzschild, *The Pursuit of the Ideal,*
PP	Kant, *Perpetual Peace and Other Essays*
PR	Hegel, *The Philosophy of Right*
R	Kant, *Religion within the Boundaries of Mere Reason*
RH	Hegel, *Reason in History*
RR	Hermann Cohen, *Religion of Reason out of the Sources of Judaism*
SR	Franz Rosenzweig, *The Star of Redemption*

Introduction

There is one part of this work that should not require elaborate defense: that we live in an age of despair. The planet is getting more crowded, and for many of its inhabitants, violence, hunger, inadequate medical care, and race hatred are commonplace. In the twentieth century, nuclear and environmental disaster became real possibilities. The threat of terrorism is now a fact of life for just about everyone and is likely to remain so for the foreseeable future. With few exceptions, the richest economies in the world still suffer from boom-and-bust cycles and confront chronic unemployment. In many, income distribution is heavily skewed toward the rich, and public debt has reached dangerous levels.

According to the most recent census, 14.3 percent of the U.S. population, or 43.6 million people, live in poverty. There are as many guns as people – perhaps more. For too many people in the inner cities, life resembles Thomas Hobbes' description of a state of nature: nasty, brutish, and short. As of this writing, no consensus has emerged on how to address these problems, which means they will probably not be addressed at all. One reason for this sorry state of affairs is that public debate has become ugly and acrimonious. Increasingly the question is not "Where are the people who can lead us out of this mess?" but rather "Are we willing to be led at all?" In its 2009 year-end issue, the *Economist* magazine wrote, "The forests are disappearing; the ice is melting; social bonds are crumbling; privacy is eroding; life is becoming a dismal slog in an ugly world."

This is not a book about how to grow more food, save the environment, pay off debt, or get the Mideast peace process back on track. I will leave such things to others not only because I lack the expertise to tackle them, but also because they are not issues to which religion has anything specific to say. Rather, this is a book about a question to which religion does have something to say: whether one is justified in looking at the evils of the present situation and being hopeful about the future. Judaism, Christianity, and Islam hold out the promise of a better future. Can a rational person accept them, or does acceptance amount to nothing but wishful thinking? I will argue for the former, making every effort to avoid the latter.

There are a number of people whose written work, critical comments, and ongoing dialogue continue to be a source of inspiration. They include Michael Morgan, Adriano Fabris, Menachem Kellner, Regina Schwartz, Lenn Goodman, David Novak, Haim Kreisel, David Shatz, James Diamond, Alan Mittleman, Gary Saul Morson, Stefano Perfetti, and Leora Batnitzky. I also would like to thank the Tikvah Project on Jewish Thought at Princeton University for organizing a highly effective working group on messianism. Its members included Michael Morgan, Steven M. Wasserstrom, Shai Held, Benjamin Pollock, Annette Y. Reed, Steve Weitzman, and Elisheva Carlebach.

I

Messianism and Mythology

The standard account of Judaism holds that its chief contribution to world culture is monotheism: the belief that everything owes its existence to a single, all-powerful deity. The truth is, however, that it is responsible for another idea that is equally profound: the belief that the future will be an improvement on the past or present. According to Maimonides, whereas the truth of monotheism can be demonstrated by reason alone, the direction of the future cannot. One can be a monotheist and also believe that human history is static, circular, or even degenerative. Despite the difference in the epistemic status of monotheism and belief in a better future, Maimonides (*MT* 14, Kings and Wars, 11.1) leaves no doubt about the importance of the latter[1]:

King Messiah will arise and restore the kingdom of David to its former state and original sovereignty.... He who does not believe in a restoration or does

---

[1] On what basis does Maimonides say that belief in the coming of the Messiah is part of the teaching of Moses? His argument is based on several passages. Among them, Deuteronomy 30:3 ("gathering you again from all the peoples among whom the Lord your God has scattered you") assumes that the people are already in exile and claims that their fortunes will be restored and they will be brought back together if they follow the commandments. Numbers 24:17, the oracle of Balaam ("I see him, but not now"), is taken as a reference to David, and the next line ("I behold him, but not near") is taken as a reference to the Messiah. Finally, Deuteronomy 19:8–9 says that if (or when) God enlarges Israel's territory, as he swore to do, Israel must add three additional cities of refuge. Because this commandment was never fulfilled, and God commands nothing in vain, Maimonides concludes it will be fulfilled in the days of the

not wait the coming of the Messiah denies not only the teachings of the prophets but also those of the Law of Moses our Teacher.

These words were written in a time of exile and oppression. They offer hope that the current state of things is not ultimate and that someday not only Israel, but also, according to Maimonides, the rest of humanity will be redeemed. It is in this sense that Pierre Bouretz is able to characterize Jewish thinkers as "witnesses for the future" in the darkest hours of history.[2]

Traditional Jews will recognize that a prayer for the coming of the Messiah is part of the *Amidah*, "The Eighteen Benedictions," recited three times a day. It also constitutes the twelfth of Maimonides' Thirteen Principles, whose acceptance, in his opinion, is necessary for salvation. In a history often dominated by death and destruction, praying for the Messiah is more than an empty ritual. As Steven Schwarzschild notes, Jews in the ghettos, in concentration and extermination camps, in Warsaw, and among partisans and Holocaust survivors made Maimonides' twelfth principle their universal anthem.[3] To be sure, the Messiah did not come, a fact they surely must have foreseen. It is important, however, that their belief that he *will* come at some point allowed them to face their plight with a measure of dignity. The human condition is not tragic; the forces of evil will not win out. Eventually suffering will end, and mankind will fulfill its destiny.

Unfortunately, belief in the coming of a Messiah is deeply problematic. From a Jewish perspective, the historical record offers overwhelming evidence against it. If despite all the tragedies that have befallen the Jewish people over the course of their history, no legitimate Messiah has stepped forward, has this belief not been shown to be groundless? Worse, the messianic zeal created by illegitimate messiahs raises false hopes and often leads to destruction and death. Yet for all the problems associated with messianism, the historical record also shows that it is an idea with enormous staying power. The prayer book mentions it on page after page. The great Jewish philosophers of the medieval

---

Messiah. Needless to say, these arguments are not intended for skeptics and would be questioned by modern scholarship.

[2] Pierre Bouretz, *Witnesses for the Future*, 11. I regret that this massive work came into my hand too late for extensive comment.

[3] *PI*, 211.

and modern periods all wrote about it. Secular thinkers in the twentieth century returned to it and reformulated it. As we have just seen, victims of the Holocaust invoked it in the last few minutes of their lives. The purpose of this book is to examine the staying power of this idea and formulate it in such a way that we retain its redemptive force without succumbing to mythology.

THE IDEA OF THE FUTURE

Even the most casual reader cannot fail to notice that the Hebrew Bible is future oriented. Without any sort of prelude or introduction, it opens with the words "In the beginning," which, on any reasonable interpretation, implies that it is legitimate to ask about the middle and end. The linear structure of the narrative is confirmed by the fact that many of the stories that follow involve journeys: Abraham's travel to a new land and to a mountain where he is supposed to sacrifice his son, Jacob's efforts to flee danger and find peace, Joseph's journey to Egypt, and the Exodus from Egypt and journey through the wilderness. Yet unlike the *Odyssey*, which also recounts a journey, these stories generally involve people going to places they have never seen before.[4]

In addition to the theme of futurity, there is also the theme of novelty. For the most part, the events narrated in the Torah are not variations on a familiar theme but turning points that change forever the way we view human behavior: the fall from Eden, the Flood, the call of Abraham, the Exodus from Egypt, and the giving of the Torah at Sinai. It is with this background in mind that we can appreciate Isaiah 43:18–19: "Do not remember the former things, or consider the things of old. I am about to do something new." In fact, the biblical view of history has become so much a part of our way of thinking that we need to step back to appreciate how things could be otherwise.

For the ancient Greeks, the world is eternal, and the order we perceive is rooted in the essential nature of things. The job of the philosopher is not to ask how the world came to be but what that nature is.[5] This approach is apparent not only in the philosophic tradition, in which

---

[4] For the comparison with Homer's *Odyssey*, I am indebted to Michael Walzer, *Exodus and Revolution*, 10–17; cf. Erich Auerbach, "Odysseus' Scar," in *Mimesis*, 13.
[5] It has been argued that Plato's *Timaeus* is an exception, but see my *Maimonides on the Origin of the World*, chap. 2, for an argument that it is not.

change (becoming) is regarded as a defect or falling away from per-
manence (being), but in the writing of history as well. In the introduction to his *History of the Peloponnesian War*, Thucydides claims,[6]

The absence of the fabulous may make my work dull. But I shall be satisfied if
it be thought useful by those who wish to know the exact character of events
now past which, human nature being what it is, will recur in similar or analogous forms. It has not been composed to win temporary applause but as a
lasting possession.

Nothing in Thucydides' account of the war rules out the possibility
that over the course of history, empires will rise and fall and the political map of the world will change. On the contrary, he is convinced
such upheavals are inevitable. His point is that, however devastating,
they will not alter human nature, so that the categories we now use to
explain it will apply equally well in other contexts. Conspicuous by its
absence in this account is any promise of a final redemption.

Thucydides' view contrasts sharply with that of the Hebrew prophets, whose overriding conviction is that despite the depths to which
human behavior has fallen, the universe we inhabit is not chaotic, and
the day is coming when justice will prevail. Whether we think of this
as a future time (the Day of the Lord) or the ascendancy of a particular person (the days of the Messiah) is insignificant. The point is
that if things can – and eventually will – get better, the way they are
now is not the way they have to be. Although mankind now lives
in deplorable conditions, and the histories of individual people may
have terrible endings, no cosmic principle guarantees that the strong
will always prevail, that the weak will always suffer, or that disaster
is inevitable.

If this were a self-help book, I would launch into a discussion of
the therapeutic effects of hope – how people with serious illnesses or
disabilities improved the quality of their lives by believing that their
situations would improve. But it is not a self-help book, and I want
to avoid such claims. My contention is that belief in the idea of the
future is not just a way of coping with misfortune. More important, it
is a presupposition of moral behavior. According to Kant, "The hope
for better times, without which an earnest desire to do something that

---

[6] Thucydides, *The Peloponnesian War*, 1.22.

benefits the general good would never have warmed the human heart, has always influenced the work of the well-intentioned."[7] Simply put, there would be no reason to work for the common good unless we believe that our efforts have some chance to succeed. This is another way of saying that our behavior will be better if we are convinced that the human condition is not inherently tragic – that the demands of morality do not impose a Sisyphean labor in which failure is the only outcome. Acceptance of this view changes significantly the way we view human behavior.

It is not enough to say that there are eternal standards of right and wrong – or even that if we live rightly, we will be better off. Beyond the question of right and wrong is the need to confront the future with optimism – to believe not only that one's own circumstances will improve, but also that suffering and oppression of any kind will be eliminated. It is in this sense that Hermann Cohen (*RR*, 261) could say that the concept of history is the creation of the prophet idea. Rather than measuring history by looking back to a Golden Age from which humanity has fallen away, the prophets measured it by looking to a future to which humanity must aspire. We can therefore agree with Karl Löwith that for the prophets history is not just a collection of facts but a story of fulfillment and salvation.[8]

THE FORMATIVE HISTORY OF JUDAISM

To understand how the prophets developed their understanding of history, it helps to view them as commentators on a narrative whose formative event is the Exodus from Egypt. The narrative begins with a band of slaves living in a strange land where they are oppressed by a cruel dictator. Their cry for help is answered when a charismatic leader comes before the dictator demanding that the people be set free. After a series of deadly confrontations, the slaves are told they are free to go. But the dictator changes his mind and sends his army to destroy them. Trapped between the advancing army and a large body of water, the people witness a miracle: The water parts, allowing them to walk

---

[7] Kant, "Theory and Practice," in *PP*, 309 (86). Cf. Reinhold Niebuhr, *Moral Man and Immoral Society*, 81: "Without the ultrarational hopes and passions of religion no society will ever have the courage to conquer despair and attempt the impossible."

[8] Karl Löwith, *Meaning in History*, 1.

to safety. After traveling through the wilderness for some time, the former slaves reach the homeland, where they can fulfill their destiny as a kingdom of priests and a holy nation.

It takes no great insight to see that the Exodus is the quintessential story of hope and redemption. As Michael Walzer remarks, our whole political consciousness is built up around it.[9] That consciousness involves everything from the fate of underdogs, to the arrogance of power, to the eventual triumph of good over evil. In addition to Passover, it is celebrated every week on the Sabbath and referred to prominently in the first commandment: "I am the Lord your God, who brought you out of the land of Egypt, out of the house of bondage."

As is often the case with biblical narratives, there is more to the story than first meets the eye. In this case, hope and redemption turn out to be complicated. According to Exodus 14: 30–1, "The Lord saved Israel that day from the hand of the Egyptians; and Israel saw the Egyptians dead upon the seashore. And Israel saw the great work which the Lord did against the Egyptians, and the people feared the Lord, and they believed in the Lord and in his servant Moses." Unfortunately, the people's mood of reverence does not last very long. Within a dozen lines of the "Song of the Sea," they become thirsty and begin to murmur against Moses. The foundation for their lack of faith is laid as early as Exodus 6:9, when Moses promises that God will liberate them and lead them to a new land: "Moses spoke thus to the people of Israel; but they did not listen to Moses, because of their broken spirit and cruel bondage." The usual explanation for this is that slavery involves more than economic oppression; over time, it crushes a person's spirit and causes one to abandon hope.

Frightened and accustomed to following orders, the slave is often reluctant to seek a better life.[10] That is why the people cannot be taken to the Promised Land right away. If redemption is to be more than a deus ex machina, the people must first discard the slave mentality and accept the responsibilities of freedom, which is another way of saying that redemption must be earned if it is to be significant. So the story prepares us for the fact that the transition from slavery to freedom will not be easy. As any reader can see, the fledgling nation is about to

[9] Michael Walzer, *Exodus and Revolution*, 7.
[10] For further discussion, see *Exodus and Revolution*, 45–9.

embark on a series of disasters. The question is this: Will they succeed in transforming themselves or continue to think like slaves?

At Exodus 15:24, we learn that "the people" murmured against Moses, leaving open the possibility that only some of them lost faith.[11] Yet at 16:2, the mood of despair widens: "The whole congregation of the people of Israel murmured against Moses and Aaron." The reason for their discontent is lack of food and water. They conclude that it would have been better to remain in Egypt ("when we sat by the flesh pots and ate bread to the full") than to die in the desert. The reference to flesh pots is important because it serves as a symbol of the slave mentality: Better to live under oppression with a full stomach than to go hungry as free men and women.

Did the people have full stomachs under Pharaoh's rule, or have the hardships of the desert made them long for "happy days" that never really existed? Whereas the early chapters of Exodus paint a picture of cruelty and oppression, by Numbers 11:4–6, the people refer to Egypt as the seat of luxury and comfort: "We remember the fish we ate in Egypt for nothing, the cucumbers, the melons, the leeks, the onions, and the garlic." The most reasonable explanation for this is that the people's memory has begun to play tricks on them. Yet whatever explanation one prefers, the fact remains that the people show little interest in the spiritual task before them and seem more concerned with the practical question of when they are going to get their next meal.

Their lack of attention to spiritual matters reaches a climax at Exodus 32, when Moses is delayed on the mountain, and they ask Aaron to make gods (*elohim*) for them. Aaron responds by collecting gold jewelry and fashioning a statue of a calf. When the people proclaim the statue divine, Aaron builds an altar around it and announces that there will be a festival to the Lord the following day. At the

---

[11] According to Exodus 12:38, a "mixed multitude" suggesting slaves, political prisoners, thieves, and anyone else who might benefit from social chaos accompanied the Israelites on the Exodus. Some Rabbinic commentators try to put the blame for the people's lack of faith on this group. Thus Rashi suggests that the mixed multitude were responsible for the golden calf. The crux of his argument is that when the statue is presented to the people at Exodus 32:4, the text does not say, "These are our gods, O Israel," but rather, "These are your gods, O Israel." Exodus 32:26 implies that not every Israelite took part in this episode. On the other hand, when the mixed multitude are at fault, as at Numbers 11:4, the text says so quite clearly.

festival, the people are told, "These are your gods [*elohim*], O Israel, who brought you up out of the Land of Egypt."

Although the golden calf is often viewed as a paradigm of Israel's lack of faith, the text is ambiguous because *elohim* has a wide variety of meanings. In some passages (Genesis 1:1), it refers to the true God, in which case it takes a singular verb. However, it can also refer to false gods (Exodus 20:3), angels and heavenly creatures (Exodus 18:11), or anyone who exercises legal or moral authority (Exodus 4:16; 21:6). So when the Israelites ask Aaron to make them *elohim*, it is unclear whether they are rejecting God, introducing an unauthorized way of worshiping God, or expressing the need for an intermediary between God and the people.

Bull worship was widespread in the Near East, and according to a tradition that derives from the book of Joshua (24:14), the Israelites practiced idolatry during the Egyptian captivity. There are, then, good grounds for viewing the golden calf as a case of backsliding. One Midrash suggests, contrary to the biblical text, that the golden calf episode was responsible for the people's having to wander in the desert for forty years.[12] Beginning with the Book of Acts (7), early Christians argued that the golden calf constituted a violation of Israel's covenant with God, making it necessary for God to establish a new covenant. On the other hand, Rabbinic commentators like Rashi and Nachmanides point out that with Moses gone, the people thought they needed something infused with the spirit of God to continue to lead the way.[13] All we can say for sure is that the people's sin is great enough to make God want to destroy them. Only a desperate appeal for mercy on the part of Moses saves the day.

By the end of the Book of Exodus, the people are disappointed because the milk and honey they were promised have not materialized, and God is disappointed because the people have put more emphasis on food than on salvation. Still, the Book of Exodus does not end on an air of desperation. By chapter 39, we learn that work on the

---

[12] *Midrash Genesis Rabbah*, 30.7.

[13] For English translations, see *Chumash with Rashi's Commentary: Exodus*, 179–81, and Nachmanides, *Commentary on the Torah (Exodus)*, 549–57. For an excellent study of how the golden calf was viewed by later traditions, see L. Smoler and M. Aberbach, "The Golden Calf Episode in Postbiblical Literature," *Hebrew Union College Annual* 39 (1968): 91–116.

Tabernacle is finished, which means that the people now have a con-crete manifestation of God's presence (Exodus 25:8). With the golden calf out of the way and the instigators put to death, there is every rea-son to think the people will direct their attention to the true God and put up with the austerity of the desert until the end of the journey.

The troubles start over again at Numbers 11:4, when the people leave the Sinai region and go deeper into the wilderness. They say again that they are tired of eating manna and want the sumptuous dishes they had in Egypt. Moses protests that he can no longer keep everyone happy. God responds by causing a bevy of quail to blow in from the sea so that the people can eat meat. Soon after they finish their meal, however, the people are smitten with a plague. In the next chapter, Miriam and Aaron incur God's anger by speaking against Moses and suggesting that they, too, are prophets. Miriam is stricken with leprosy.

The theme of disloyalty becomes critical in chapter 13, when Moses sends spies to survey the land and report back on what they find. Most of the spies say the land is indeed flowing with milk and honey, but that the current inhabitants are strong and the cities well fortified. Chapter 14 describes how the people reacted:

Then all the congregation raised a loud cry; and the people wept that night. And all the people of Israel murmured against Moses and Aaron; the whole congregation said to them, "Would that we had died in the land of Egypt! Or would that we had died in the wilderness! Why does the Lord bring us into this land, to fall by the sword? Our wives and our little ones will become a prey; would it not be better for us to go back to Egypt?" And they said to one another, "Let us choose a captain, and go back to Egypt."

Joshua and Caleb encourage the people to have faith, but the people respond by trying to stone them.

From this point on, it is clear that the generation of the Exodus will never forge a new identity for themselves. Faced with a choice between comfort and freedom, they will invariably choose the former. All the signs and wonders that God wrought for them are to no avail. In anguish, God asks Moses (Numbers 14:11), "How long will this people despise me?" Again God threatens to destroy the entire nation and start over. Again Moses asks for mercy; but this time God cannot forget what the people have done. Those who complained at every hint of danger or discomfort are deemed hopeless. Simply put, the generation of the Exodus is deemed unworthy of redemption. If the Israelites are to enter the Promised Land, it will have to be with a new generation unaccustomed to slavery.

The Book of Deuteronomy opens with renewed hope based on the prospects of a generation that did not experience slavery. From a literary perspective, Deuteronomy is more a history lesson than a narrative. Moses describes the failures of the previous generation in great detail and warns their children not to follow in their footsteps. This sets the stage for the final chapter of the story. Because Moses himself will not be allowed to enter the Promised Land, a typical ending would have God tell him that his years of wandering in the desert were not in vain – that even though the first generation could not pull itself together, the second was about to do just that. On this reading, the tragedy would be that Moses could not actually see the outcome; like an old man planting a tree that will not bear fruit until he is dead, Moses could only imagine what the future had in store. According to this account, he would approach the end of a happy if not totally fulfilled life.

From a political perspective, the success of the second generation would legitimate the struggle to bring about a new order. From this point of view, Maimonides (*GP* 3.32, p. 528) argues that God made the people wander in the desert to toughen them up until a generation was born that was not accustomed to slavery and servitude. Along similar lines, Walzer claims we can look on the experience in the wilderness as a school for the soul. The instruction might be long and hazardous, but it would not be futile. The picture of a transformed people living in a new land would allow us to say that not only slavery can be overcome but the slave mentality as well. It may not happen in one lifetime, but in the end, even the most despondent people can rise to new heights.

It is here that our expectations dictate a sudden turn of events: The people repent, Moses weeps, and God brings about a miracle even more dazzling than the parting of the Red Sea. Yet this is how God asks Moses to prepare for death in the actual story (Deuteronomy 31:16–18):

Behold, you are about to sleep with your fathers; then this people will rise up and play the harlot after the strange gods of the land, where they go to be among them, and they will forsake me and break my covenant which I have made with them. Then my anger will be kindled against them in that day, and I will forsake them and hide my face from them, and they will be devoured; and many evils and troubles will come upon them, so that they will say in that day, "Have not these evils come upon us because our God is not among us?" And I will surely hide my face in that day on account of all the evil which they have done, because they have turned to other gods.

The rhetoric of this passage is the harshest in the Torah, for it claims that the people are no better than a common prostitute and will continue to break faith with God.[14] For all its beauty, the Promised Land does not bring about a transformation. As Ezekiel (20:28–31) put it years later, the Promised Land turned out to be the scene of a whole new round of provocations.

The closest Moses gets to a happy ending is the blessing of Deuteronomy 33, which culminates in the following verse: "Happy are you, O Israel! Who is like you, a people saved by the Lord, the shield of your help, and the sword of your triumph! Your enemies shall come fawning to you; and you shall tread upon their high places." Yet these lines are hardly strong enough to overturn the negative tone of Deuteronomy 31 and Moses' own prediction (31:27): "For I know well how rebellious and stubborn you are. If you already have been rebellious toward the Lord while I am still alive and among you, how much more so after my death." This means, in effect, that history cannot help but repeat itself.

The end of the story is so far out of line with our expectations that it cannot help but call attention to itself. Why does an epic based on the themes of deliverance and redemption end on such a sour note? Modern scholarship answers by saying that the Book of Deuteronomy is a later addition to the Torah and thus contains "predictions" of what already happened. I have no reason to dispute this except to say that it leaves the basic question unanswered. Assuming the ending is a later addition, why pick such a sour one?

Unfortunately, the fundamental question raised by the story is never answered: If the miracle at the Red Sea, the giving of the Torah at Sinai, guidance by the greatest prophet who ever lived, and entry

---

[14] Israel's harlotry is a familiar theme in prophetic literature. See Hosea 1–3; Isaiah 1:21; Jeremiah 3:1; 4:30–1; Ezekiel 23: 1–45.

into the Promised Land were not enough to achieve reconciliation between God and Israel, what else is needed? If, as Moses predicts, history is going to repeat itself, are we not left with despair? The prophetic answer is no. Although Moses predicted disaster after the people entered the Land, he also predicted a return to the Land and general prosperity *if* the people first return to God (Deuteronomy 30:3–5). So if the current situation is bleak, the reason is that the story of God's involvement with Israel is yet to be completed. The time is coming when a redeemer will emerge who accomplishes what Moses could not.

We can see the outlines of this response in the origin of the concept of the *Messiah*: literally the anointed one of God. Originally, it referred to a king or priest set apart from the rest of the people. At Exodus 29:41, Moses is told to anoint Aaron's sons as priests. Anointed priests are also mentioned in Leviticus 4. Later (e.g., 1 Samuel 2:10; 2 Samuel 5:3 and 23:1; Psalm 89:20), "Messiah" is used to designate a present king. In the hands of the prophets, however, it came to mean a future king or redeemer, usually from the House of David, who will restore political sovereignty and end the oppression of Israel. Thus according to Isaiah 11:1–2, "A shoot shall come forth from the stump of Jesse, and a branch shall grow out of his roots. The spirit of the Lord shall rest upon him." And Jeremiah 23:5 states, "The days are surely coming, says the Lord, when I will raise up for David a righteous branch, and he shall reign as a king and deal wisely, and shall execute justice and righteousness in the land." Eventually the future redeemer came to be called "the Messiah," and hope for a better future took on the character of an eschatology.

Even the most hardened of readers cannot fail to be moved by the force and incomparable beauty with which Isaiah (11:9) proclaims, "The earth shall be full of the knowledge of the Lord, as the waters cover the sea," or as Ezekiel (37:5) tells the bones in the desert, "I will cause breath to enter you and you shall live again." In time, these images and the sentiments behind them became an essential part of the Western philosophic tradition – so much so that in the introduction to the *Critique of Pure Reason*, Kant could say that the central questions of philosophy are three in number: "What can I know?" "What should I do?" and "What can I hope for?" If the first two would have made perfect sense to an ancient Greek audience, the latter may well have struck them as silly. By contrast, the latter is for Kant the synthesis or culmination of the first two.

HOPE AS GRAND BUT UNREAL

Compelling as they are, prophetic utterances about the future mask a serious problem. If hope for a better future has its upside in preventing people from falling into despair, it also has a downside. "There is something grand about living in hope," wrote Gershom Scholem, "but at the same time there is something profoundly unreal about it."[15] Needless to say, the history of Judaism is littered with false hopes, false messiahs, and wild speculation about the circumstances in which the true one will appear. Christianity faces the same problem in connection with the second coming of Christ. Although hope is needed when things get difficult, it is precisely when things get difficult that people are most susceptible to folly. Such folly expresses itself in either of two ways.

The first is the vision of apocalypse, which carries with it an "us-versus-them" mentality and a vision of divine vengeance against "them." For many of the prophets, the current situation is so awful that justice cannot be done until every sin is exposed and every sinner punished. This will require nothing less than a miracle of stunning proportions. Thus Amos (8–9) – the first but by no means the last prophet to offer dire predictions about the days ahead – claims that the Day of the Lord will not be a joyous time but a bitter, awful one, when no light will shine and famine will destroy the land. The punishment will be so severe that no one, from those in Sheol to those at the top of Mt. Carmel, will escape. Jeremiah (4) tells us the earth will be waste and void, the heavens will have no light, the mountains will quake, cities will lie in ruins, and "disaster will follow upon disaster." Isaiah (6) goes so far as to ask God to stop up the people's ears and shut their eyes so that cities will lie in waste and the land will be totally desolate.

Although these passages may strike the modern reader as excessive, the logic behind the prophetic view of the future is clear. Religion

---

[15] *MIJ*, 35. Cf. Norman Cohn, *The Pursuit of the Millennium*, 19: "Precisely because they were so utterly certain of being the Chosen People, Jews tended to react to peril, oppression and hardship by phantasies of the total triumph and boundless prosperity which Yahwey, out of his omnipotence, would bestow upon his Elect in the fullness of time."

but why?

directs one's attention to the absolute. The more one is focused on the absolute, the more human behavior appears as wanting. The more human behavior appears as wanting, the more devastating corrective measures will have to be. Again from Scholem, "Jewish messianism is in its origin and by its nature ... a theory of catastrophe."[16] Though it is questionable whether centuries of Jewish messianic thinking can be grouped under one category, Scholem's observation has ample precedent in the Bible. Recall that God destroyed most of humanity during the Flood, destroyed the cities of Sodom and Gomorrah, and threatens to destroy the Jewish people after the golden calf episode. In view of the severity of this line of thinking, it is hardly surprising that the rabbi sometimes express reservations about the Messiah, for example, "Let the messiah come, but let me not live to see it."[17]

Scholem's generalization is also overstated in that "Jewish messianism" is too broad a term to allow for easy generalizations, and visions of catastrophe are not limited to Jewish sources. In the Christian Bible, the wars, famines, and earthquakes described at Matthew 24:7 are said to be just the beginning of what will happen. False prophets will arise, many people will be tortured or put to death, lawlessness will increase, but "The one who endures will be saved." To continue (Matthew 24:29–34),

The sun will be darkened, and the moon will not give its light; The stars will fall from heaven, and the powers of heaven will be shaken. Then the sign of the Son of Man will appear in heaven, and then all the tribes of the earth will mourn, and they will see "the son of Man coming on the clouds of heaven" with power and great glory. And he will send out his angels with a loud trumpet call, and they will gather his elect from the four winds, from one end of heaven to the other ... Truly I tell you, this generation will not pass away until all these things have taken place.

Jesus' image calls to mind that of Daniel 7:13 ("I saw one like a human being coming with the clouds of heaven"), a critical text for apocalyptic thinkers in both traditions.

The second source of folly is the vision of what will follow the apocalypse: a world totally unlike this one, where peace will reign,

---

[16] *MIJ*, 7. See Joseph Klausner, *The Messianic Idea in Israel*, 242–3, for a more nuanced view.

[17] *Sanhedrin* 98a.

death will be overcome, haughtiness and pride will be eliminated, and idolatry will give way to worship of the true God. Eventually this vision was extended to include the restoration of a divinely appointed king from the house of David, political sovereignty for Israel, the ingathering of the exiles, the rebuilding of the Temple in Jerusalem, and, following Daniel, resurrection of the dead. The problem is that false hopes not only leave people disappointed but also, in many cases, make a bad situation worse.

History records that the Roman occupation of Judea was brutal and that two attempts at revolution failed miserably. In regard to the first, Josephus writes,[18]

Their chief inducement to go to war was an equivocal oracle also found in their sacred writings, announcing that at that time a man from their own country would become Monarch of the world. This they took to mean the triumph of their own race, and many of their own scholars were wildly out in their interpretations.

This led to the destruction of Jerusalem, civil war between competing Jewish factions, numerous massacres and crucifixions, and a large number of people being taken away as slaves. In the second attempt, the Jews were led by Bar Kochba ("son of the star"), who ruled as king (*nasi*) for a short period but was eventually defeated by a scorched-earth policy meant to teach the Jews a lesson for all time. As one might expect, there were multiple claimants to the title of Messiah during such troubled times, the two most notable being Jesus and Bar Kochba himself.

The failure of the second attempt at revolution raised the same question over again: What is the proper response to catastrophe – despair or hope? If the former, what is left of the tradition that began with Abraham? If the latter, why has hope gone unanswered? Given the speculative nature of the question, and the dire circumstances in which the Jews found themselves, the rabbis of the Talmud were unable to reach a single answer. On the one hand, there are rabbinic texts that claim that the Messiah will come if Israel mends its ways: repent for a single day or observe a single Sabbath in accordance with the

---

[18] Josephus, *The Jewish War*, 6.312– 13. As Josephus goes on to say, the oracle was actually about Vespasian.

Torah.[19] The rationale for this view is clear: It is not enough to wait for God to intervene; people can hasten the coming of the Messiah by improving the quality of their behavior. Rather than a Herculean effort, what is required is a sincere desire not to repeat past mistakes.

On the other hand, *Sanhedrin* 97a tells us, in the name of various rabbis, that the Messiah will come when things have reached their lowest ebb: scholars will be few in number and each evil will follow quickly on the back of the previous one, the house of assembly will be for harlots, Galilee will lie in ruins, God-fearing men will be despised, young men will insult the old, daughters will rise up against their mothers, impudence will increase, esteem will be perverted, and the whole kingdom will be converted to heresy.

Again the rationale is clear: No matter how bad things may get, one should never abandon hope that the Messiah is on his way.[20] Behind this tradition are passages from Isaiah (13:6–8; 26:17–18) that compare the coming of the Messiah to the pain of a woman in labor. We can therefore appreciate the view of Rabbi Yohanan, who concluded that the Messiah will come in a generation that is *either* totally righteous *or* totally corrupt.[21] Whichever one it is, apocalyptic thinking typically expresses itself in absolutes. The existing order is rotten to the core. The new order will correct all ills and put human life on a completely new footing.

Along the same lines, some rabbis pictured cosmic upheavals, the return of Elijah to announce the arrival of the Messiah, or a war between Gog and Magog.[22] Some speculated that in the days of the Messiah, wine will be plentiful, grain and fruit will grow more quickly, women will be more fertile, and in general people will live a life of leisure. The greatest miracle of all will be the resurrection of the dead. Against this, *Sanhedrin* 91b claims that the only difference between this world and the days of the Messiah is that Israel will regain political sovereignty. Yet another tradition maintains there will be two Messiahs: the Messiah ben Joseph, who will win many victories but ultimately be slain, and the Messiah ben David, who will avenge the death of the first Messiah

---

[19] See, for example, *Sanhedrin* 97b and Taanit 64a. Cf. *Yoma* 86b; *Shabbat* 118b.

[20] Cf. Levinas, *DF*, 77: "even if the world is absolutely plunged in sin, the Messiah will come."

[21] *Sanhedrin* 98a.

[22] For the original reference, see Ezekiel 34:11. Cf. *Megilla* 11a; *Sanhedrin* 97b.

(possibly resurrecting him) and secure the ultimate victory over evil.[23] By contrast, *Sanhedrin* 98a raises the possibility that the Messiah will be a leper at the gates of Rome bandaging his sores.

It is clear that the rabbis are deeply ambivalent about messianism. Given the horrors of exile and oppression, they were not in a position to squelch a belief that gave the people hope. At the same time, they could not be completely comfortable with a doctrine that had led to two disastrous wars, spawned a rival religion, and on some interpretations puts more emphasis on military prowess than it does on observance of the commandments. In this respect, they were neither the first nor the last people in history to see that messianic fervor can be dangerous. The problem is that, while dangerous, it can also be inspiring. As Heinrich Graetz put it, messianism is both Pandora's box and the elixir of life.[24]

How does one deal with such a pronounced dichotomy? Traditionally there are five ways: (1) inflate the idea of the Messiah, (2) deflate it, (3) marginalize it, (4) internalize it, or (5) defer it. Each has obvious strengths and weaknesses.

Inflation consists of raising the bar of acceptance so high that for all intents and purposes, it can never be crossed. If Elijah has not come to herald the Messiah's arrival, if the exiles have not returned to Zion, if the Temple has not been restored, if there has not been a groundswell of repentance or Sabbath observance, if there has not been a cataclysm or apocalypse approaching that described by the prophets, and if no one has been resurrected, the Messiah has not come, and we will just have to wait. In fact, waiting for the Messiah in the sense of adopting a hopeful or trusting attitude toward God is a virtue.[25] To think that

---

[23] The origin of this tradition is unclear, but see Klausner, *The Messianic Idea*, 400–1, 520–1. For a rabbinic precedent, see *Sukkah* 52a. For recent discussion, see J. Liver, "The Doctrine of the Two Messiahs," *Harvard Theological Review* 52 (1959): 149–85. Some speculate that this doctrine is analogous to the second coming of Jesus. According to Maimonides, *MT* 14, Kings and Wars, 11.1, the only Messiahs are David and the one who will restore the Davidic dynasty.

[24] Graetz, "The Stages in the Evolution of the Messianic Belief," in *The Structure of Jewish History and Other Essays*, 151–2.

[25] Habakkuk 2:3, *Sanhedrin* 97b. Cf. David Patterson, "Though the Messiah May Tarry: A Reflection on Redemption," *May Smith Lecture on Post-Holocaust Christian Jewish Dialogue*, 21: "The Messiah, therefore, does not end history; rather, the endless wait for the Messiah even though he may tarry, *is* history."

we can force God's hand is presumptuous.[26] So barring a nation-wide decision to repent, all we can say is that the Messiah will come when God decides to send him.

I will not have a great deal to say about inflation because of its reliance on mythology. To the degree that mythology enters the picture, philosophy leaves it. There is, however, one major advantage to this view: Inflating the concept of the Messiah makes it all but impossible for pretenders to the title to make a case. The problem is that without a realistic hope for redemption in the future, life becomes frozen in the present. If this is true, we have no choice but to live our lives as if the present state of things is all we have and all we will ever have. Levinas calls this "the sterile passivity of so-called orthodox piety lying in wait for a miraculous Messiah."[27] In a later chapter, we will see that like politics, theology makes for strange bedfellows and that the vision of a Messiah who enters history from a position beyond it became popular among secular Jews in the early part of the twentieth century.

Deflation is the opposite: Lower the bar of acceptance so that the expectations people have for the Messiah will be lowered as well. The best-known proponent of this view is Maimonides, who is famous for arguing, in connection with *Sanhedrin* 91b, that when the Messiah comes, the course of nature will remain as it now is, the only difference being that Israel will be at peace with the other nations and regain political sovereignty. Thus any reference to cosmic upheaval, new revelations, or radical changes in human nature are systematically eliminated. But deflation comes with a cost as well. If the bar of entry is lowered, it becomes easier for pretenders to make a case.[28]

Marginalizing the Messiah means arguing that the main challenge we face is and has always been faithful observance of the commandments; everything else is a distant second. One can do this either by saying that the Messiah has already come or by downplaying the importance of his arrival. Thus second Isaiah (45:1–7) claims that a non-Jew, Cyrus of Persia, was the Messiah in the original sense of being the anointed one of God. Centuries later Rabbi Hillel, a descendant of

[26] *Sanhedrin* 97b.
[27] Levinas, *DF*, 227.
[28] This consequence is discussed by David Berger in "Some Ironic Consequences of Maimonides' Rationalist Approach to the Messianic Age," in *The Legacy of Maimonides: Religion, Reason and Community*, 79–88.

the great Hillel, went so far as to say there will be no Messiah for Israel because he has already come during the time of Hezekiah.[29] Similarly Rav, a third-century Talmudic master, proclaimed that the appointed dates for the Messiah have come and gone, so that at this point, all that remains are repentance and good deeds.[30] A good way to understand this response is to say with Jacob Neusner that the purpose of religious life is not salvation, understood as a future event, but sanctification, understood as an ever-present possibility.[31] More fully, "If people wanted to reach the end of time, they had to rise above time, that is, history, and stand off at the side of great movements of political and military character."

Neusner has shown that this strategy is prominent in the Mishnah, which was composed at a time when memories of two failed attempts at revolution were still fresh in people's minds. It is not that the rabbis of the Mishnah ignored the idea of the Messiah but that, to stay with Neusner, they said as little about it as they could except insofar as it provided a further reason to obey the commandments.[32] This approach is less true of the Babylonian Talmud, when time and distance caused unpleasant memories of revolt to fade and Messianic speculation began to reassert itself. We have seen that such speculation raised more questions than it answered and left people wondering when the Messiah would come and what he would do. In any case, the notion that Israel is or ought to think of itself as standing "outside of time" gained new life in the twentieth century in the hands of Franz Rosenzweig, who argues (*SR*, 138) that the Jewish people stand apart from others because they have already entered eternity, the point where "time no longer has a right to a place between the present moment and consummation."

---

[29] *Sanhedrin* 99a.

[30] *Sanhedrin* 97b.

[31] Jacob Neusner, "Messianic Themes in Formative Judaism," *Journal of the American Academy of Religion* 52 (1984): 357–74. One of the central claims of Neusner's argument is (p. 357), "The conception or category, Judaism's Messianic Doctrine, as a systematic construct, yields only confusion." In arguing that there are five distinct ways to respond to the problems raised by messianism, it is obvious that I agree. Also see *Messiah in Context: Israel's History and Destiny in Formative Judaism*, 74–8.

[32] Neusner, *Messiah in Context*, 177: "If Israel at large yearned for the redemption and the end, then telling them to attain that goal by doing what the rabbis wanted would vastly strengthen the rabbinic system."

At the beginning of the twenty-first century, David Hartman took a similar position. Citing Hillel's claim that the Messiah has already come during the time of Hezekiah, Hartman draws attention to the fact that the Talmud was able to include the voice of someone who thought that historical redemption is no longer an essential part of Jewish tradition.[33] In Hartman's words, "I am convinced that something else besides messianism served as the carrier of the living God in their [the Jewish people's] everyday lives. And that, I suggest, was the shift in the tradition from an event-based to a text-centered theology."[34]

Internalization involves claiming that the Messiah should not be understood as a historical figure but rather as an allegory for the transformation of even a single person from a life of sin to a life of holiness. In this way, each of us has the ability to bring – or even to *be* – the Messiah by undergoing a radical change of heart. The problem with internalization is that it severs any connection between messianism and the larger question of historical redemption. Important as it is, the change of one heart is not enough. The prophets longed for a day when the hearts of an entire nation would be changed and the results visible in the public square. Once messianism loses any historical significance, it loses much of its compelling force.

Finally, deferral means putting off the coming of the Messiah so that his arrival will come only in the distant future, by some accounts only at infinity. Philosophically speaking, the Messiah will not come at a specific point in history but represents an ideal or perfect state that history approaches asymptotically.[35] According to Cohen (*RR*, 314–15), "his coming is not an actual end, but means merely the infinity of his coming, which in turn means the infinity of development." In this way, the messianic age is always ahead of us. Hence Schwarzschild: "the Messiah not only has not come but also will never have come ... [rather] he will always be coming."[36] *Deferral* is a

---

[33] David Hartman, *Israelis and the Jewish Tradition*, 96.

[34] *Ibid.*, 104.

[35] For the reference to asymptotes, see Kant, *C1*, A663/B691. This view will be discussed in detail in Chapter 4.

[36] Steven Schwarzschild, *PI*, 211. Cf. Patterson, "Though the Messiah May Tarry," 16: "the Messiah is by definition *the one who tarries*, signifying a redemption that is *always yet to be*, always future, because what we do now is never *enough*." This idea can also be found in post modernists like Blanchot and Derrida, who stress that the future must always contain an element of openness or undecidability so

misleading description of Cohen's position if we take it to mean that the coming of the Messiah is an event that keeps getting put off in the way one puts off going on a diet. Rather the Messiah is a symbol for the attainment of moral perfection. In philosophic terms, the demands imposed by morality can be approximated but never realized. As we will see, this raises the question of *why* they cannot be realized and what sense it makes to strive for a goal that is forever out of reach.

It should be clear that these approaches are not mutually exclusive. A person could hold, as Cohen and Schwarzschild do, that the coming of the Messiah is a way of talking about the process of self-sanctification *and* that the completion of this process is an infinite task. By the same token, one consequence of inflation is deferral, if not for an infinite amount of time, at least for enough time that the suddenness or immediacy of the Messiah's coming is, to use Scholem's word, neutralized.[37]

The fact that there are five ways of dealing with the need for hope versus the danger of false optimism shows it is misleading to talk about *the* Jewish position on this subject or to think that all the arguments point in a single direction. Even if we leave out philosophic speculation, the picture is so complicated that, commenting on the rabbis of the Talmud, Ephraim Urbach could say there are times when the diversity "exceeds the standards of normal differences of opinion and reaches down to fundamentals."[38] The result is that many of the doctrines amount to the complete negation of others.

---

that the Messiah can never actually *be* present. See Maurice Blanchot, *The Step Not Beyond*, 108, 137, and Jacques Derrida, *Specters of Marx*, 81–2. The difference is that for Schwazschild, the messianic has the content of a Kantian regulative idea, while for Derrida, who upholds the notion of the "messianic without messianism," it has no content. For Derrida, then, there is no set doctrine or structure that will be realized at a future point, only an eternal openness to the possibility of what could be. For further comment, see John D. Caputo, *The Prayers and Tears of Jacques Derrida*, 77–81 and especially 119: "For Derrida has all his life been praying and weeping over some coming messiah, over something coming, something or other, I know not what, that is coming." For the relation between Derrida and Jewish tradition, see Martin Kavka, *Jewish Messianism and the History of Philosophy*, 195–8.

[37] *MIJ*, 176–202.

[38] Ephraim Urbach, *The Sages*, 649. Cf. Scholem, *MIJ*, 51: "As long as the Messianic hope remained abstract ... it was possible for it to embody even what was contradictory, without the latent contradiction being felt." For an earlier account of the variation in Jewish conceptions of the Messiah, see Heinrich Graetz, "Stages," 151–72.

The purpose of this study is to examine the philosophic implications of these approaches in the hope of arriving at a coherent account of what belief in a Messiah ought to involve. As with Maimonides' treatment of prophecy and providence, where demonstration is not possible, there is no choice but to proceed dialectically in an attempt to construct a workable solution. I hope to show that beneath the visions of tragedy and triumph in the sacred literature, there is a rationally defensible view of how to look at human history. Unfortunately tragedy has been a much more common theme in Jewish history than triumph. The Roman destruction of Judea was but one of a host of disasters that history forced us to confront. The prevalence of disaster raises important questions about what we take history to be. For the prophets, it is the unfolding of God's will. For Thucydides, it is an account of the consequences or effects of human nature. For Hegel, it became the progressive embodiment of rationality.

The problem with philosophies of history is that they inevitably run up against the hard facts of history itself. In the case of Judaism, those facts range from defeat to exile to massacre to a full-blown Holocaust. It makes no sense to discuss messianism in the abstract and ignore the painful reality of these events. Do the disasters that have confronted the Jewish people really constitute the unfolding of God's will? Do we have reason to think that human nature is invariant? Can the horrific events of the twentieth century be reconciled with the idea that history is moving toward a final redemption?

Mention has already been made of the fact that victims of the Holocaust invoked Maimonides' words on the coming of the Messiah. How is it possible to do justice to the horror these victims faced and still hold that messianism makes sense? These are the questions I wish to address. In rough outline, I will proceed in chronological order, taking up ideas and events in the order in which they appeared. I will end with a vision of what redemption should be like.

EVOLUTION OR REVOLUTION

Broadly speaking, there are two ways to look at redemption. According to the first, if a spiritual transformation is to occur, it can only be produced by a change of heart and a renewed effort not to repeat past mistakes. While the coming of the Messiah will usher in a period unlike any that has occurred before, it will not involve a disruption of the natural order analogous to the parting of the Red Sea. All that will happen is that human beings will come to their senses and finally achieve the spiritual growth of which they were always capable. According to the second, the story of the Exodus and the subsequent failure to achieve reconciliation with God show that no amount of human effort will be sufficient to bring about the kind of change that is necessary. In the end, the only thing that will is some form of divine intervention. The first approach is essentially that of Maimonides, the second that of apocalypticism in either its Jewish or Christian forms.

Let us briefly consider the apocalyptic alternative. Although exhorting people to improve their lives may be a good thing, history teaches that if after all this time, reconciliation between God and Israel has still not been achieved, something more than human effort is needed. Left to its own devices, human behavior is flawed and will remain so. The notion that little by little the human race can lift itself out of the desperate straits in which it finds itself flies in the face of overwhelming historical evidence to the contrary. That is why nothing short of a cataclysm is needed to set humanity on a new course.

As Scholem puts it, "The Bible and the apocalyptic writers know of no progress in history leading to the redemption."[39] Instead they foresee a time when redemption will come from an outside source leading to a world completely unlike this one. We will see in what follows that apocalypticism is more than just a biblical relic. In the early part of the twentieth century, it became a popular position among Jewish intellectuals traumatized by World War I and the failure of German society to address the many ills that plagued it.

It will come as no surprise that my sympathies are with Maimonides. Not that I want to return to animal sacrifice in a rebuilt Temple but that I want to maintain a strict interpretation of the principle that *ought* implies *can*. If it is not within the power of human beings to do something, they cannot be obliged to do it. Conversely, if it is within

---

[39] *MIJ*, p. 10. While this may be true of biblical and apocalyptic writers, we have seen that it is not always true of rabbinic.

their power, they bear full responsibility for their success *or* failure. In short, reconciliation with God does not require miraculous intervention or a second revelation or an effort to supersede the Torah. We have everything we need right now. The fact that it has not yet occurred has no tendency to show that it cannot or will not. The future course of history is entirely in our hands.

2

Maimonides and the Idea of a Deflationary Messiah

Faced with a prophetic tradition containing visions of upheaval and a rabbinic tradition that had no set doctrine about the coming of the Messiah, Maimonides sought to imbue the discussion with a healthy dose of conceptual rigor. Citing Ecclesiastes 3:14 ("Whatever God does shall be forever"), he argues that nothing God has made admits of excess or deficiency.[1] Thus all references to cosmic upheaval in the works of the prophets should be read as references to the overthrow of political regimes, not to disruptions of the natural order. Similarly, Isaiah's vision at 11:6 ("The wolf shall dwell with the lamb...") should be interpreted as a metaphor for the fact that Israel will live in peace amid its neighbors.[2] In fact, Maimonides follows a rabbinic view according to which the only difference between life now and life then is that Israel will be at peace, regain political sovereignty, and be able to focus its attention on study and worship.[3] In regard to everything

---

[1] *GP* 2.28, p. 335.

[2] *MT* 14, Kings and Wars, 12.1.

[3] *Perek Heleq*. *MT* 14, Kings and Wars, 11.3, 12.1. For rabbinic sources, see *Berakhot* 34b; *Shabbat* 63a, 151b; *Sanhedrin* 91b, 99a. Maimonides' account of the days of the Messiah stands in marked contrast to that of Saadia, *The Book of Beliefs and Opinions*, 8.6. 241–47, 304–12, who imagines a cataclysm, military victory, and the accumulation of enormous wealth. It is well known that Maimonides presents a more traditional view of messianism in his "Epistle to Yemen," a letter written to a Jewish community in distress. In that letter, he claims there will be cosmic upheavals and that the Messiah will work wonders and goes on to suggest that it is possible to predict when the Messiah will come. I follow David Hartman, *Crisis and Leadership: Epistles*

else, he writes, "Do not think that the King Messiah will have to perform signs and wonders, bring anything new into being, revive the
dead, or do similar things. It is not so."[4]

WHAT THE MESSIAH WILL DO AND WHY

Not surprisingly, Maimonides has nothing but contempt for those
who think that rivers will flow with wine, the earth will bring forth
baked bread, or people will become angels. In *Perek Helek*, he tells us
that even in the days of the Messiah, there will still be rich and poor,
strong and weak.[5] Although it will be easier to provide for the neces-
sities of life, people will still have to sow and reap. In his view, then, the
Messiah will be a religious and political leader who works according
to natural means. In time, the Messiah will die of natural causes.

Not only does this take the miraculous element out of messianism,
as Cohen remarks, but it also purges it of hedonistic overtones.[6]

---

    of Maimonides, 172, in saying that "The *Epistle to Yemen* cannot be treated as a para-
digm of Maimonides' theory of messianism or history."

[4] *MT* 14, Kings and Wars, 11. 3. As many people have noted, this raises a question
about resurrection, which is not only a miracle, but in Maimonides' opinion also a
fundamental principle of Jewish belief. Because Maimonides' view of resurrection is
a subject unto itself, I will not dwell on it here except to say that even if we take his
Letter on Resurrection as genuine, as I am inclined to, Maimonides' argument is that
once we accept creation, we have accepted the possibility of miracles and therefore of
resurrection as well. A God who can bring an entire universe into being can also give
new life to the body. He insists, however, that the sort of miracle involved in resurrection would be short-lived – like the changing of a rod into a serpent – and would
leave the permanent order of nature unchanged. That is what enables him to say that in the
days of the Messiah there will still be rich and poor, strong and weak. The problem
is that if he admits the possibility of a temporary disruption of nature like the raising
of the dead, why should he not also admit the possibility of a temporary cataclysm?
After all, a God who can bring an entire universe into being can also move mountains
or dry up oceans. Maimonides' answer is religious: Jewish tradition mandates belief in
resurrection but not belief in a cosmic upheaval. Maimonides' rejection of a miraculous element in messianism may also seem to conflict with his claim (*MT 14*, Kings
and Wars, 12.3) that the Messiah will identify the true descendents of the priestly class
with the aid of the Holy Spirit.

[5] By contrast, Maimonides says at *MT* 14, Kings and Wars, 12.5, that during the days
of the Messiah, there will be neither jealousy nor strife. Because he is not more explicit,
it is difficult to know exactly what he has in mind. My interpretation, to be defended
at greater length later, is that although human behavior will be greatly improved, it
will not be perfect.

[6] *RR*, 311.

Although restoring sovereignty to Israel will make it easier to earn a living, Maimonides insists that the purpose of doing so will not be to enjoy material comforts, but rather to have the time to pursue spiritual and intellectual goals. The Messiah will put an end to the persecution of Israel *so that* Israel can fulfill the commandments, devote itself to study and worship, and lead the rest of humanity in the same direction. In the words of *Mishneh Torah* 14, Kings and Wars, 12.4, "The sages and prophets did not long for the days of the Messiah that Israel might exercise dominion over the world, rule the heathens, or be exalted by the nations, or that it might eat, drink, and rejoice. Their aspiration was that Israel be free to devote itself to the Law and its wisdom."[7] According to Cohen, this also liberates messianism from *utopianism*, which is nothing but a fantasy image based on the pursuit of happiness.

The phrase "the Law and its wisdom" in the foregoing citation is revealing because it shows that the Messiah will not just usher in a better age than the present one, but will mark the fulfillment of the Torah and, by implication, the perfection of the human species. At present Israel is in exile and cannot fulfill all the duties God has assigned it. The exile has also led to persecution by other nations and a general neglect of science and learning.[8] Not only does Israel suffer from such neglect, but the other nations do as well because they devote themselves to imaginary goals like wealth and power rather than the pursuit of wisdom. The result is that humanity is unable to reach the end for which it is naturally suited.

The Messiah will change this, not by going to war, but by ushering in conditions that allow Israel to fulfill all the commandments – including the laws of sacrifice and the observance of the Sabbatical and Jubilee years.[9] Because the Law as a whole aims at the perfection of the body *and* soul, and because the latter consists in acquiring correct opinions and developing the rational faculty, fulfillment of the

---

[7] Cf. *MT* 1, Repentance, 9.2: "Hence all Israelites, their prophets and sages, longed for the advent of Messianic times, that they might have relief from the wicked tyranny that does not permit them properly to occupy themselves with the study of the Torah and the observance of the commandments; that they might have ease, devote themselves to getting wisdom, and thus attain to life in the world to come."

[8] *GP* 1.71: 175; 2.11: 276.

[9] *MT* 14, Kings and Wars, 11.1.

Law will result in a general increase in wisdom.[10] Such wisdom will not be limited to Israel but will spread to the other nations as well, insofar as they decide to live in peace. Thus (*MT* 14, Kings and Wars, 12.5) "The one preoccupation of the whole world will be to know the Lord."

In saying "the Messiah will change this," I do not mean to imply that for Maimonides, the messianic age will arrive all of a sudden. Having done away with the idea of a sudden upheaval, Maimonides thinks in terms of steady improvement. In the words of Menachem Kellner, the messianic era is better understood as a process rather than an event.[11] We can see this in two ways.

First, Maimonides tells us that the task of identifying the Messiah will proceed in stages. Rather than relying on astrological or numerical predictions, we will have to determine whether the person in question is a king from the House of David who meditates on the Torah, observes the commandments, prevails upon all of Israel to do so, and "fights the battles of the Lord." If all this comes to pass, Maimonides claims we can *assume* he is the Messiah.[12] If he does all of this, rebuilds the Temple, and gathers in the exiles, we can be *sure* he is. Not only will this take time, but it will require active participation from a wide range of people who will have to cooperate before his true identity is known. Second, Maimonides allows for the possibility that Christianity and Islam will play a role in educating people and, to use Kellner's expression, *monotheizing* the rest of humanity.[13] Again, this is to be done by natural means, which is to say that it will be accomplished by a gradual process of teaching and learning rather than a sudden upheaval.

Maimonides never doubts that perfection of the intellect is "the true human virtue." Although he does not cite Aristotle in this regard, he easily could have referred to the beginning of the *Metaphysics*: "All men by nature desire to know." This means that acquiring knowledge is not just something people like to do; it is the most basic need we

---

[10] *GP* 3.27.

[11] Kellner, *Science in the Bet Midrash*, 291, and "Messianic Postures in Israel Today," in *Essential Papers on Messianic Movements and Personalities in Jewish History*, 504–9.

[12] *MT* 14, Kings and Wars, 11.4.

[13] This text, which was once censored, comes from the end of *MT* 14, Kings and Wars, 11.

have – what makes us human as opposed to merely animate. It also means, as Aristotle recognizes (*Metaphysics* 1072a27), that God is both the primary object of knowledge and the primary object of desire.

Maimonides also thinks that the acquisition of wisdom by the rational faculty has practical overtones, because it shifts one's focus from the satisfaction of material needs to the satisfaction of spiritual.[14] According to *Guide* 3.11, the great evils that people inflict on one another all stem from ignorance. If ignorance could be replaced by knowledge, "they would refrain from doing any harm to themselves and to others. For through cognition of the truth, enmity and hatred are removed and the inflicting of harm by people on one another is abolished." He follows this remark by quoting Isaiah 11:6 and 11:9: "The earth shall be full of the knowledge of the Lord."[15] When this happens, and only when this happens, human nature will finally perfect itself.

The standard way of interpreting Maimonides is to follow Scholem by distinguishing between a restorative and a revolutionary conception of the Messiah, assigning Maimonides to the first group.[16] This reading is accurate in the sense that Maimonides believes that the laws of the Torah are true for all time, so that the perfect state will be a theologically oriented kingdom centered on animal sacrifice in a rebuilt Temple. It is also accurate in the sense that no matter how much time is devoted to science and philosophy, Maimonides is convinced that no one will equal, let alone surpass, the level of understanding achieved by Moses.

Unfortunately, the second point is harder to see. When Maimonides says that the one preoccupation of the whole world will be to know the Lord, he goes on to say that the Israelites will be very wise and "will know the things that are now concealed." What does this mean? Concealed from the majority, from the select few who are schooled in these matters, or from everyone including Moses and the patriarchs? Elsewhere in the *Mishneh Torah* (1, Repentance, 9.2), he is more specific: "Because the king who will arise from the seed of David will possess more wisdom than Solomon and will be a great prophet,

---

[14] Cf. *GP* 3.27, 511, 3.54, 634–8.
[15] Cf. *MT* 14, Kings and Wars, 12.5.
[16] Scholem, *MIJ*, 24–31.

approaching Moses our Teacher, he will teach the whole of the Jewish people and instruct them in the way of God; and all nations will come to hear him." This says that although the Messiah will acquire knowledge that was concealed from Solomon, he will approach but not surpass that acquired by Moses.

I take the latter as Maimonides' considered view because he lists as a fundamental principle of Judaism that Moses' prophecy is unique and will never be duplicated.[17] If someone were to rival Moses, he would be in a position to add or subtract from the Torah and thus to deny its eternal validity. So although most people will learn things they did not know before, no one will take humanity to entirely new ground. Instead, people will learn and relearn lessons that have been around for a long time.

The need for science as well as philosophy is justified by Maimonides' conviction (*GP* 1.34, 74) that human beings are incapable of knowing God directly and must settle for knowledge of what God has made or done. This means that the only way we can know God is by examining the consequences or effects of divine activity as manifested in the created order. Because we cannot fulfill the commandment to love God without acquiring knowledge of God, we are obliged to study the created order, which means to pursue science. Although Maimonides believed that scientific progress had been made since the time of Moses, he had no conception of the sort of revolutions we associate with Galileo, Darwin, or Einstein. For him, progress meant slightly better astronomical predictions, new medical treatments, or the discovery of a new plant or animal species. There is, however, no question that for him the pursuit of science constitutes the fulfillment of a sacred obligation.

We may conclude that although the Messiah will be a deep and accomplished thinker, the only way he will surpass Moses is in the political realm. For all his wisdom, Moses did not succeed in making peace with the rest of the nations or in convincing Israel to abandon idolatry. As we saw, God told Moses shortly before his death that the people would forget the lessons he taught them and undertake a whole new round of provocations. Not only will the Messiah teach these lessons more effectively, because humanity has learned the fruitlessness of

---

[17] *Perek Helek*, principle 7, and *MT* 1, Basic Principles, 7.6.

war, but also the Messiah will be able to reach a wider audience. This will enable him to put an end to the superstitions and injustices that prevailed when, in Maimonides' opinion, history veered off course and Israel went into exile.

Again we may question whether the Messiah himself will be responsible for these developments or whether he simply will preside over the achievements of others. The strength of Scholem's interpretation is that the lessons taught by the Messiah will not be new; all they will do is spread eternal wisdom to a wider and more receptive audience. In the *Mishneh Torah*, Maimonides goes so far as to say that in the days of the Messiah, all people "will accept the true religion." Whether this means monotheism in general or Judaism in particular is open to question.[18]

Still, Scholem is perceptive enough to see that the utopian element in Maimonides' messianism does not completely disappear.[19] Aside from rebuilding the Temple and gathering in the exiles, is it realistic to suppose that humanity will one day recognize that wealth and power are not the ultimate end of human life and devote itself to study? Maimonides' answer would be that realism is not the issue if that means making a prudent calculation of when all this will happen. From a philosophic perspective, the question is not "How likely is it the Messiah will come?" but "Is there anything in principle that prevents the Messiah from coming?" To the latter question, Maimonides' answer is no.

We saw that for Maimonides, human perfection consists first and foremost in the perfection of the intellect. With the perfection of the intellect, the rational soul is able to leave this world at death and pass into the next world, where it will cease to be bothered by bodily distractions and contemplate eternal truth forever. Given the state humanity is now in, such a perfection is beyond the reach of most people. This point is worth emphasizing because Maimonides does not think perfection is beyond the reach of all people. One can achieve human perfection without the arrival of the Messiah. The problem

---

[18] For further discussion of this point, see Kellner, *Maimonides' Confrontation with Myticism*, 241–50. I will have more to say about this issue and Kellner's development of it in the last chapter of this book.

[19] Note Bouretz's description of Maimonides' position as resembling "an anti-utopian utopia" at *Witnesses*, 269.

is that doing so requires time and resources that are not available to people who are struggling merely to survive. That is the tragedy of the human predicament: The opportunity to study is not widely available, thus most people are left to wallow in ignorance.

Our predicament is analogous to that of a pack of horses where all but a small minority are lame, thus they cannot do that for which they are naturally suited. It is then the present situation – not the messianic era – that sins against nature, because its emphasis on pleasure and power prevents most of humanity from achieving its natural end. Although it may strain human capacity to right this wrong and give all people the opportunity to study, nothing in Maimonides' philosophy suggests that doing so transcends that capacity.[20]

Although Maimonides is clearly following in the footsteps of the rabbis, it is noteworthy that unlike many of his predecessors, he has not set the bar for the Messiah so high that no one can cross it. On the contrary, by doing away with the miraculous dimension of messianism, he has lowered the bar to the point where the expectations we have for it could possibly be fulfilled. To be sure, they are not easy to fulfill and would require historical progress unlike anything witnessed thus far. But difficulty is one thing, possibility another. As long as there is possibility, there are grounds for hope. How firm those grounds are remains to be seen.

It is also noteworthy that Maimonides does not take the internalist approach. There are, and perhaps always will be, a few gifted and highly motivated people who have so transformed themselves that their minds are turned to God no matter what they are doing.[21] Yet the existence of such people is not identical with the coming of the Messiah. In Maimonides' view, the latter is a political event that involves all of Israel and large portions of the rest of humanity. The same is true for infinite deferral. Although the coming of the Messiah will set a new standard for human achievement, Maimonides never suggests it can only be realized at infinity. By lowering the bar of acceptance, he has gone out of his way to suggest it will be an actual event in history, not

---

[20] Cf. Aviezer Ravitzky, "'To the Utmost Human Capacity': Maimonides on the Days of the Messiah," in *Perspectives on Maimonides*, 232–3: "Even in the future, 'They will attain an understanding of their Creator according to the utmost human capacity (*kefi koah ha-adam*)' i.e. without transcending human limitations."

[21] GP 3.51, 620ff.

a catastrophe that puts an end to history or an ideal that perpetually transcends it.

THE NATURE OF HUMAN PERFECTION

To understand Maimonides' naturalism in greater detail, we must go deeper into his view of human perfection. Rather than discuss moral or epistemological issues in the abstract, I propose that we look at the people he puts forward as paradigms of human excellence. The first is Adam. As Maimonides sees it, Adam had perfect metaphysical knowledge in the Garden of Eden – or as perfect a knowledge as is possible for a human being. Such is his interpretation of the verse that claims God made man in his likeness (*GP* 1.2, 24). With this knowledge, Adam was able to distinguish truth from falsity. What Adam could not do at this stage is distinguish right from wrong. Following Aristotle, Maimonides argues that right and wrong are "generally accepted things" (*al-mashhurat* = *endoxa*) and thus not apprehended by the intellect. Because all Adam had was his intellect, he did not recognize that it is right to cover one's genitals and wrong not to.

Adam's downfall occurred when he decided to forsake the intellect and eat the fruit that the Bible describes as *a delight to the eyes* (Genesis 3:6). His punishment is that he was deprived of his intellect and "became absorbed in judging things to be bad or fine."[22] On this view, ethics is inferior to metaphysics because it cannot furnish us with necessity. Although people should cover their genitals, it is impossible to demonstrate this in the way one can demonstrate that pi is irrational.

Maimonides' account of Adam's fall is based on the conviction that intellectual apprehension is superior to right conduct. The problem is that, unlike Adam before the fall, we are not in a position to ignore considerations of right and wrong. Although prophets may renounce everything other than God, begrudge the times in which they are turned away from God, and be ashamed of their bodily functions, they cannot completely escape the fact that they live in a social environment.[23]

---

[22] Unlike Aristotle, Maimonides does not recognize the category of practical reason in the *Guide* and talks about the imagination instead. As far as the *Guide* is concerned, then, the only kind of reason is theoretical reason.

[23] *GP* 3.51, 620–2; 3.52, 629.

Put otherwise, there is no hope of returning to the state Adam occupied before the fall – as long as we remain in this life. In *Perek Helek*, Maimonides expresses contempt for those who think the Messiah will somehow lead us back to the Garden of Eden. Although the Messiah will help create conditions that enable us to *attain* the next life, there is no question he will have to deal with issues pertaining to right and wrong in this one. As we saw, his chief virtue is that he will be a political leader who ushers in a period of extended peace.

The second figure is Abraham. Maimonides claims that Abraham possessed valid proofs of the existence and unity of God and passed them on to Isaac and Jacob.[24] Abraham had to deal with war and famine and the problems of running a household, but his prophecy did not include commandments dealing with festivals, dietary laws, songs of praise, and other issues associated with standardized worship. The result, according to Maimonides, is that during the Egyptian captivity, the Israelites forgot the monotheism Abraham taught them and adopted the pagan religion of their captors. In Maimonides' opinion, Abraham's religion failed not because it was based on false premises, but because it was too metaphysical and did not take into account the need for standardized worship.

This fault was corrected by the third figure, Moses. Although Moses remained with God for forty days without any consideration for his body and, as far as we know, any formalized prayer or ritual, he realized that unless religion paid attention to these things – unless it became political as well as spiritual – it would be forgotten all over again. So in addition to establishing a close relation with God, Moses was a lawgiver and political leader. Although it may be true, as Maimonides suggests, that he served other people with his limbs only, the fact is that he did serve them.[25] We saw, however, that Moses too was not entirely successful. The people did not heed his message, and he did not succeed in making peace. We also saw that for Maimonides there is no chance that the Messiah or anyone else will rise to the level of Moses.

The fourth figure, Rabbi Akiba, is unique, because unlike the first three, he is not a prophet. Whatever knowledge he has comes from the

---

[24] *MT* 1, Idolatry, 1.2.
[25] *GP* 3.51, 624.

analysis of texts and arguments, not the voice of God. Maimonides mentions him in connection with *Hagigah* 14b, which recounts the legend of the four rabbis who entered paradise (*pardes*).[26] Maimonides interprets "paradise" as exposure to esoteric subjects. The legend tells us that one Rabbi died, one went mad, one became an apostate, and only Akiba entered in peace and went out in peace. Maimonides invokes the legend to drive home a strong sense of epistemological humility:

> For if you stay your progress because of a dubious point; if you do not deceive yourself into believing that there is a demonstration with regard to matters that have not been demonstrated; if you do not hasten to reject and categorically to pronounce false any assertions whose contradictories have not been demonstrated; if, finally you do not aspire to apprehend that which you are unable to apprehend – you will have achieved human perfection and attained the rank of *Rabbi Akiba*.

This should not be read as an antiphilosophic polemic. Later in the same chapter, Maimonides concludes by saying that the prophets and sages did not want to close the gate of speculation but simply to point out that "the intellects of human beings have a limit at which they stop."

Although Akiba was not a political leader and erred grievously by proclaiming Bar Kochba the Messiah, he serves as a model insofar as he recognizes his epistemological limits and does not aspire to exceed them. I take this to mean that although his mind was active, always considering new arguments and objections to old ones, there is no sense in which he was involved in an infinite quest. No doubt Maimonides' picture of Akiba is tied up with his negative theology. I will have more to say about that later. For the present, let me simply say that the thrust of Maimonides' negative theology is that not only will an infinite quest toward understanding God not succeed, but also, on the contrary, it will only lead to frustration and incoherence. At *Guide* 1.59, p. 137, he proclaims,

> Glory then to Him who is such that when the intellects contemplate His essence, their apprehension turns into incapacity; and when they contemplate the proceeding of His actions from His will, their knowledge turns into ignorance; and when the tongues aspire to magnify Him by means of attributive qualifications, all eloquence turns into weariness and incapacity!

[26] *GP* 1.32, 68–9.

Rather than occupy a position at the top of a metaphysical hierarchy, Maimonides' God is separate from the world and totally unlike it. The wisest among us is therefore the one who recognizes this and contemplates God's complete transcendence over anything in the created order. What the Messiah can do is help people reach this point.

Maimonides does allow for the possibility of prophets following the restoration of sovereignty to Israel. Although we must pay heed to them, he hastens to add that their role will be severely restricted.[27] They cannot introduce new commandments or take away existing ones. Nor can they invoke their relationship with God to interpret the Law or resolve disputes that arise within it. When it comes to problems of interpretation, they must give way to the likes of Akiba, who, as we have seen, had no access to divine revelation. Prophets can always urge obedience. They can tell us where to build a wall or when to go to war; but beyond that, they have no substantive role to play.

Maimonides' position rests on Deuteronomy 30:12 ("Torah is not in the heavens"), which he takes to mean that anyone who claims to bring new Torah from heaven is a false prophet.[28] I will have more to say about this passage in a later chapter as well. Note, however, that Maimonides' interpretation of the passage and his restriction on the role of future prophets is in keeping with his overall strategy of downplaying the role of the miraculous. Even if new prophets arise, legal disputes will still have to be settled by rational argument rather than appeal to heavenly voices or wondrous events. Even when it comes to Moses, the greatest of the prophets, Maimonides argues that the people did not believe in him because of the wonders he performed, because it is possible to perform wonders through magic or sorcery.[29] Although miracles may attract attention, in Maimonides' opinion, they do little to perfect the intellect. That is why it makes no sense to expect miracles from the Messiah.

---

[27] *MP* 1, Basic Principles, 9.1–4.
[28] For the classic rabbinic interpretation of this passage, see *Baba Metzia* 59 b, where the rabbis reject God's intrusion into a legal dispute. For further discussion, see my *Autonomy in Jewish Philosophy* (New York: Cambridge University Press, 2001), chap. 3.
[29] *MT* 1, Basic Principles, 8.1. Cf. David Hartman, *Israelis and the Jewish Tradition*, 85: "If one's whole sense of faith depends upon a miracle-based conception of the biblical promises of reward and punishment, then one risks exchanging God for alternative sources of well-being and security."

LIFE IN THE DAYS OF THE MESSIAH

We are now ready to consider the implications of Maimonides' theory. From what we have seen, one claim underlies everything he says about the Messiah and Judaism in general: that the laws of the Torah are valid forever. From a textual standpoint, the Torah says this about itself at Deuteronomy 13:1 and 29:28. Yet Maimonides' view also rests on an argument that can be reconstructed as follows: (1) the first two commandments affirm eternal truths, (2) all the other commandments deal with human nature as it is after the fall of Adam,[30] and (3) human nature is unchanging.[31] If human nature is unchanging, and the Torah exists to show us how to perfect that nature, then the Torah cannot change either. Along these lines, we saw that so far from introducing new laws, the Messiah will bring about conditions that allow us to fulfill the laws we already have.

To appreciate what this means, we must read Maimonides' claim about the eternal nature of the Torah in conjunction with another: that many of the laws of the Torah are concessions to human fallibility. Recall that from an intellectual perspective, Abraham's religion was perfect. The problem is that it failed to make provisions for the human need for spectacle, ritual, and sacrifice or prayer. At *Guide* 2.32, 526, Maimonides writes that it would be unrealistic for a prophet to say, "God has given you a Law forbidding you to pray, to fast, to call upon Him for help in misfortune. Your worship should consist solely in meditation without any works at all." I take this to mean that although the laws governing spectacle, ritual, and sacrifice or prayer are not necessary in themselves, they are necessary *given the human condition as we know it*. In other words, these commandments are a concession to human fallibility. If the entire human race were like Abraham, they would be unnecessary, and the Torah would not include them.

To take an obvious example, Moses did not need jewelry, fine linen, or a luxurious sanctuary to speak with God. Yet the fact that God issues commandments dealing with these things indicates the majority of people do. Why? Maimonides answers that they became accustomed to these things during the Egyptian captivity and that a sudden

---

[30] *GP* 2.40, 382.
[31] *GP* 2.28, 335–6; 2.29, 344–5; 3.32, 529.

transition from paganism to strict monotheism would have confused them.[32] Recognizing this, God commanded them to construct a luxurious sanctuary and adorn a high priest to preside over it. The difference is that whereas the divinely ordained sanctuary contained things that attracted the people's attention, it did not contain images that would tempt the people to return to idolatry.

To take another example, Maimonides argues that festivals where people come together to rejoice are indispensable for human beings and useful for establishing friendship, a necessary feature for people living in a social context.[33] In regard to the festival of Sukkot, he points out that the plants used in the ceremony are beautiful to look at and pleasant to smell, possibly a veiled reference to the fruit of Genesis 3:6, which was responsible for the fall.

A more telling example still is repentance. No one ever wrote more elegantly or insightfully on the need for repentance than Maimonides did in Book One of the *Mishneh Torah*. By the time he gets to the *Guide* (3.37, 540), however, he admits that our acts of repentance have no effect on God. The justification for repentance is its social utility: to keep people from falling into despair. As Maimonides recognizes, a person cannot help but sin or fall into error – either through ignorance or because he is overcome by desire or anger.[34] If human nature remains the same during the days of the Messiah, this will still be true. So confessions, sacrifices, and fasts will still be needed to allow people to feel they have a chance to start over.

We can infer that even in the days of the Messiah, spectacle and ritual will serve a purpose: People will still need to gather for sacred assemblies, to mourn the dead, and to call upon God in times of distress. No amount of study or reflection will change this. And there will still be occasions for confessing sin and seeking repentance. All this is a way of saying that Maimonides did not conceive of the days of the Messiah as a time when people will shed their earthly nature and become angelic. That will occur only when they pass from this world to the next. The general thrust of Maimonides' position is therefore that the days of the Messiah and the World to Come are

---

[32] *GP* 3.32, 525–6.

[33] *GP* 3.43, 570.

[34] In view of *GP* 3.11, it is not clear whether Maimonides considered the two explanations for sin given here to really be true.

separate. In the first, human nature remains as it is, and natural laws continue to apply; it is only in the second that neither is any longer the case.

We saw that during the days of the Messiah, there will still be rich and poor, strong and weak. If so, there will still be a need to respond to social problems and ask ourselves whether we have done everything to root out injustice. Taking the next step, we may conclude that there will still be wills to adjudicate, marriages and divorces, legal disputes, and questions about how to allocate limited resources. On a personal level, there will still be what Hamlet referred to as the thousand natural shocks that flesh is heir to.

What there will not be is constant preparation for war. From a biblical perspective, kingship was not originally the preferred form of government because, in a sense, God was supposed to be the king. When the idea of kingship was first broached, it was seen as a rejection of God (1 Samuel 8:1–22). The primary argument in favor of kingship was military: The people need a king to organize themselves for war. So when Maimonides says that the Messiah will make peace, he is saying the Messiah will be a king who negates the reason kingship was established. As James Diamond argues, we will come to a point when kingship "has weaned itself out of existence" because there will be no military problems to solve.[35] Yet there will be social and personal problems to solve. This is another way of saying that even if humanity were to redeem itself, there would still be a need for political and spiritual authority. Although the state may serve different functions from what it now does, on Maimonides' view, it will not wither away.

What does it mean for humanity to redeem itself? Human behavior in this life does not have to achieve a level of absolute perfection in which all forms of error or frailty evaporate; all it has to do is conform to, and eventually see the wisdom in, a Law that was formulated with the limitations of human nature clearly in mind. In fact, even this may be too strong. If, as Kellner argues, Maimonides believed that non-Jews like Aristotle have a place in the world to come based on the level of their intellectual achievement, conforming to the Law

---

[35] Diamond, "Maimonides On Kingship: The Ethics of Imperial Humility," *Journal of Religious Ethics* 34:1 (2006): 113–14.

may not be necessary for everyone.[36] In other words, it is not true that everyone will have to embrace Judaism. Although Maimonides does say (*MT* 14, Kings and Wars, 12.1) that all of humanity will return to (or accept) the true religion, it is unclear whether this means Judaism in particular or monotheism in general. Whatever the case may be, the general tenor of Maimonides' view is in keeping with the first part of Deuteronomy 30:11: "Surely this commandment which I am commanding you today is not too difficult for you."

We saw that Paul denies this. If the only path to salvation were through Law, the human situation would be tragic. But Maimonides is not Paul. Although human nature may make it difficult to fulfill the Law, difficulty is not the same as impossibility. When error occurs, there are procedures for setting things right. As far as Maimonides is

---

[36] Kellner, *Maimonides on Judaism and the Jewish People*, 72, and *Maimonides' Confrontation*, 239, n. 63, 242. Kellner's position is based on the passage from *Perek Helek* in which Maimonides claims that in the world to come, the righteous will sit with crowns on their heads enjoying the radiance of God's presence. If, as Maimonides goes on to say, "with crowns on their heads" refers to the acquisition of philosophic knowledge, there is no reason to suppose that entry into the world to come will be limited to Jews. Against this, there is the famous passage in *MT* 14, Kings and Wars, 8.11, in which Maimonides says (on one rendering) that if a gentile observes the seven Noachide commandments as a result of a reasoned argument and not because God commanded them to Moses, he is not a resident alien (*ger toshav*), or one of the pious gentiles, or (*velo*) one of their wise men. This rendering has long been disputed and is often replaced by the claim that such a person is not a resident alien or one of the pious gentiles, but (*ela*) one of their wise men. For discussion of the controversy surrounding the passage and an interpretation that brings it into line with the universal tenor of Maimonides' philosophy, see Eugene Korn, "Gentiles, the World to Come, and Judaism: The Odyssey of a Rabbinic Text," *Modern Judaism* 14 (1994): 265–87. In a nutshell, Korn follows Rav Kook by arguing that the point of the passage is that *wise gentile* constitutes a higher category than *pious gentile* and that Maimonides does not exclude either from the world to come. Cf. Joel Kraemer, "Maimonides' Messianic Posture," in *Studies in Medieval Jewish History and Literature*, Vol. 2, 140–1, who supports the *ela* reading, but still concludes that a gentile who does not accept the commandments on the basis of revelation may be a sage but has no share in the world to come. In a more recent study, Haim Kreisel, "Maimonides on Divine Religion," in *Maimonides after 800 Years: Essays on Maimonides and His Influence*, 151–66, argues that although there is no systematic way in which Maimonides could exclude someone like Aristotle from the world to come, given the historical situation in which he wrote – one in which Judaism had lost ground to both Christianity and Islam and faced the danger of having people convert – Maimonides had to emphasize the inherent superiority of Judaism over other religions. If, for example, a person could share in the world to come based on philosophic speculation alone, why should a Jew who is philosophically gifted obey all the commandments?

concerned, if Israel were to regain its sovereignty and the Temple were rebuilt, there would be nothing in principle to prevent the Law from being fulfilled in its entirety. This is another way of saying that for Maimonides, the standard used to measure human action, although divine in origin, is decidedly human in conception.

IMITATIO DEI: A BRIEF FORAY INTO METAPHYSICS

If the standard used to measure human action is human in conception, we face the question of how to reconcile that belief with Maimonides' understanding of the principle of *imitatio Dei*. Maimonides was well aware there is ample precedent for the principle in both biblical and rabbinic literature.[37] Many of the standard prayers would make no sense without it. There is even a precedent for it in Aristotle.[38] The problem is how to make sense of this principle if the vast majority of the commandments of the Torah deal with conditions specific to human beings. How, for example, can God serve as a model for laws governing sacrifice, festivals, diet, sexual relations, or repentance?[39] The problem is complicated by Maimonides' negative theology, which holds there is absolutely no resemblance in any respect between God and the created order.[40] Thus any words used of both God and us are purely equivocal. If there is no resemblance in any respect between God and us, what is one to make of the commandment to imitate God?

We can begin with the treatise on "Character Traits" in the *Mishneh Torah*, where Maimonides argues that Deuteronomy 28:9 ("You shall walk in His ways …") should be understood as commanding us to pursue a mean between behavioral extremes.[41] Although the doctrine derives from Aristotle, Maimonides does not hesitate to say that it is implied by the sacred literature of Judaism, which, in his opinion, forbids extreme or excessive behavior. It follows that as God

---

[37] Leviticus 11:44; Deuteronomy 6:6; 28:9; *Sotah* 14a; *Shabbat* 133b; *Sifre Deuteronomy*, 85a.

[38] Aristotle, *Nicomachean Ethics*, 10.7–8.

[39] Cf. Aristotle, *Nicomachean Ethics*, 1178b11–12: "Will not the gods seem ridiculous if they have to make contracts and return deposits?"

[40] *GP* 1.35, 80.

[41] *MT* 1, Character Traits, 1.5.

is called gracious, we should be gracious; as God is called merciful, we should be merciful; as God is called holy, we should be holy; and so on.[42] Putting negative theology aside for the moment, this passage raises the question of how and under what circumstances God acts. If, as Maimonides emphasizes earlier in the *Mishneh Torah* (1, Basic Principles, 11) and in greater detail in the *Guide of the Perplexed*, God is timeless, unchanging, and radically simple; there is no sense in which God can have emotions, moral dispositions, or other qualities that would normally be associated with gracious or merciful behavior.[43]

Maimonides' most rigorous treatment of this issue occurs at *Guide* 1.54 and is based on his interpretation of Exodus 33. In that passage, Moses is alone with God on the mountain and turns to him, saying, "Show me your glory." God replies by saying that no mortal can see the face of God and live, but he offers Moses a consolation by saying that if he stands behind a rock, God will cause all of his goodness to pass by. Maimonides identifies the goodness on display with that mentioned at Genesis 1.31: "And God saw everything that he had made, and, behold, it was very good." I take this to mean that everything God made has a reason to be and exists in harmony with everything else. It follows that although Moses could not know God directly by knowing his essence, he was able to know God indirectly by directing his attention to the *ways and works* of God. It follows that, strictly speaking, the subject of the predicate "good" is not God himself but the range of things God has made or done. Maimonides refers to such predicates – in effect everything Moses was allowed to see – as *attributes of action* (note the use of the plural).

Viewed from a global perspective, nature is a well-designed system in which each species is given the means necessary to protect itself and obtain food. Thus it is well known that nature does nothing that is frivolous or in vain. So interpreted, the principle of *imitatio Dei* claims that we should imitate God's attributes of action rather than God himself. For example, nature is structured so that the embryos of living things are protected from destruction. As a result, God is called

---

[42] The reference is likely to *Sifre Ekev*, 11:22. Note the precise nature of Maimonides' formulation: God *is called* gracious, not God *is* gracious. More on this point later.

[43] *GP* 1.1.35.

merciful. Because a father who shows pity or compassion to his child is called the same thing, a good father should strive to embody these qualities. Maimonides elaborates (*Guide* 1.54): "The meaning here is not that He possesses moral qualities, but that He performs actions resembling the actions that in us proceed from moral qualities – I mean from aptitudes of the soul; the meaning is not that He ... possesses aptitudes of the soul." Even this is misleading if we take *actions* to mean that God makes day-to-day decisions about the governance of the world. Instead, what we are supposed to see is that God's unchanging activity creates and sustains an order in which one can detect gracious or merciful features in the overall design.

Owing to human linguistic practice, when gracious or merciful features proceed *from* God, the predicates "gracious" or "merciful" are applied *to* God, hence the descriptions found in prayers and hymns. Here, as in the *Mishneh Torah*, Maimonides strives for greater rigor by avoiding the claim that God *is* merciful or gracious, saying instead that God is *called* merciful or gracious. The difference is significant. To say that God *is* merciful would imply that God has a merciful disposition or has developed the habit of acting mercifully over a period of time. This way of speaking is clearly anthropomorphic and sins against negative theology. Because God has no material component, it is impossible for God to have dispositions or affections.[44] By limiting ourselves to what God is called, we make no claim about God himself and direct our attention to how we characterize God.

There is no question that the sacred literature of Judaism encourages us to view God as a judge who listens to pleas of mercy and grants clemency. Maimonides' point is that however useful this language may be in encouraging people to repent, strictly speaking, it cannot be true. In fact, the denial of habits and dispositions in God leads Maimonides to conclude that if a person really wants to imitate God, she should act in a completely dispassionate way. According to *Guide* 1.54, "It behooves the governor of a city, if he is a prophet, to acquire similarity to these attributes, so that these actions may proceed from him according to a determined measure and according to the deserts of the people who are affected by them and not merely because of his following a passion." If a judge is going to grant mercy, the reason should not be

---

[44] *Guide* 1.35.

that she has developed merciful feelings toward the criminal, but that the criminal on his own deserves merciful treatment.

By the end of the *Guide* 3.54, Maimonides goes further. Human perfection consists in apprehension of God to the degree that is possible, as well as knowledge of God's providence as it extends over creatures and is manifested in the acts of creation and governance. After achieving this apprehension, Maimonides continues, such a person will always have in view loving-kindness, righteousness, and sound judgment.[45] Again, we must give up the idea that God governs the universe in the way a mayor governs a city. Yet even if we do, problems remain. How does one go from the apprehension of metaphysical perfection in a timeless being to acts of loving-kindness in a temporal one? The question is not new, and much has been written on it. A helpful suggestion in the recent literature is that after viewing the cosmos in its totality, Moses was able to "translate" his vision into the laws of the Torah.[46] I take this to mean that although there is no way to deduce the laws of the Torah from a global vision of nature, it is still possible to describe those laws as an expression of or response to it.

Consider an analogy. It is not for nothing that Gothic cathedrals are designed to look as if they are reaching up to the sky and that laboratories or research centers are designed to have a sleek, uncluttered look. In each case, architecture creates a kind of environment, and environments can have an impact on how people act. There is no logical inference that can take one from knowledge of how things are to knowledge of how they ought to be, but there is likewise nothing that says a metaphysical vision cannot *inspire* a moral outlook.

[45] This passage has led to considerable discussion on whether Maimonides rescinded his intellectualism at the end of the *Guide* by saying that the person who apprehends God will assimilate moral qualities. In fact, all he says is that *after* one apprehends God, one will apprehend God's governance of the created order. The apprehension of God is negative: knowing that we cannot know. Still, Maimonides has said nothing to imply that apprehension of God is not the highest human perfection. I will have more to say on this point later. For further understanding of the issues involved, see David Shatz, "Maimonides' Moral Theory," in *The Cambridge Companion to Maimonides*, 167–92.

[46] Lawrence Kaplan, "Maimonides and Soloveitchik on the Knowledge and Imitation of God," in *Moses Maimonides (1138–1204): His Religious, Scientific, and Philosophical Wirkungsgeschichte in Different Cultural Contexts*, 491–523. Also see Howard Kreisel, *Maimonides' Political Thought*, 15.

Having seen the ordered world that God created, a world that avoids excesses and deficiencies, Moses was inspired to propose a body of law that emphasizes orderly behavior, purity of purpose, and control of the emotions. Put otherwise, if God acts for a purpose and does nothing that is frivolous or in vain, it makes sense to say that we should act in a similar way. Note, however, that by adhering to the laws of the Torah, we are not imitating God as much as the features of God's governance. In this way, our imitation of God is never simple or direct. If Maimonides is right, the person who succeeds in such imitation will have no desire to act in a selfish, arrogant, or unforgiving manner. He will insist on fairness above all else and see to it that the various parts of his realm live together in harmony. The result will be that just as God is called merciful or gracious, he will be called the same thing.

It follows that the extent to which we can imitate God is highly attenuated. In the words of Alan Mittleman, "It makes eminent sense for Aquinas to describe God as virtuous while it makes no sense – indeed, it is the height of blasphemy – for Maimonides."[47] We can continue to speak of divine mercy or graciousness as standards of behavior provided we do not draw unwarranted conclusions from them. Between God as he is in himself and the consequences or effects that proceed from God, there is no similarity. One is simple, the other complex; one necessary, the other contingent; one the *creator*, the other *creation*. It is only the latter to which we can assimilate our behavior. Although Maimonides often speaks of getting close to God, we must keep in mind that "closeness" in this context involves a measure of irony: we are close to God to the degree that we recognize the unbridgeable nature of the gap that separates us. Accordingly (*GP* 1.59, p. 138),

[A] man sometimes has to labor for many years in order to understand some science and to gain true knowledge of its premises so that he should have certainty with regard to this science, whereas the only conclusion from this science in its entirety consists in our negating with reference to God some notion of which it has been learnt by demonstration that it cannot possibly be ascribed to God.

This is the highest level of contemplation we can have. Although the knowledge it gives us is negative, Maimonides is adamant that it still

---

[47] Cf. Mittleman, *Hope*, p. 50, n. 27.

counts as knowledge. Once it is achieved, we can proceed from God to God's governance of the created order; but in so doing, we run the risk of speaking in anthropomorphic terms and spreading confusion. In the end, the correct way to understand our situation is that we are enjoined to cultivate mercy and graciousness not because God has cultivated them, but because God has blessed us with a world in which signs of mercy and graciousness are clearly visible.

We may conclude that although Maimonides' worldview is obviously God centered, there is no standard of comparison to which both God and humans are subject, and therefore nothing that requires human beings to answer to a divine level of perfection. It is otherwise for Christianity, which holds that at a particular moment in history, God entered the human sphere, felt emotion, and resisted the lure of sin. In this context, one can use a divine standard to measure human behavior and avoid the metaphysical problems to which Maimonides calls attention. Yet there is no question that Maimonides himself thought that these problems are unavoidable. The result is that human beings are asked to live up to the standard appropriate for their species: the standards set forth in the laws of the Torah. The fact that God has revealed them means only that they are based on a correct assessment of what the human species can or cannot accomplish. To the degree that Akiba can be taken as an exemplary member of the species, an important part of that standard involves observing limits and staying within them.

MESSIANISM AND MYTHOLOGY REVISITED

To return to the Messiah, Maimonides is not in the business of giving odds or predicting how political forces will play out. Like Plato, who argued in the *Republic* (499b) that a philosopher-king is not impossible, all Maimonides can do is show that a Messiah, who is conceived along the lines of a philosopher-king, is not impossible either. No cataclysm is necessary to bring him, no change in human nature, no new revelation from above. Simply put, we have everything we need – except, of course, the motivation to act.

Does this mean that Maimonides thought that a Messiah would actually arrive? There is nothing in his writing to indicate that he did not. That belief in the coming of a Messiah cannot be demonstrated is beyond question. Maimonides' argument in favor of it is therefore textual: It is implied by certain passages in the Torah.[48] Beyond that, he would most likely fall back on considerations similar to those that motivated Kant: Hope for a better future is justified on the basis of its social utility because without such hope we would wallow in despair. As with Maimonides' views on prophecy and providence, the absence of a demonstration does not imply the absence of commitment. It follows that if human beings have not perfected themselves, if after centuries of pursuing false or imaginary goals, mankind still devotes its energies to the acquisition of wealth and power, the reason is not that God is waiting to send the Messiah but that we have not come to our senses.[49] To the degree we have not put ourselves on the right path, there is little that a Messiah can do to help.

This takes us back to the *ought* implies *can* principle. If we ought to hope for a messianic age – and not only hope for one but work for it as well – then a messianic age must be possible. If we ought to obey the Law whose fulfillment will bring that age, it must also be possible for the Law to be fulfilled. As Maimonides sees it, fulfillment of the Law and dissemination of its wisdom are the only things that will put an end to the current miseries.

Not only is there no room for divine intervention in this picture, but there is no room for a force analogous to Hegel's "cunning of reason" (*List der Vernunft*) either.[50] The closest Maimonides comes to the latter is the passage from the *Mishneh Torah* in which he suggests that Jesus and Mohammed can be seen as helping to spread the truth of monotheism and thus to prepare the way for a world devoted to study and worship. Although it offers an enlightened view of religious pluralism, this passage leaves entirely open the question of whether humanity will actually come to that point.

To some people, Maimonides' added rigor has taken away whatever appeal the idea of the Messiah was supposed to have. Surely, it could

---

[48] See Chapter 1, n. 1.

[49] Cf. Kellner, *Maimonides on the "Decline of the Generations" and the Nature of Rabbinic Authority*, 70: "[T]he Messiah will come when humans have *brought* him, not when God *sends* him."

[50] *RH*, 43–4. For a different view, see Amos Funkenstein, "Maimonides' Political Theory and Realistic Messianism," *Miscellanea Mediaevalia* 11 (1977): 92–3. For an extended rejection of Funkenstein's position, see Hartman, *Crisis and Leadership*, 202–3.

be said, the whole point of that idea is that God will not let human fortunes descend to the point where life is completely unbearable. If the only means the Messiah has at his disposal are natural, then, for all intents and purposes, he is powerless to confront the overwhelming forces aligned against him. That Maimonides understood this objection is evident from the degree to which he himself gives in to it in the "Epistle to Yemen."[51]

The fact is, however, that for all its appeal, the idea of a Messiah possessing supernatural powers is nothing but a return to mythology. In the world of mythology, the line separating the divine from the human is thin. Humans become gods, and gods become human. Some humans are endowed with supernatural powers, and gods intervene in human affairs to ensure they get their way. Maimonides opposed this picture so vehemently he ran the risk of being called an atheist. In fact, he *was* called an atheist by rabbis in Southern France, and would still be regarded as one in some circles today if his doctrines were presented as clearly as he formulated them. In his view, however, the consequences of hoping for a Messiah who makes rivers flow with wine or single-handedly rids the world of evil are so awful they must be avoided no matter what the cost.

[51] See n. 3.

3

Internalism: The Messiah Within

In the previous chapter, we saw that Maimonides distinguishes between personal salvation, which is achieved through the acquisition of knowledge, and the coming of the Messiah, which is a political event that takes place on the grand stage of world history. Internalism seeks to undermine this distinction by claiming that the latter is an allegory for understating the former. If there are upheavals or transformations, they are to be understood as events in the life of a particular person. There is a clear precedent for this in Jewish tradition. According to *Pirkei Avot* (4.1), strength is not something connected with battlefields but is the ability to control one's evil impulses; wealth is not something one deposits in a bank but is being satisfied with one's lot. From a philosophic perspective, the appeal of internalism is that it allows one to demythologize the idea of the Messiah and thus avoid having to answer questions like who? when? or how?

Scholem argues that internalism was the essence of the Hasidic response to the failure of Sabbateanism.[1] Unlike Bar Kochba, Sabbatai Zevi's messianism did not express itself in military terms. However, it did involve millions of people and led to heightened expectations about the coming of a new age. Unfortunately, the enthusiasm was short-lived. Faced with the choice of martyrdom or conversion to Islam, Sabbatai chose the latter. Although some of his followers justified his decision on the grounds that the Messiah has to descend to the netherworld before

[1] *MIJ*, 176–202.

he can complete his mission, the vast majority became disenchanted. This raised the question of how so many people could be taken in so quickly by a man who was emotionally unstable and whose teachings contained a strong antinomian strain. Suffice it to say that more than 1,500 years of exile, oppression, and expulsion coupled with daily prayers asking God to send a redeemer constitute a sufficient explanation for what was by any estimation a national disgrace.

Scholem's argument is that although early Hasidim continued to say the usual prayers and repeat the usual formulas, their focus turned inward. Instead of redemption *from* exile, the goal became redemption *in* exile, by which they meant the sanctification of the individual soul culminating in *devekut*, or union (adhesion), with God.[2] This at least was within human capability; although they did not deny that redemption could occur on a grand scale, events of this kind are in the hands of God.

Yet there is more to internalism than dissatisfaction with the failure of Sabbateanism. Levinas finds a similar move expressed as early as the Talmud.[3] The key passage is from *Sanhedrin* 98a, which Levinas renders as follows: "R. Nahman said: If he [the Messiah] is of those living [today], it might be one like himself, as it is written, *And their nobles shall be of themselves, and their governors shall proceed from the midst of them* (Jeremiah 30:21). Rav said: If he is of the living, it would be our holy Master; if of the dead, it would have been Daniel the most desirable man." Levinas reasons that the Messiah should not be identified in terms of his relation to us but in terms of his own essence. The Messiah is the one who suffers. This follows from *Sanhedrin* 98b, where the idea that the Messiah carries leprosy is proved with reference to Isaiah 53:4: "Surely he has borne our griefs, and carried our sorrows: yet we esteemed him a leper, smitten by God." From the identification of the Messiah with the one who suffers, Levinas concludes that each age has its own Messiah. Thus secular history is no longer relevant. The Messiah might be me. In connection with the citation from Jeremiah, Israel will no longer be governed by a foreign king. Levinas takes this to mean that the Messiah is "the absolute interiority of government."

[2] *MIJ*, 195.
[3] *DF*, 87–90.

The ultimate exemplar of interiority is the self (*Moi*), from which it follows that "The Messiah is Myself [*Moi*]; to be Myself is to be the Messiah." What does it mean to be myself? The answer is to accept moral responsibility and take on oneself the suffering of everyone. In this way, the Messiah is not a king who sits on a throne or overthrows foreign rulers in the manner of Bar Kochba. Nor is it someone who ushers in a new ideology. It is simply the one who comes to the realization of what it is to be a human being. Edith Wyschogrod draws a parallel between Levinas's messianism and Luke 17:20–1: "The kingdom of God is not coming with things that can be observed; nor will they say: 'Look, here it is!' or 'There it is!' For in fact, the kingdom of God is among [within] you."[4]

Internalism, then, is more than a Jewish obsession. It tells us that the real drama of history is not played out on battlefields but within the human soul. Rather than an apocalypse, what is needed is an inner transformation. Along these lines, Plato argued that true learning is not a matter of taking in another person's opinions, but rather the recollection of what the soul once knew but forgot. Paul looked into his soul and was honest enough to admit he saw something he did not like. In the history of thought, Augustine, Anselm, Descartes, Leibniz, and Kant all espoused some form of this doctrine. So too did Maimonides if one emphasizes *Guide* 3.51, in which he talks about contemplating God in solitude. Plato is, of course, the father of the internalist school, and I will have more to say about him in the next chapter. For present purposes, however, the central figure for this discussion is Kant. Recall that it was Kant who made the question "What can I hope for?" a central theme of his philosophy.

HOPE AS A MORAL IDEAL

We can begin our consideration of Kant by returning to the redemptive force of belief in a better future. To argue that hope is a moral ideal is to distinguish it from wishful thinking. We saw that Kant's

---

[4] Edith Wyschogrod, *Emmanuel Levinas: The Problem of Ethical Metaphysics*, 205–6. It is not clear whether the text from Luke should be read as meaning "among" or "within." Also see Martin Kavka, *Jewish Messianism*, 197: "Messiah will here be the metaphor of subjectivity itself, the drawing of the boundaries of the self."

claim about hope for better times amounts to more than the observation that if I approach the future with optimism, my fortunes are likely to improve. It is rather that hope for better times will make us more likely to work for the improvement of the common good. His strategy is therefore to transform the concept of hope from a feeling involving luck or fortune that can blind people to the true nature of things to a concern for the welfare of humanity. Hope, then, is a way of helping us fulfill our obligations. Beyond that, it has no philosophic significance.

To take this a step further, hope is normally directed to something whose prospects are neither assured nor impossible. Under normal circumstances, it makes no sense to hope that the sun will rise in the east tomorrow or to hope that someone will square the circle. Hope then is limited to things that could happen but may not. Because no finite agent can know how history will turn out, a hopeful attitude is one of trust in or expectation of a desirable outcome. But not any desirable outcome will do. There is nothing praiseworthy about hoping for a World Series victory or a winning lottery ticket.[5] Not only must all of humanity benefit, but also, more importantly, the outcome must be one that furthers the interests of morality.

However necessary, these restrictions raise a serious question. How do we know whether our trust or expectation has been fulfilled? Kant argues at some length that although we can hope that the human condition will improve over time, we will never be in a position to know that it has.[6] This means that historical evidence alone is never decisive. Sometimes it appears that the human situation is getting better, sometimes that it is getting worse, sometimes that it is going along in the same old way. In Book Two of *Jerusalem*, Mendelssohn argued that although individuals may make progress, the human race as a whole exhibits "no steady progress in its development that brings it ever closer to perfection."[7] In truth, no one is in a position to assess all of history and say which view is right. However, Kant replies, unless it can be shown with certainty that human behavior is getting worse,

---

[5] Note, as Alan Mittleman does in *Hope in a Democratic Age*, 32–3, that in this sense, hope is morally neutral. To use his example, if the Allies hoped for victory in World War II, the Axis Powers hoped for it just as passionately.

[6] See Immanuel Kant, *The Conflict of the Faculties*, 141–71.

[7] Mendelssohn, *Jerusalem*, 97.

from a practical point of view, we have a duty to assume that progress is possible.[8]

Indeed, once we look at history from a global perspective and introduce a distinction between the conscious intentions of the protagonists and the historical consequences of the their actions – what Hegel referred to as "the cunning of reason" – it becomes difficult to say which actions advance the cause of human progress and which do not. Joseph's brothers committed evil by selling him into slavery, but as he himself comes to see (Genesis 45:5), the ultimate effect of this action was to save life[9] – so too, one might argue, the destruction of the Second Temple, the conviction of Albert Dreyfus, or the Japanese bombing of Pearl Harbor. Even if we were to take a single moment in history and ask whether things were moving in a positive direction, to answer with certainty, one would have to look into the souls of the actors and assess the purity of their motives, an impossible feat for anyone but God.

Kant responds with the following argument. Morality demands that we work to promote the highest good, a condition in which happiness, understood as the satisfaction of desire, is proportioned to desert – where all those worthy of happiness receive it to the degree that they merit. Because we cannot know for certain whether our efforts to promote the highest good are succeeding, or, for that matter, whether they even have a chance to succeed, morality requires that we adopt beliefs that theoretical reason alone cannot establish: that the world was created by a benevolent God and that the moral quality of the human condition is improving. It is not that theoretical reason is currently deficient and may improve over time, but that in principle it cannot validate these claims and any attempt to do so would be deficient and serve the cause of skepticism.

Kant's claim therefore is limited: There are good grounds for *regarding* human history as proceeding on an upward path, or we should view it *as if* the human condition were improving. What are these grounds? Unless we believe moral improvement is possible, we would not be motivated to work toward it. Even this may be too weak. We must believe not only that the highest good is possible in principle

---

[8] Kant, "Theory and Practice," *PP*, 309 (86).
[9] Here I am indebted to Aviezer Ravitzky, *Messianism, Zionism, and Jewish Religious Radicalism*, 112.

but also that our efforts to achieve it have some likelihood of success. According to Kant (R 6:5), although the question "What is to result from this right conduct of ours?" is not, strictly speaking, the concern of morality, neither can it be viewed as a matter of indifference. His point is this: The obligation to act morally is unconditional. We are obliged to obey the moral law even if we are convinced our actions will not change anything. The fact is, however, that such a conviction would have a devastating effect on human behavior. It follows that belief in historical progress, though it may not be justified on theoretical grounds, is justified on moral ones.

No discussion of Kant's practical philosophy would be complete without the oft-repeated claim that *ought* implies *can*. Unless something is within our power to do, we cannot be obliged to do it. He therefore concludes that morality asks us to take a positive perspective on human history even though we can never be certain that that perspective is right. Does this amount to wishful thinking? Kant would answer that it does not, but to see why, we have to take a further step. If I am not in a position to know whether the human condition is improving, how can I know it is possible for it to improve? The simple answer is that the possibility of improvement presupposes the existence of a benevolent creator.

Briefly stated, Kant's argument for a benevolent creator goes as follows. The highest good is a condition in which virtue is accompanied by happiness. As he understands it (C2 5:110), virtue is the supreme (*supremum*) good in the sense that it is unconditioned and thus subordinate to nothing. Thus virtue is never pursued for the sake of something else. Yet it does not follow that virtue is the perfect (*perfectissimum*) good in the sense that nothing greater than virtue can be imagined. Kant's claim is that we can imagine a greater good than virtue alone: namely, a condition in which virtue is joined with happiness. Again, this does not mean that virtue is pursued *for the sake of* happiness – that would imply hedonism – only that virtue *together with* happiness is preferable to virtue *simpliciter*.

This conclusion follows from the fact that human beings have a dual nature: In addition to the rational side, there is also a material side that seeks the satisfaction of desire. Although critics often object that Kant ignores the material side of our existence and denigrates the desire for happiness, this is not true. He is clear that although happiness cannot provide the motive of our actions, it is unrealistic to expect human beings to give it up altogether. Thus "man is not expected to *renounce* his natural end, happiness, when the issue of obeying his duty arises; for he cannot do that, no more than any finite rational being in general can."[10]

Contrary to the way he is often portrayed, Kant is not a Stoic. Accordingly, he argues that a situation in which a person who is worthy of happiness does not receive it is morally repugnant and that no rational person can be satisfied with it. Simply put, this amounts to the claim that no rational person can be satisfied with the prospect of innocent suffering. If so, we are obliged to see that it does not happen.[11] This means we are obliged to look beyond our own happiness and promote the happiness of people – wherever they may be – whose moral character makes them worthy of it.

The importance of the highest good for Kant cannot be exaggerated. It is discussed in all three *Critiques* as well as *Religion*. In the first place, it allows him to say that moral life is not a series of unrelated obligations but a system that culminates in a single end, the unification of virtue and happiness or freedom and nature. In his words (*R* 6:5), "It cannot be a matter of indifference to morality, therefore, whether it does or does not fashion for itself the concept of an ultimate end for all things ... for only in this way can an objective practical reality be given to the combination, with which we simply cannot do without, of the purposiveness [deriving] from freedom and the purposiveness in nature."

In the second place, the idea of a highest good forces us to rethink the duties we face as moral agents. As Yirmiyahu Yovel expresses it,

---

[10] Kant, "Theory and Practice," *PP*, 278.

[11] Not everyone is convinced that Kant succeeds in showing we have a duty to pursue the highest good. Hermann Cohen certainly was not. See *Kants Begründung der Ethik*, 352–3. In modern times, see Nicholas White Beck, *A Commentary on Kant's Critique of Practical Reason*, 244–5. For an opposing view, see John Silber, "Kant's Conception of the Highest Good as Immanent and Transcendent," *Philosophical Review* 68 (1959): 469–92. For recent discussions sympathetic to Kant's attempt to establish such a duty, see Yirmiyahu Yovel, *Kant and the Philosophy of History*, 29–80, and Beiser, "Moral Faith and the Highest Good," in *The Cambridge Companion to Kant and Modern Philosophy*, 588–629. I am in basic agreement with Beiser's claim, 616: "What Kant is looking for is not rewards for moral intentions and actions, but the motivation to persist in moral action at all."

the goal is not just to make myself good but to make the world good as well.[12] Not only must I answer the dictates of my own reason, but I must also help create an environment in which all people worthy of happiness are able to live satisfying lives. As we will see, this requires a change in outlook from private to public, from what it is right for me to do to how I can join with others to bring about the perfection of the human race.

The only way happiness can be apportioned *according to* desert is if the world is so constituted that happiness is compatible *with* desert. To put it another way, we cannot be obliged to make the world a better place unless it is capable of being made better. Because no finite agent has the power to guarantee the convergence of nature with freedom, the only way to account for its possibility is to assume that the world was fashioned by an all-powerful being acting on the basis of noble motives.

A few words of caution are in order. Here too Kant insists that certainty is denied us. Because no proof of the existence of God is valid, we will never be in a position to know that the all-powerful being required by morality actually exists. For Kant, dogmatism on such matters is neither possible nor desirable.[13] This does not mean that we are justified in adopting a personal relation with God á la Kierkegaard. Rather, it means that if we limit ourselves to what can be known for certain, we cannot accept the assumptions on which moral action is based. An atheist could accept the idea of the highest good. But if Kant is right (C3 5:452), all he will see around him are natural phenomena completely indifferent to the demands of morality: want, disease, and untimely death. Based on what he sees, the atheist would have no reason to think his efforts to promote the highest good would make any contribution to realizing it and so would lack sufficient motivation to act. Without God, then, the idea of the highest good would be empty, and striving for it a practical impossibility.[14]

We may conclude that the issue is not one of predicting the outcome of historical events on the basis of empirical generalizations. Even if human history up to this point has been a disaster, postulating the

---

[12] Yirmiyahu Yovel, *Kant and the Philosophy of History*, 74.

[13] According to C2 5:125, there cannot be a *duty* to assume the existence of a thing, for this concerns theoretical as opposed to practical reason.

[14] C2 5:143.

existence of a benevolent creator offers some hope that the future can and will be different. As we saw, historical evidence alone is never decisive. All it tells us is what is – or has been – the case. By postulating the existence of a benevolent creator, we are given a way to bridge *is* with *ought* and to hope that for all its atrocities, human history is moving toward a morally acceptable end.

ETHICS AS SELF-SANCTIFICATION

That brings us to the internalist dimension of Kant's thought. According to the *Groundwork*, the moral worth of an action does not depend on the object realized by the action but merely on the principle of volition by which it is undertaken. Because the principle of volition by which an action is undertaken cannot be seen, and no one can plumb the depths of his own incentives, we can never be certain that our motivation for doing something is pure. Kant insists, however, that the question for ethics is not whether this or that action was undertaken for the right reason but whether reason itself independently of all experience commands that human action *ought* to be undertaken for the right reason. In short, ethical imperatives are valid a priori. Even if all the evidence around us indicates that people are inherently selfish, it would still be true that reason demands that we act for the sake of principle.

In *Religion* (R 6:159), he draws a connection between this view and the teachings of the gospel. Citing Matthew 5:20–48, Kant claims that Jesus taught that it is not the observance of outer civil or statutory duties that makes one pleasing to God but "the pure moral disposition of the heart." He follows this up with a citation of Matthew 5:48 ("Be perfect, therefore, as your heavenly Father is perfect"), which he takes to mean that, in general, holiness is the goal toward which everyone should strive.[15]

We can understand this better by turning to the *Critique of Practical Reason* (5:122), where Kant defines holiness as "complete conformity of the will to the moral law." In this way, we are asked to purify ourselves to the point where we obey the command of reason without any taint of selfishness. Returning to *Religion* (R 6:65), Kant writes, "The Law says: 'Be ye holy [in the conduct of your lives] even

---

[15] Cf. *The Metaphysics of Morals*, 240/446.

as your Father in Heaven is holy.' This is the ideal of the Son of God which is set up before us as our model." In the next chapter, we will see that Kant is convinced that no one can attain such an ideal in this life. However, he assures us, we will be judged not on the basis of what we do but on whether we have a firm disposition to improve ourselves. In effect, God will credit us for what we were trying to be rather than for what we actually are. Because dispositions are not observable, only God can tell whether the effort to improve ourselves is really sincere.

Not surprisingly, Cohen (*RR*, 205) expresses complete agreement with Kant's internalist posture. Although he is best known for stressing the need for correlation between people and between humans and God, all this stems from a need to reflect on one's own spiritual progress. In regard to prayer, he writes (*RR*, 272), "For all spiritual, for all moral action, the mind needs to withdraw into itself; it needs the concentration of all its inner forces and Prospects. As the solitude of the soul becomes a necessity in opposition to the whirl of sense impressions, so the soul psychologically is in need of withdrawal into itself, into its most inner depth, if it is to rise to the dialogue with the godhead." It follows that the fundamental task of human life is the need to become holy – or, as Cohen puts it on the basis of Leviticus 11:44, to sanctify oneself.

Although both thinkers refer to the idea that the law of morality is written on the heart, Cohen's familiarity with Jewish sources is much deeper than Kant's with Christian sources.[16] He therefore argues that Deuteronomy 30:11–14 ("the Law is not in heaven but in your mouth and in your heart") indicates the "internalization" of revelation into the spirit of man. He puts it thus (*RH*, 101): "The teaching is not in heaven but in man's mouth, in his faculty of speech and in his heart, and therefore also in his mind. It did not come to man from without; it originated with him. It is rooted in his spirit which God … has put into man as the holy spirit, the spirit of holiness."

This does not mean that morality is "man-made" as we usually use that term. Cohen's point is that God imbued man with the moral law by a kind of internal revelation – just as it might be said that God "planted" a priori knowledge in our minds. We do not have to consult

---

[16] *R* 6:181; *RR*, 81.

anything external to ourselves to recognize the validity of the moral law any more than we have to consult something external to recognize the validity of the laws of logic.

The question is whether we will live up to the demands morality places on us. This takes us back to the process of self-sanctification, which Cohen (*RR*, 205) identifies with repentance. Morality speaks to us not as an external voice but as the voice of our own heart. Yet we know that we fall short of it. The process of turning ourselves around and trying to do better is what it means to seek sanctification. Although only we can sanctify ourselves, Cohen (*RR*, 209) insists that "*The forgiveness of sins becomes the special and most appropriate function of God's goodness.*" From his perspective, all of this is what reason itself requires. Reason, in other words, puts before us the task of self-sanctification and the idea of a God who looks into the heart and forgives sin. Without this, the human propensity to sin would present an insurmountable obstacle to moral progress.

Enter messianism. One of Kant's great achievements in the *Critique of Pure Reason* was to show that by its very nature, reason seeks the unconditioned. It is the function of reason to unify and thus bring to completion the knowledge gained by understanding. Accordingly, reason assumes that if the conditioned is given, the whole series of conditions, which culminates in the unconditioned, is given as well. We can see this in the cosmological argument for God's existence. If *A* is caused by *B*, and *B* by *C*, reason assumes that a cause for the entire series must be found, which is to say an unconditioned cause for God. According to Kant, this is no accident but an "unavoidable" fact that gives rise to a "natural and inevitable illusion": the tendency to confuse the subjective necessity of our ideas with an objective necessity descriptive of things in themselves (*C1* A297/B353). From the fact that reason posits the unconditioned, it does not follow that we are required to believe in it.

Although the unconditioned cannot serve as a legitimate object of knowledge, it can serve as a goal of action. By that I mean that reason in its practical capacity not only can but also does establish moral ends that we are obliged to pursue. For Cohen, this means that reason is messianic, pointing in the direction of an ideal that is yet to be fulfilled. This is another way of saying that by its very nature, reason is not satisfied with the world as it is. Like the prophets, it sees much in the world that is wrong and offers a conception of something better. It is reason, for example, that gives us the idea of a perfect democracy in contrast to the give and take that go on every day at city hall. Moreover, it is reason that tells us that we do not have to be satisfied with the give and take at city hall, but that we should strive for something better. From Cohen's perspective, the same is true of the self. Citing Ezekiel 18:31 ("Cast away from you all your transgressions ... and get yourself a new heart and a new spirit"), he concludes (*RR*, 194) that reason demands that we turn away from sin. In doing so, it gives each of us the possibility to become master of ourselves – that is, autonomous agents.

Although most people would say that messianism is founded on hope, Cohen's claim is stronger: It is founded on the nature of what it is to be rational. His argument is this: Monotheism upholds belief in a unique God. From the idea of the unique God comes the belief that all people have a common source in God. From this it follows that all human life is sacred in the eyes of God, so that all people must be treated with respect. The duty to treat all people with respect is both the origin of the idea of humanity and the ideal toward which it strives. "In monotheism," Cohen (*RR*, 119) tells us, "lies the origin of the history of man." Again from Cohen (*RR*, 255, 293), messianism is the "straightforward consequence" of monotheism, its "summit," and its "purest fruit."

This means that messianic hope cannot be tied to a particular person who appears in the course of history to redeem or restore sovereignty to a particular people. To limit it in that way would be to take it out of the realm of rational necessity and put it back into that of mythology. Rather than a person who walks the earth, the Messiah refers to the moral perfection of the human race, which is to say the human race insofar as it has managed to sanctify itself.

Although Cohen does not go so far as to say that the Messiah is Myself (i.e., my ideal self), broadly speaking he and Levinas are not far apart. Both reject the idea of a historical person who comes to fulfill the prophetic visions. Both insist that messianism requires a transformation, or, to use Levinas's term, a *twisting back* on oneself. More importantly, both reject the identification of the Messiah with happiness or triumphalism. Following Isaiah's suffering servant vision, both thinkers argue that the Messiah bears the suffering of humanity on himself. For Cohen, suffering is the essence of humanity.[17] Thus (*RR*, 266) "The ideal man suffers. The Messiah is seized by the distress of mankind in its entirety."

The ideal person therefore sets out to relieve suffering by making the world worthy of God's goodness. Again, the ideal person is not a historical figure but the ideal toward which all of humanity are supposed to strive. It is by taking the suffering of others on ourselves that we become our *true* selves. Behind this conclusion is the conviction, shared by both thinkers, that the "other" person, whoever that might be, is defined by his poverty and vulnerability. Citing Isaiah 58:7 ("When you see the naked, cover him, and do not hide yourself from your own kin"), Cohen concludes (*RR*, 147), "the poor man is your own flesh."

Although a long way from Bar Kochba or Sabbatai Zevi, Cohen's position is not a long way from Jesus – as Kant understood him. Kant had no interest in the historical details of Jesus' life or in the fine points of Christology. For him, the notion that Jesus descended from heaven in a supernatural fashion is of no practical relevance, because all that matters are the moral qualities he exemplifies (*R* 6:61): "the idea of a human being willing not only to execute in person all human duties, and at the same time to spread goodness about him as far wide as possible through teaching and example, but also, though tempted by the greatest temptation, to take upon himself all sufferings, up to the most ignominious death, for the good of the world and even for his enemies."[18] Rather than the authority of the Gospels, it is practical reason – something found in ourselves – that commands us to emulate the example Jesus set.[19] We can therefore agree with Denis Savage, that just as Adam is not a specific person for Kant but a symbol of the fall from innocence that each of us experiences in choosing to act, Jesus is not so much a specific person as a symbol of moral perfection.[20] This

---

[17] *RR*, 146.

[18] The significance of Jesus' ability to overcome temptation rather than be free of it will be discussed in the next chapter.

[19] See *G* 4:408: "Even the Holy One of the gospel must first be compared with our ideal of moral perfection before he is recognized as such." Cf. Cohen, *RR*, 78: "[T]he tendency of revelation is to detach its meaning from the *fact* on Sinai and base it rather on the *content*."

[20] Denis Savage, "Kant's Rejection of Divine Revelation and His Theory of Radical Evil," *Kant's Philosophy of Religion Reconsidered*, 73.

explains Kant's invocation (R 6:42) of Horace's adage: "Change but the name, of you the tale is told."

THE TRUTH OF INTERNALISM

The usual way of accounting for Kant's view and Cohen's elaboration of it is to say that it is an outgrowth of Lutheranism.[21] For Luther, religion stands or falls on the moral purity of the individual worshipper. Perhaps this is what led Scholem to reflect thus[22]:

> Judaism, in all its forms and manifestations, has always maintained a concept of redemption as an event which takes place publicly, on the stage of history and within the community. It is an occurrence which takes place in the visible world and which cannot be conceived apart from such a visible appearance. In contrast, Christianity conceives of redemption as an event in the spiritual and unseen realm, an event which is reflected in the soul, in the private world of each individual, and which reflects an inner transformation which need not correspond to anything outside.

Historically speaking, there is much to recommend this.

Whatever it may have accomplished spiritually, the ministry of Jesus did little to change the political circumstances in which first-century Jews found themselves. Roman imperialism was still a fact of life, and by the year 70, the Temple was in ruins. How could this happen if the Messiah had already come? It is hardly surprising, then, that for Jews, messianism meant a return to national sovereignty. For Christians, politics is not the issue. As Jesus says (Mark 12:17), "Render unto Caesar what is Caesar's and unto God what is God's." If the revolt against Rome failed, it is because Jews have put their trust in the wrong things and once again have incurred the wrath of God.

---

[21] Kant clearly thought that Protestantism represented the high point of historical religion. See R 121–3. For the classic study of Kant's relation to Luther, see Heinrich Ostertag, "Luther and Kant," *Neue Kirchliche Zeitschrift* 36 (1925): 765–807. For a more recent study, see Bernard Wand, "Religious Concepts and Moral Theory: Luther and Kant," *Journal of the History of Philosophy* 9 (1971): 329–48. For Cohen's dependence on Protestant theology, see David N. Myers, "Hermann Cohen and the Quest for Protestant Judaism," *Leo Baeck Institute Year Book* 46 (2001): 195–214, and more fully *Resisting History* (Princeton: Princeton University Press, 2003), chap. 2. Note, in particular, Cohen's claim (p. 60) that Maimonides was "the standard-bearer of Protestantism in medieval Judaism."

[22] *MIJ*, 1. Also see Klausner, *The Messianic Idea*, 10–11, 519–31, for the same sentiment.

Moreover, it is important to remember that for many Jews, poverty, oppression, and religious intolerance were seen as symptoms of something more fundamental: exile. To this way of thinking, redemption implies first and foremost the return of sovereignty. We can see this in Maimonides. The Messiah will restore the Davidic dynasty, thus allowing Jews to earn a living, live in peace, and return to the ways of the Torah. The return of sovereignty is by definition a political, and therefore public, event. To be sure, political sovereignty will enable people to devote their time to study and worship, which will result in perfection of the soul. However, as he conceives it, the political aspect of redemption is a necessary condition for everything else.

Yet Scholem's generalization overlooks two points. Whereas some Jews in late antiquity looked forward to a Messiah who would throw off the yoke of Roman oppression, others – for example the Essenes – stressed spiritual purity and awaited an internal redemption. Moreover, Scholem overlooks the extent to which later Jewish and Christian thinkers either borrowed from one another or came to similar conclusions by independent routes. As we will see, both Cohen and Rosenzweig conceived of redemption as apolitical.

In addition to visions of apocalypse, one of the dangers of messianism is its tendency to become a personality cult. What will the Messiah say? What will he look like? From what family will he derive? How will he make himself known to us? All such questions encourage useless speculation and direct attention away from the central issue: What does belief in a Messiah demand of us? We can therefore appreciate Levinas's conviction that "[o]ne has failed to say anything about the Messiah if one represents him as a person who comes to put a miraculous end to the violence in the world, the injustice and contradictions which destroy humanity but have their source in the nature of humanity, and simply in Nature."[23]

Along similar lines, Maimonides argued that the specifics of the Messiah's activity – for example, whether he will be preceded by Elijah – are beyond human comprehension so that thinking about them does nothing to promote the fear or love of God.[24] We saw that Kant's

---

[23] *DF*, p. 59.
[24] *MT* 14, Kings and Wars, 12.2. Note, however, that Maimonides continues to refer to the Messiah as a descendent of David. Cf. Lenn Goodman, *On Justice*, 166: "[A] cult of personal messiahship never did succeed among Israelites.... Messianism

view of the historical Jesus follows the same path: The Messiah is important for what he teaches, not who he is.

Yet the truth of the Messiah's teaching can never be the whole story. One of the central themes of this book is that no matter how true it might be, no moral teaching can be indifferent to its realization. Moses taught a set of valid moral rules at Sinai; we saw, however, that he did not succeed in bringing about reconciliation between God and Israel. From a philosophic perspective, even if we agree that ethical imperatives are valid a priori, there is still the question of whether people will be motivated to follow them.

The strength of the internalist position is that the arrival of a Messiah would be pointless unless it is accompanied or preceded by a moral transformation in the hearts of the people who receive him. In the words of Ezekiel (11:19), the heart of stone must be replaced by a heart of flesh. Understood negatively, this means, as Lenn Goodman points out, that the Messiah is not a deus ex machina, and that the messianic era will not arrive simply with the passage of time.[25] Understood positively, it means that human effort is all-important. If only God looks into the heart, only we can produce a lasting change in what he finds. To put this another way, neither God nor the Messiah can bring about redemption single-handedly. As we saw in the story of the Exodus, redemption presupposes a change of heart. It is in this context that one can understand the rabbinic belief that repentance brings the Messiah.[26]

How does one affect such a change? Goodman argues that laws, rituals, and educational opportunities go only so far:[27] "[T]he most real and lasting changes come from within. Even the Torah, as a document, symbol, or ritual form, cannot substitute for moral change. The transformation of character is not equivalent with adherence to Law. Rather it is the practical aim toward which the whole Law drives." To obey the Law is one thing; to obey it with the right focus or intention is another. Yet even proper focus or intention may not be enough.

---

is a function, not a personality, and at bottom Jews always knew this." Although I agree with Goodman's view of how messianism ought to be understood, his assessment of what Jews always knew seems overly optimistic.

[25] *On Justice*, 172–81.

[26] *Sanhedrin* 98a.

[27] *On Justice*, 189.

Beyond the reach of any legal system are character traits like sympathy, compassion, humility, and gentleness toward others. The problem is, as Maimonides remarks at *Guide* 3.34, that by its very nature, law deals with general cases rather than specific circumstances. It can mandate forms of behavior that are likely to instill desirable traits in most people, but it cannot tell one exactly how to respond to the specific circumstances in which one finds oneself. For the latter, one needs to understand what the Law is aiming at and adopt it as one's own personal goal. So Goodman is right to say that the Law – at least divine law – *aims* at the transformation of character.[28]

Yet even this is not enough. It is one thing to aim at something, another to realize it. Obviously, one cannot solve this problem by adding another law to an already existing body of laws. Cohen tried to solve the problem by arguing that beyond the question of obedience is that of compassion, and that one would not feel compassion unless she is willing to suffer. Buber tried to solve it by looking for a moral transformation in the immediacy of the I-Thou encounter. Levinas looked for a moral transformation in the vulnerability of another person's face. Whatever way we think of it, moral transformation is not something that can be dialed up, by which I mean that there is no simple procedure for bringing it about. If there were, it would be not moral but mechanical.

Although it may be harder to affect a moral change than to move a mountain, the internalist argues that the impetus for moral change must come from within. In Kant's words (R 6:44), "The human being must make or have made *himself* into whatever he is or should become in a moral sense, good or evil." With this sentiment in mind, we can appreciate the realism of early Hasidism, at least as characterized by Scholem: Focus your attention on what you can accomplish and leave grand events to God. The meaning of saying that each person should regard herself as the Messiah is that each person must take it upon herself to do what is necessary to bring redemption. As we saw, each person has the Law written on her heart – not just as an array of dos and don'ts but as a teaching about how to sanctify life. If Kant is right, it makes no difference whether we think of this teaching as emanating

---

[28] The qualification *divine* law is necessary because it could be argued that secular law has no such aim.

from God or from practical reason. The point is that each of us has the potential to answer the call of morality. To that extent, each of us legislates not only for ourselves but also for humanity at large. In effect, each of us becomes a kind of Messiah.

According to one rabbinic legend, the Messiah will come if all Israel celebrates the Sabbath for two weeks running.[29] The legend is important not as an empirical prediction but as a way of dramatizing what is involved in seeking redemption. Because no natural law prevents this from happening, no violation of the order of nature is needed to realize it. Nor would one need superhuman effort: All that is asked is that one observe a day of rest. Still, one would be foolish to expect something like this to happen without massive preparation and a spiritual awakening of unprecedented proportions. In either case, the decision rests with us. As Goodman writes, "no charismatic figure can achieve this goal of history *for* us. Only homely inward self-transformation can accomplish it."[30] In short, there is a sharp divide between what is possible in principle and what is likely to happen in fact.

FROM THE PRIVATE TO THE PUBLIC SPHERE

For all of the truth it contains, internalism leaves two important questions unanswered. To understand the first, let us return to Scholem's claim that Judaism conceives of redemption as a public event and Christianity as a private one. The internalist tradition is right to say that any meaningful concept of redemption has to include some private, that is, inward, dimension. However, Scholem is right to say the traditional concept of redemption was not *exclusively* private. We can understand the difference by returning, however briefly, to Maimonides. We saw that it is possible for an individual to achieve perfection without the Messiah. The problem is that doing so requires time and resources that are not available to most people. On Maimonides' view, the Messiah will be a political figure who helps make the necessary time and resources available to everyone. There is an internal dimension

[29] *Shabbat* 118b. According to another legend (*Taanit* 64a), only one Sabbath is needed.
[30] *On Justice*, 183.

to Maimonides' messianism to the degree that nothing can substitute for the intellectual perfection needed to enter the world to come. Yet there is an obvious public dimension as well. The world will come to see the folly of war and devote itself to worship and study. Take away the public dimension, and you take away much of what we typically mean by *messianic*.

In modern terms, messianism typically involves a claim about the course of history. It is not just that this or that person will redeem himself but that humanity as a whole will redeem itself. According to rabbinic legend, the two are related. *If* Israel repents or celebrates the Sabbath two weeks running, *then* the Messiah will come. Likewise for Maimonides: *If* humanity comes to its senses, *then* a leader will emerge who makes peace and educates us about the important things in life. In short, internalism must either reject the public dimension of messianism or say more about how private and public are related.

The second unanswered question has to do with achievability. Questions of difficulty aside, can a person redeem herself in the way the internalists describe, or is redemption an infinite task whose goal can only be approached but not achieved? Kant, Cohen, and to some degree Levinas all come down on the side of infinity and thus all fall into the category of infinite deferral. Because infinite deferral is the subject of the next chapter, let us return to the relation between public and private.

We saw that for Kant, the moral history of the human race is measured by the idea of the highest good: a condition in which all those worthy of happiness receive it. This is clearly a greater good than my own personal salvation or a condition in which I alone receive the happiness I merit. As a moral agent, I am obliged to work for the happiness of people other than myself. Unless I do, I myself have not achieved all that I am capable of. It follows that the highest good, or what Kant calls the Kingdom of God, is clearly a public phenomenon.[31] Kant (*R* 6:97) is deeply skeptical that we can achieve

---

[31] *C2* 5:128; *R* 6:122, 151. On this issue, see Yovel, *Kant*, 31: "[T]o realize it [the highest good] now means to imprint the demands of the moral idea upon the whole range or totality of empirical environment, transforming the patterns of our psychological dispositions, our social and political institutions, as well as the surrounding physical and ecological systems – insofar as they relate to the sphere of human needs and moral interests." Note, however, that throughout his study, Yovel draws a sharp

it working as isolated individuals and compares this condition to living in a state of nature. In his view, like-minded people must band together to form a "system of well-disposed human beings, in which and through whose unity alone the highest moral good can come to pass." To be "well-disposed," a person must first make a concerted effort to improve her behavior.

However, even if everyone underwent such a transformation and like-minded people did join together to work toward moral ends, the highest good would still be out of reach unless there was some reason to think that our efforts to improve the human condition had some chance to succeed. In the words of Frederick Beiser, "The achievement of the highest good, therefore, does not depend on the will alone, but on factors well beyond its control, on nothing less than the structure of the cosmos and the course of history itself."[32]

That is where God comes in. Logically there is no connection between virtue and happiness (C2 5:124). One belongs to the realm of freedom, the other to the realm of nature. If the two are to be brought together, it can only be because some agent worked to unite them. This can happen only if the world has been fashioned so that they *can* be united, and the only one who can ensure this is God. It should be understood that Kant is not talking about divine intervention into human history. As he sees it (R 6:134), the mention of apocalypses in scripture are intended only for the purpose of "stimulating greater hope and courage." All God does is guarantee that there is no principle in nature that would cause it systematically to thwart our attempts to bring it into harmony with freedom. This is compatible with saying that the job of making the needed improvement, of reshaping nature in conformity with moral ends, belongs to us.

Unfortunately, Kant does not say much about what it would mean for nature to cooperate or not cooperate with our efforts at moral progress. From the standpoint of empirical science, nature is morally neutral. Even from the standpoint of morality, nature seems indifferent to who lives and who dies, who is stricken with grief, and who lives a happy and fulfilling life. It would have been helpful if Kant had given

---

contrast between Plato and Kant. In the next chapter, I will suggest there is an important sense in which Kant thought of himself as following in Plato's footsteps.

[32] Frederick Beiser, "Moral Faith," 598.

us a clearer picture of what it would be like for nature to thwart our efforts to bring it into harmony with freedom and of what it would be like for it to cooperate. Is it that nature is orderly, so that improved science allows us to harness it? Is it that the earth offers a hospitable climate? Or will nature itself make some sort of contribution to our efforts?

Whatever the case may be, Kant's position is subject to a critical ambiguity. Is he saying that God guarantees the *possibility* that the realm of nature can be brought into harmony with that of freedom – that the two are compatible – or that we have reason to think nature *will* be brought into harmony with freedom? The former says human history can be perfected, the latter that it will be. Again, Kant is not as clear as we might like. The *Second Critique* talks only of possibility. Nowhere does it say that the existence of God as a postulate of moral reason means that history can only move in one direction or that we can be certain that one day it will reach its desired end.

However, in his historical writings, and in certain passages in the *Third Critique*, he takes another direction. For example, in "Universal History," he speaks of a hidden plan of nature to bring about a perfect moral constitution.[33] In "Perpetual Peace," he is more explicit. Nature takes it upon itself to will (i.e., to work for) the same ends that practical reason establishes as a duty.[34] Thus war, acts of violence, and other self-seeking inclinations, although evil when taken by themselves, may serve a moral purpose to the degree that they cancel one another out and in so doing teach the virtues of civility and moderation. To take an obvious example, wars are costly. Recognizing this, a person intent on providing himself with material comforts may well conclude that peace is the better option. To use a familiar metaphor, it is as if an invisible hand is somehow pushing humanity past war and hatred to civility. Kant concludes that nature "irresistibly *wills* that right should finally triumph."

In the *Third Critique* (5:433), he argues that nature has been fashioned to "give us that education that opens the door to higher ends than it can itself afford." Again consider the atrocities of war. Awful as they are, Kant sees reason to hope that they will encourage people to

[33] Kant, "Universal History," in *PP* 27.
[34] Kant, "Perpetual Peace," in *PP* 364–8.

work toward a civil society in which human talents can direct themselves to the building of culture rather than its destruction. According to what commentators now call "the cunning of nature," we cannot fail to recognize that art and science will eventually prevail over rudeness and violence. Although art and science do not necessarily lead to morality, Kant derives some comfort from the fact that they make one civilized and thus prepare the day for a sovereignty in which reason alone will hold sway. This is Kant at his optimistic best. Aside from the fact that humanity seems not to have learned the lessons that Kant thought nature is trying to teach it, there is the question of whether Kant has any right to speak of nature this way. His entire position presupposes that God is the author of nature.

However, as Kant thinks he has shown, it is impossible to prove that God exists. All we can say is that there are moral grounds for believing that he does. The same is true of the claim that nature exhibits a moral teleology. As we saw, regarding it so gives us the motivation we need to fulfill our moral obligations. Whether this is true of nature in fact – independent of all human interests or concerns – is another question.

Accordingly, Kant begins his discussion of nature as a teleological system in the *Third Critique* (5:429) by pointing out that although there are grounds for a reflective judgment to this effect, there are no grounds for a determinant judgment.[35] This means that though viewing nature as a teleological system may be unavoidable from our standpoint, it does not give us the right to make an ontological claim. What is more, as Yovel points out, the most we can expect from the cunning of nature is a political system designed to keep hostile actions in check.[36] As we will see shortly, this system is very different from the ethical commonwealth Kant envisions, which, in his opinion, is necessary for the realization of the highest good. By establishing order, a political system serves the ends of enlightened self-interest. Because it serves moral ends, an ethical commonwealth can be established only by the free association of like-minded individuals, a process in which natural forces have no role to play.

---

[35] Reflective judgment moves from particulars in nature to universals. For the limitations of reflective judgment, see C3 5:185–6.
[36] Yovel, *Kant*, 173–5.

The problem of how to understand God's role in determining the course of human history is complicated by the fact that Kant's treatment of God is uneven. From a practical standpoint, he never doubts that God serves as a moral paradigm. Thus the only way we can please God is to improve the quality of our behavior. Beyond God's practical significance, Kant thinks God is completely mysterious. Although it is rational to believe that God will cooperate with us in the achievement of the highest good, the extent of God's cooperation, if any, is impossible to know. Kant argues thus (R 6:139):

And here there opens up before him [humanity] the abyss of a mystery regarding what God may do, whether *anything* at all is to be attributed to him and *what* this something might be in particular, whereas the only thing that a human being learns from a duty is what he himself must do to become worthy of that fulfillment, of which he has no cognition or at least no possibility of comprehension.

The upshot is that we are not in a position to know whether God does anything more than guarantee the possibility that the highest good can be realized. We can view nature as providing assistance but will never be in a position to say for sure whether it is an ally in the effort to perfect the human condition or merely a neutral bystander. By the same token, we can view God as an active partner in establishing his kingdom on earth but will never be in a position to know the extent of his involvement.

To sum up (R 6:101), "Each must, on the contrary, so conduct himself as if everything depended on him." This amounts to Kant's version of "focus your attention on what you can accomplish and leave grand events to God." The advice is true whether we think of our efforts privately, as an inner commitment to abide by the moral law, or publicly, as establishing a moral commonwealth of which all of humanity are citizens.

However we understand God's role, it is clear that internal transformation must express itself publicly for messianism to have any meaning. If the heart of stone is going to be replaced by a heart of flesh, each of us must abandon a self-centered view of the world and work toward the happiness of others. Kant writes (R 6:95), "Inasmuch as we can see, therefore, the dominion of the good principle is not otherwise attainable ... than through the setting up and the diffusion of a society in accordance with, and for the sake of, the laws of virtue – a society which reason makes it a duty of the entire human race to establish in its full scope." Although such a society can – indeed must – exist within a political commonwealth, in principle the two are distinct in that a political commonwealth is founded on coercion and seeks civil order, whereas an ethical commonwealth is founded on virtue alone.

The establishment of an ethical commonwealth takes us back to the central question raised by messianism: Will this be an act of God, an action undertaken by a historical figure, or a joint action undertaken by humanity as a whole? Unaccustomed to working out the details of messianic expectation, Kant is exceedingly vague. We are told that the establishment of an ethical commonwealth presupposes a higher moral being, namely God, but, again, it is unclear what role God is supposed to play. Unlike a political commonwealth, an ethical one cannot take its laws from the people but must take them from a being whose commands are at the same time ethical duties (R 6:99), "one who knows the heart." We must keep in mind, however, that according to Kant, and internalists in general, God's commands are written *on* the heart, so an ethical commonwealth would not qualify as a *theocracy* if that means that a king or priesthood enforces its will on an unenlightened population.

Running true to form, Kant affirms that although only God can found an ethical commonwealth, we must proceed as if everything depended on us. In effect, his ethical commonwealth is a church that stresses the need for moral action and does everything possible to eliminate statutory laws. As a rational ideal, its realization may lie outside of history and serve as a model against which historical churches can be measured.

One way to understand Cohen's messianism is as an attempt to fill in the ambiguities left by Kant. For Cohen, the ethical commonwealth that Kant speaks of already exists in the form of Israel – at least as understood by the prophets. Israel is distinguished from the rest of the nations not only because it is has no homeland, but also, most importantly, because it has given up any concern with its own self-interest and taken upon itself the moral improvement of the entire human race. True, Israel suffers; but in that suffering it becomes symbolic of the rest of humanity, whose essence, as we saw, is to suffer. As Cohen sees it (*RR*, 149), "Israel is in its history the prototype of suffering, a symbol of human suffering, of the human creature in general. God's love for Israel, no less than God's love for the poor, expresses God's love for the human race." As the suffering servant of the monotheistic God – the God who rules over all the earth – Israel is uniquely motivated to alleviate poverty and work for the betterment of the human race. For Cohen, this involves the establishment of a new political order founded on democratic socialism.[37] God remains a moral paradigm, as originally conceived by Kant, and enters history only to the extent that people seek his forgiveness or strive to emulate his perfection. In this way, the miraculous dimension of messianism has been completely eliminated along with any suggestion of a nationalistic resurgence.

THE INNER LIFE RECONSIDERED

Let us return to the internalist's view of moral life. Kant's whole project is to prevent that life from succumbing to despair. How much innocent suffering does a person have to witness before she decides to look after her own interests and abandon any hope of affecting the course of history? The sad part of Kant's response is that theoretical reason has no consolation to offer her. From a biblical perspective, it took Job many long chapters to realize this. Kant's answer is to say that God can do what neither theoretical reason nor ordinary human experience can: offer enough confidence to overcome despair. God can bridge the gap between virtue and happiness, even though we are at a loss to know how. To skeptical eyes, this is all too neat and makes it look as if we are calling God into existence to help us do what we cannot do on our own.

If Kant had followed Maimonides and Aquinas in thinking that God's existence could be demonstrated, this objection would have no force. God exists whether we are sanguine about our moral strivings or depressed. Note, however, that not only does Kant object to the validity of the standard proofs, but he also goes on to claim that even if they worked, they would not give us what we want. Briefly stated, they would give us a first cause for necessary being, but not a being

---

[37] For Cohen's socialism, see Schwarzchild, "The Democratic Socialism of Hermann Cohen," *Hebrew Union College Annual* 37 (1956): 417–38.

who helps bridge the gap between virtue and happiness.[38] Yet this too makes it seem as if we are writing a job description for God. In the next chapter, we will see that not only does Kant's God bridge the gap between virtue and happiness by offering the gift of grace, but he also bridges that between performance and accountability. This too is something it is reasonable to hope for. Although it is true that hope gives us the courage we need to face what often appears as a cold and morally indifferent world, we may well ask whether the hope Kant offers is too ad hoc to do what is expected of it.

We can begin to construct Kant's answer by recognizing that the question "What can I hope for?" is different from either "What can I know?" or "What should I do?"[39] "What can I know?" is a theoretical question, "What should I do?" a practical one. By contrast, "What can I hope for?" is both, because it combines a moral question, namely, "How can I be worthy of happiness?" with an empirical one, that is, "What things will make me happy?" Kant argues that the structure of the answer to the question "What can I hope for?" is essentially this: Something is because something ought to happen. What ought to happen can be determined by reason a priori. Yet the inference from what ought to happen to what is, although questionable under any circumstances, is all the more so when *what is* refers to a being whose nature is mysterious and who can never be given as an object of experience.

In the *Second Critique* (5:142–8), Kant argues that our assent to such a being arises from "a need of pure reason." Without such a being, the harmony of *is* with *ought*, of theoretical with practical reason, would be impossible, which means that reason would be subject to an irreducible bifurcation. As the faculty whose job it is to seek unity, reason would have to admit failure and face the prospect of incoherence. We have seen that from a personal standpoint, the result would be despair and with it, lack of motivation to act in a moral fashion. Such a result would undermine Kant's entire philosophic project. If the universe is such that moral action makes no sense, then from his perspective life is not worth living.

Kant expresses this by saying (*1CR*, A828/B856) that there is only one condition under which the end of obeying the moral law can

[38] *C1*, A816/B844 – A818/B846.
[39] *C1*, A805/835 – A806/B834.

connect with all other ends, namely, that God exists and that there is a future life. He continues,

Since, therefore, the moral precept is at the same time my maxim (reason prescribing that it should be so), I inevitably believe in the existence of God and in a future life, and I am certain that nothing can shake this belief, since my moral principles would thereby be themselves overthrown, and I cannot disclaim them without becoming abhorrent in my own eyes.

Kant's wording is significant: It is not that a logical absurdity would result, but that he would become abhorrent in his own eyes, making it impossible for him to live with himself. Kant's confidence in the existence of God finds an obvious parallel in Cohen, who argued (*RR*, 21) that against the confidence that morality will be established in the human world, "no skepticism, no pessimism, no mysticism, no metaphysics, no experience of the world, no knowledge of men, no tragedy, and no comedy can prevail."

Yet the foregoing objection can be reformulated. However satisfying it may be, confidence alone does not win arguments. Why should we assume that something exists merely because reason needs it to complete its work and we need it to make sense of our lives? To be sure, Kant is not talking about need in the sense in which a person might say she needs a two-week vacation. The need he has in mind is moral and systematic. A lesser thinker would have solved the problem in one of two ways. Either she would have said that theoretical reason *can* establish the existence of God, so that the unity of *is* with *out* is guaranteed, or she would have invoked a kind of faith that carries with it absolute conviction. To his credit, Kant will have nothing of either alternative. Reason cannot establish the existence of God without overstepping its boundaries. By the same token, to think that one can command belief in God as an article of faith is to succumb to dogmatism.

That leaves us with a faith – or better yet, a hope – that the universe has a rational structure and that moral striving is not for naught. To the objection that such a hope may be unfounded, Kant would answer yes. Not only would he answer this way, if my interpretation is right, but he would do so proudly and with conviction. We can imagine a philosopher who lamented the fact that God's existence cannot be demonstrated and searched high and low to find a demonstration that worked. Maimonides thought the creation of the world de

novo could not be demonstrated and went to great lengths to find a
deuteros plous.

The fact is, however, that Kant thinks reason's inability to demonstrate God's existence or to command it as an article of faith is something to celebrate, not despair over.[40] Simply put, Kant has staked his
entire philosophy on the contention that systematic unity and belief
in the efficacy of human action are things that have to be chosen, not
demonstrated. Rather than claims we accept because their opposites
are inconceivable, they are claims to which we have to commit ourselves. We *choose* to believe there is something to hope for, even though
the opposite is possible. As he puts it at the end of the *Second Critique*
(5:143), "I *will* that there be a God, that my existence in this world be
also an existence in a pure world of the understanding beyond natural
connections, and finally that my duration be endless; I stand by this ...
and I will not let this belief be taken from me." What Kant has shown
is that such a choice is not arbitrary. As he goes on to say in the passage just cited, it is the only case where interest determines judgment.
We entertain hope not to feel better about our personal situation but
to answer the call of morality. Such is the conclusion we arrive at if we
commit ourselves to religion *within the limits of reason alone*.

It is significant that religion within the limits of reason alone is
decidedly messianic. Although it is a long way from the Hebrew prophets to the author of the three *Critiques*, the idea that human thought
is future oriented and strives for moral perfection takes center stage in
each. In defense of this tradition, it is remarkable that for all its pitfalls
and excesses, the idea that history has a moral teleology runs deep in
the human psyche. It has survived centuries of exile and frustration,
including Bar Kochba, Sabbatai Zevi, and countless other pretenders –
even the horrors of Auschwitz. Without going into the historical basis
for this conviction, Kant came to the same conclusion. Moral teleology
runs deep not only in the human psyche but also in its highest forms of
reflection. For people in this tradition, to think is, in a sense, to hope –
or, as we have seen, to choose to hope. More than anything else, it is
this choice that is supposed to bring the Messiah.

---

[40] Here I follow Hilary Putnam, *The Many Faces of Realism*, 46–50.

4

Infinite Deferral

Recall that internalism left two questions unanswered: whether an internal transformation expresses itself publicly and whether redemption is an infinite task whose goal can only be approached but not achieved. I now turn to the second of those questions. If all we can do is approach a messianic age – if, as Schwarzchild put it, the Messiah not only has not come but also will never have come; rather he will always *be* coming – then he will never come in finite time. No matter how much progress humanity makes in creating the conditions necessary for his arrival, there will always be an infinite amount of progress yet to achieve. As we saw, this commits one to the view that the coming of the Messiah is not an event as much as the recognition that morality presents us with an infinite task.

Yet even if we keep this qualification in mind, the doctrine in question is a strange one. If nothing else, belief in the coming of the Messiah is supposed to provide hope. Thus Saadia argued that whatever punishment the Jewish people may have incurred, it cannot be endless, thus redemption must be on its way.[1] But if the Messiah will always *be* coming, then, to cite Schwarzchild at an early stage in his career (*PI*, 19), far from encouraging us about the prospects for success, infinite deferral would seem to provide a guarantee of relative failure. From a philosophic perspective, the problem with infinite deferral is that it conflicts with the *ought* implies *can* principle. On good Kantian

---

[1] Saadia, *Beliefs and Opinions*, 8.230–1, 291.

grounds, Cohen asserts (*RR*, 205) that God cannot assign a labor of Sisyphus. However, if redemption is impossible to achieve in finite time and can be reached only at infinity, is this not exactly what we get? Along these lines, Rosenzweig objected that what only comes at eternity does not come for all eternity.[2] Simply put: If the Messiah is not coming for all eternity, then he is not coming.

The obvious response is to say that although no finite agent can be obliged to achieve moral perfection, a finite agent can still be obliged to strive for it. In Kant's words (*MM*, 241), "It is man's duty to *strive* for this perfection, but not to *reach* it (in this life), and his compliance with this duty can, accordingly, consist only in continual progress." Similarly (*C2* 5:123), "For a rational but finite being only endless progress from lower to higher stages of moral perfection is possible."[3] What is true of individual agents is also true of humanity as a whole. It can strive for the Kingdom of God but not realize it by undertaking a finite series of steps.

The obvious advantage of this view is that it completely demythologizes our idea of the Messiah. If the Messiah will never actually walk the earth, then all questions asking how we will identify him, what he will do, or where he will reside become meaningless. In Kantian terms, the Messiah becomes an idea of reason, not an actual person. Yet the difficulty of infinite deferral remains: Not only are we obliged to work for a goal we cannot achieve – the Kingdom of God – but we are also told not to lose hope in the process. Is this credible? Before answering that question, it would be helpful to examine the assumptions on which the idea of infinite deferral rests.

FOOTNOTES TO PLATO

It was Plato who first made a principled distinction between an intelligible world of forms and an imperfect sensible world that strives to be like it but falls short.[4] To be sure, *strives to be like* is a metaphor.

---

[2] Franz Rosenzweig, *Briefe und Tagebücher*, Vol. 2, 1150. Cf. Ernst Bloch, *The Spirit of Utopia*, 178, who argues that Kant's view of the infinity of practical reason gives us an ocean without a shore, and then asks what comfort this offers for travelers if no arrival is possible.

[3] Cf. C2 5:32–3, 5:128; R, 6:67.

[4] *Phaedo* 74d–e.

Plato's point is not that equal sticks and stones make an effort to be like equality itself, the intelligible form, but that only by understanding equality itself can we understand how sticks and stones can be classified as equal, albeit in a deficient way. With one significant exception, Kant accepts this view of the world.[5] That exception is that Kant is talking about moral claims, not metaphysical. It is not that reason intuits a realm of separately existing things that it recognizes as archetypes, but that it posits ideal standards to which no empirical reality can ever be adequate (C_1, A313/B370):

> Plato made use of the expression "*idea*" in such a way as quite evidently to have meant by it something which not only can never be borrowed from the senses but far surpasses even the concepts of the understanding ... inasmuch as in experience nothing is ever to be met with that is coincident with it. For Plato ideas are archetypes of things themselves, and not, in the manner of the categories, merely keys to possible experiences.

The job of understanding Plato better than he understood himself consists in pointing out that the chief area in which Plato applied his theory was the practical realm. Abandoning any use of the theory in the speculative or theoretical realm, Kant argues that to derive our idea of virtue from experience would be to make it an "ambiguous monstrosity." That no one will ever act in a way that is adequate to our idea of virtue has no tendency to show that our idea of virtue is faulty. The reason for this is that our idea of virtue is not supposed to tell us how people actually behave but how reason of its own determines that they *ought* to behave.

So morality depends on reason's ability to formulate ideas, and, as Kant goes on to argue, so does our ability to approach the study of nature in a systematic way. Because ideas cannot be derived from experience, they have no constitutive role to play in the growth of knowledge; but they do have a regulative role to play: "directing the understanding towards a certain goal upon which the routes marked out by all its rules converge, as upon their point of intersection" (C_1, A644/B672).

---

[5] For a brief but insightful discussion of Kant's Platonism, see Paul W. Franks, "Jewish Philosophy after Kant: The Legacy of Salomon Maimon," in *The Cambridge Companion to Modern Jewish Philosophy*, 54–7.

In this way, reason directs the understanding not to think in terms of isolated laws or concepts but in terms of a unified whole. We have already seen that it is the job of reason to seek the unconditioned or absolute. If so, the ideas of reason always contain more than what experience is capable of providing. They are projections rather than generalizations. We saw that this is true with respect to God, an idea whose essence is shrouded in mystery but which reason finds absolutely indispensable. In a decisive passage (C_1, A663/B691), Kant claims that we follow such ideas "only as it were asymptotically, i.e. ever more closely without ever reaching them – they yet possess, as synthetic *a priori* propositions, objective but indeterminate validity."

Eventually the suggestion of an asymptotic approach to an unobtainable idea became more than an epistemological principle; it became a way of understanding the whole course of human history. For Kant, too, history is a story of fulfillment and salvation. It is in this sense that his thought qualifies as messianic. Reason does not just direct the understanding; it directs by establishing goals that contain more than experience can furnish. Yet rather than viewing the situation statically, as Plato did, Kant asks us to view it temporally. Religion has advanced from primitive forms to more advanced forms that stress the inner life and the freedom of the individual to transform it. Political history has marched, however slowly, toward the institution of a democratic republic founded on equal rights and equal protection for all citizens. Most important, humanity has begun to throw off the bonds of its self-incurred tutelage and to embrace the idea of enlightenment.

All this can be understood along the lines of humanity's approach to the ends practical reason sets for it. However, in keeping with Plato's bifurcation of the intelligible world from the sensual, it cannot be understood as actually achieving them. If achievement is infinitely far off, then the only way to make sense of historical progress is by invoking the analogy of an asymptote. As students of modern Jewish thought will recognize, this analogy became central for Cohen (*RR*, 255), who used it to explain the coming of the Messiah, which is to say perfect morality and the unity of all mankind.

Although Plato may have been the first to propose such a bifurcation, he is not the only source of Kant's view of moral progress. The other source is Christianity. As Beiser remarks, it cannot be stressed enough that Kant saw his ethics as Christian doctrine.[6] We will see that there are places where he seems to take Christianity in an unorthodox direction. One place where he is in agreement with that doctrine is that mankind exists in a fallen condition. Even someone with as little knowledge of Christianity as Maimonides would agree – except that he took *fallen* to mean that we cannot focus all of our attention on metaphysics and must busy ourselves with matters pertaining to right and wrong.

Needless to say, Kant would disagree. Given his view that moral responsibility rests squarely on the shoulders of individual moral agents, he cannot maintain that we inherit the sin of another person. I will have more to say about Kant's view of evil in the next section. For the present, the important point is that creatures in a fallen state cannot achieve holiness, which he defined as complete fitness of the will to the moral law.[7] As Kant sees it, there is always some element of self-interest in what we do and thus a moral deficiency. Because we are obliged to pursue holiness but cannot achieve it in this life, Kant concludes (C2 5:122) that we must have infinite time in another life to accomplish what morality demands of us.

Kant's great worry is that, knowing we cannot achieve holiness in this life, we will lower the standard of morality to suit our own needs. Doing so would fly in the face of his conviction that the demands of morality are established a priori and have nothing to do with human efforts to fulfill them. It follows that the only standards that are valid are those that issue from a "strict and inflexible command of reason" (C2 5:123). Kant argues that unlike Epicureanism and Stoicism, Christianity recognized this and proposed a law that is noteworthy for its purity and strictness (C2 5:127). Thus Christianity "destroyed man's confidence of being wholly adequate to it, at least in this life."[8] Like Paul in Romans 7:18 ("I can will what is right, but I cannot do it"), Kant puts us in a

---

[6] Beiser, "Moral Faith," 593.

[7] Although it is tempting to equate "holiness" with "the holy will," the two are different. The former refers to a completely pure intention; the latter refers to a will that is purely rational in the sense that it does not experience inclination and thus has no need of moral imperatives.

[8] This suggests, as Reinhold Niebuhr put it in *Moral Man*, 68, that "man is convicted, not any particular breaches against the life of the humanity community, but of being human and not divine."

position where the law, although valid, is always beyond our reach. The most we can achieve in this life is virtue, which Kant understands as "a law-abiding disposition resulting from respect for the law." However, he adds, virtue is needed precisely because we cannot rid ourselves of the propensity to transgress the law or defile it.

In return for destroying our confidence that we can fulfill the law, Kant's account of Christianity fosters the hope that if we do everything in our power, assistance will come from "another source" – namely God. We saw that if we develop a firm disposition to do our duty and rise above selfish motives, God will credit us as if we succeeded even though strictly speaking we did not (*R* 6:74–5). To the degree that we get more than what we have earned – or could earn – on our own, the gift of grace is incomprehensible although still rational in the sense that it offers hope that our inability to do what morality demands of us will not lead to despair. Note, however, that if this is true, our plight resembles that of Sisyphus, except that unlike him, we can hope for the grace of God to close the inevitable gap between disposition and deed.[9]

With this background in mind, Kant concludes (*C2*, 5:128) that all we can achieve on our own is "a self-esteem combined with humility." The mention of humility is important because it indicates how deeply Kant's ethical thought is infused with religious commitments. We saw that elsewhere in the *Second Critique* (e.g., 5:32–3, 5:122), he describes complete fitness of the will to the moral law as *holiness*. His choice of terms indicates that the standard against which we are being measured is divine. In *Religion* (6:66), he justifies his choice of terms by citing Matthew 5:48: "Be you holy, as your Father in Heaven is holy."[10] Once

---

[9] It is often said that Kant's view of grace is Pelagian in character because to the extent that we must make a concerted effort to develop a firm disposition to do our duty, it would seem that grace is earned rather than freely given. See, for example, Karl Barth, *Protestant Thought from Rousseau to Ritschl*, 187. A more recent version of the criticism can be found in Nicholas Wolterstorff, "Conundrums in Kant's Philosophy of Religion," in *Kant's Philosophy of Religion Reconsidered*, 40–53. For a defense of Kant, see Jacqueline Marina, "Kant on Grace: A Reply to His Critics," *Religious Studies* 33 (1997): 379–400. Note, however, how Marina's Kant begins to sound more Catholic than Protestant. I will argue later that the problem with Kant is not that he shows traces of Pelagianism, but that he is not Pelagian enough.

[10] The exact wording of the text is "Be perfect, therefore, as your Father in heaven is perfect." Cf. Leviticus 11:44.

we take this into account, it is clear why Kant wants to say that the standard is beyond our reach. Who would be so bold as to claim that her moral progress had taken her to the level where she had actually become holy? Surely the safe thing to say is that only a divine being can be holy in the true sense of the term.[11] To recognize this is to embody humility. To act out of respect for the moral law is to embody virtue. Anything beyond that takes us outside the realm of what human action can achieve. In Schwarzschild's words (*PI*, 223), "Divine norms are, by definition, infinite." If so, finite agents, even finite agents acting together, will never be able to satisfy them in finite time, so that perfection will always be infinitely far off.

THE SOURCES OF EVIL

What exactly does it mean to say that mankind exists in a fallen state? Or, to put the question differently, how do we know that a finite agent cannot fulfill the demands of the moral law in this life? Kant's answer is that there is in all of us a propensity (*Hang*) to subvert the moral law, or what he calls *a perversity of the heart* (*R* 6:30). A propensity is distinguished from a predisposition (*Anlage*) on the grounds that the former can be represented as acquired or as something we bring on ourselves. The perversity that we manifest is both radical, because it corrupts the ground of all maxims, and inextirpable by human power. The problem is that if it is going to be deemed evil, it must result from a free exercise of the will. This means it cannot be blamed on our sensuous nature, something over which we have no control. Nor can it be blamed on a corrupt feature of moral reason, because that would set reason against itself and thus deny its authority. If we act to subvert the moral law, the only acceptable explanation is that we have *chosen* to do so. In support of his view, Kant cites Paul from Romans 3:9–10 ("They are all under sin, there is none righteous [in the spirit of the law]"), which is taken from Psalm 14:1–3.

It is clear, then, that Kant accepts some version of the doctrine of original sin. Rather than saying that Adam's sin is passed on to us, he

---

[11] "Divine being" is ambiguous and raises the question of Kant's view of Jesus. I will argue later that whereas Kant's Jesus embodies holiness, insofar as he feels inclination, he is not the same as the holy will.

takes the claim "in Adam all have sinned" as indicating that Adam's sin represents a paradigm case of the decision all of us make to rebel against the demands of morality. As he puts it (R 6:41), "Every evil action must be so considered, whenever we seek its rational origin, as if the human being had fallen into it directly from the state of innocence," which is to say that "the action can and must always be judged as an *original* exercise of his power of choice." In effect, we all choose of our own free will to repeat Adam's mistake.

How does this happen? According to Kant, the reason is that as rational beings who are also subject to inclination, we are beset by two maxims: one to do as morality directs, the other to seek our own happiness. Of the two, only one can be primary. Evil thus results when we subordinate the first to the second (R 6:36). Yet this re-raises the question of why we do this. If we could choose to act from purely noble motives, making obedience to the moral law the supreme condition of our action, why do we always choose to make our primary maxim one that incorporates selfishness?

There are passages where Kant comes dangerously close to answering this question by falling back on the recalcitrance of matter, as when he asks (R 6:100), "How could one expect to construct something completely straight from such crooked wood?" Yet clearly this will not do. He cannot invoke a metaphysical principle to account for a moral failing, because this would mean the source of the problem is beyond our control and would exempt us from responsibility. The same applies to his claim (R 6:30) that even in the best of people, evil is somehow "woven" into human nature, which, if misinterpreted, would put the responsibility for evil on God's shoulders.

Eventually Kant responds by saying that the cause of evil is inscrutable (R 6:43). The only thing from which a propensity to evil could originate would be an evil maxim that serves as the ground of all other maxims. Yet this would only put the question off. Why do people repeatedly adopt such a maxim? Although it is perfectly natural for us to seek an explanation, Kant concludes thus: "[T]here is for us no conceivable ground from which the moral evil in us could originally have come." I take this to mean that although there is no possibility of a *systematic* explanation for the propensity to pervert the moral law, and nothing that can be derived from the concept *humanity* as such, there is no denying that all of humanity has such a propensity. As he puts it (*R* 6:30), the propensity to evil is universal and can be predicated of man as a species even though it cannot be inferred from the *concept* of his species. At bottom, evil exists because each of us of his own accord wills to do it.

To see this problem in another way, note that for Kant, freedom involves spontaneity. If I choose to do something freely, there can be no external force operating on my will. It follows that if each of us chooses evil of his own accord, it must be possible for us to choose goodness as well, a possibility that Kant readily grants (*R* 6:37). In view of this, we would expect some actions – perhaps the majority – to be evil but some not. In the words of Gordon Michalson, "discrete acts of human freedom undertaken by countless multitudes of moral agents provide no connecting thread that would account for this universality."[12] Kant insists, however, that the propensity to evil exists in man *by nature*. This does not mean we are endowed with an evil disposition in the way we are endowed with a liver, but that owing to our fallibility, we always choose to put our own interests above those of morality. If evil exists in man by nature, then to establish the Kingdom of God means that human nature will have to undergo a profound change. That is why the process requires infinite time to complete. When it is completed, we will no longer be human but will have taken on the character of the divine.

In large measure, Cohen agrees. Unable to cite the gospels as proof of his position, he turns to the Hebrew Bible. Although we are commanded to sanctify ourselves, it is nonetheless true that man "always feels himself to be innately infirm and defective" (*RR*, 211). In support of this, Cohen cites Psalm 51:7: "In sin did my mother conceive me." In the same way, human merit is always defective, as shown by Ecclesiastes 7:20 ("For there is not a righteous man on earth, who does good and sins not").

Like Kant, Cohen resists the suggestion that a predisposition to evil is somehow planted in our hearts (*RR*, 181–3). If sin is ubiquitous,

---

[12] Gordon Michalson, *Fallen Freedom: Kant on Radical Evil and Moral Regeneration*, 69. Cf. Philip L. Quinn, "Original Sin, Radical Evil and Moral Identity," *Faith and Philosophy* 7 (1984): 36: "But it seems very improbable that a propensity to moral evil should be both a product of freedom and universal among mankind."

it is because we have chosen to do it. The difference between Kant and Cohen is that Cohen could not go along with what he took to be the eudaimonism implied by Kant's conception of the highest good. Rather than providing a guarantee of the compatibility of virtue with happiness, Cohen's God is simply the ground and archetype of perfect virtue. Despite that difference, he agrees with Kant that God presents humanity with an infinite task.

The infinity of the task remains whether we conceive of it as personal or political. For the individual, it is a matter of self-sanctification. However, Cohen goes on to say that the idea of God must contain more than the forgiveness of humanity's sins; in particular it must contain the idea that God will bring about (*RR*, 293) "the complete disappearance of sin from the human race," because "the cessation of political and historical sin committed in wars and the cessation of the social injustice of pauperism clearly governs the hopes of the messianic prophet." Again, hope is critical. Cohen is in no position to say that history is moving in a moral direction. As with Kant, his point is that morality asks that we regard it as if it were so. We can assess the course of history by comparing it to our idea of its moral fulfillment, but that fulfillment is and will always remain an aspiration rather than an empirical observation. We will never actually *see* the cessation of political and historical sin, even though we are obliged to pursue it in everything we do.

Much the same is true of Levinas, except that for him, it is not God who assigns the infinite task but the face of the other person.[13] The other person is revealed to me as completely transcendent and outstrips any attempt I may make to comprehend him.[14] As Michael Morgan expresses it, the face of the other person presents itself to us "as an imperative entering *into* the *finite* from the outside."[15] The imperative calls my entire existence into question by assigning me a responsibility that is infinite. I owe more to the other person than he does to me or I do to myself. I can never do enough to fulfill this

---

[13] Levinas, "Ethics as First Philosophy," in *The Levinas Reader*, 82–4.

[14] I for one think Levinas has gone too far. No doubt, there is an imperatival force connected with the face of another person. But we are too good at knowing what the other person is thinking, how the other person is feeling, or what the other person is likely to do for him to be as other as Levinas insists.

[15] Michael Morgan, *Discovering Levinas*, 92–3.

responsibility and thus cannot avoid a feeling of shame.[16] Again, a standard has been set, and I cannot help but fall short of it.

What exactly does it mean to say that we feel ourselves to be innately defective? If it means that over the course of a human life, a person cannot help but do things he regrets or that others judge to be wrong, few would quarrel. We saw that Maimonides says as much in his treatment of repentance. The same is true if it means there are always ethical challenges to meet. Yet Kant's claim is stronger: Not only can no one lead a morally pure life all the time, but we can also never achieve complete fitness of the will to the moral law *in any action we take*. The qualification is clear from the *Second Critique* (5:122), in which Kant says that such fitness "is a perfection of which no rational being of the sensible world is capable at any moment of his existence." This remark is followed by a similar one in *Religion* (6:66), in which Kant says that the distance between the goodness we ought to do and the evil from which we start "is not exhaustible in any time."

Thus no action we can take will ever measure up to the demands morality puts on us. This is true even of the best of people (*R* 6:30). That is why morality presents us with an infinite task: No matter how hard we try to act for purely noble motives, putting the demands of morality ahead of our desire for happiness, the perversity of our heart prevents us from doing so. In the end, we all choose to subordinate the demands of morality to our own interests in pursuing happiness, which is to say that even if we do the right thing, we do not do it for purely moral motives.

This raises the question of how anyone can be in a position to know this if, as Kant admits, only God looks into the heart. His only alternative is to say while we cannot know this a priori, it is confirmed by the overwhelming weight of experience. Accordingly (*R* 6:33–4), "We can spare ourselves the formal proof that there must be such a corrupt propensity rooted in the human being, in view of the multitude of woeful examples that the experience of human *deeds* parades before us." Allen Wood takes this to mean that Kant's view of the evil

---

[16] Levinas, "Philosophy and the Idea of infinity," in *Collected Philosophical Papers*, 57–8. Cf. Cohen, *RR*, 316: "The merit of man must consist exclusively in the activity of his giving an account he can never balance."

is based on his anthropology.[17] It is not that we are born with a propensity to evil, but that as social beings who judge our own happiness or unhappiness in comparison with others, we cannot help but be exposed to greed, envy, and hostility.

This is what induces us to subordinate the demands of morality to the need to satisfy our own desires. The culprit, if one may call it that, is reason, insofar as it puts us into contact with potential rivals. In this capacity, reason creates desires for things that no one would want if humanity were left in its natural state. It is reason that introduces people to status, refined taste, outward signs of wealth, professional advancement, and other things that come with complex social organization. Unfortunately, to attain these things, one often has to gain an advantage over others – hence the emergence of envy and competition. On the other hand, it is reason that brings with it our sense of ourselves as beings who incur moral obligations.

Although Kant is right to say that experience puts countless instances of evil before our eyes, he still faces the problem of how to establish a religious doctrine on the basis of empirical evidence. In the essay "Theory and Practice," he himself claims that "the argument that something has until now been unsuccessful and therefore shall never be successful does not justify abandoning even a pragmatic or technical intention ... much less a morally obligatory one, unless, of course, its attainment is demonstrably impossible."[18] In particular, the existence of widespread evil in human history does not establish that the propensity to evil in the human species is universal.[19] As we saw, those who chose to act in an evil fashion could just as easily have chosen to act in a virtuous way. This would lead one to conclude that although evil may predominate, there are always likely to be significant exceptions. Even if evil were universal at this juncture, Kant would not have established that human effort is incapable of overcoming it. If we

---

[17] Wood, *Kant's Ethical Thought*, 287–90. See *R* 6:33–4.

[18] Kant, "Theory and Practice," in *PP*, 87.

[19] Cf. Michalson, *Fallen Freedom*, 67: "But of course there is utterly no way Kant, above all, could legitimately generate a claim about intrinsic features of human nature from even the lengthiest list of empirical examples." For a reply to Michalson (and by implication to me as well) based on Kant's moral rigorism, see Chris L. Firestone and Nathan Jacobs, *In Defense of Kant's Religion*, 134–41.

have freely chosen to bring evil on ourselves, why can we not also lift it from ourselves?

This question, which is perfectly fair given Kant's emphasis on individual freedom, was raised centuries earlier by Pelagius in an essay entitled "On the Possibility of not Sinning."[20] Pelagius begins with a strong statement of the *ought* implies *can* principle. Just as we would condemn a master who ordered his servant to complete in one day a journey that requires four, it would be unjust for God to issue commands that exceed human capabilities.

One way to avoid this conclusion is to follow Luther by challenging the *ought* implies *can* principle as it is normally interpreted. Against Erasmus, Luther argues that exhortations in the Bible like "Choose life!" say only what ought to be done, not what can be done.[21] In support of this claim, he points out that it is not uncommon for a parent to exhort or admonish a child by making a request that the child is not in a position to fulfill. Suppose, for example, a parent, upon hearing that a child had begun to read her first Platonic dialogue, were to say, "You should read Plato in the Greek." The remark would be meaningful even if the child did not read Greek and was unlikely ever to do so.

Yet it is clear that Kant cannot follow Luther, because his position is that divine commands are not just admonishments or exhortations but full-fledged obligations. Unlike an exhortation, an obligation involves a claim of necessity. As such, the possibility of the fulfillment of divine commands is implied by the very fact that practical reason – or God acting as the spokesperson for practical reason – commands them.

To continue with Pelagius, if, as some suppose, sin is unavoidable, we need to rethink what we mean by calling it *sin* at all. If sin results from free choice of the will, then it must be possible to obey God's commands or not. To argue that they cannot be obeyed is to say, in effect, that they are pointless. If they are pointless, no sin is involved in disobeying them. If they are just, then either obedience or disobedience

---

[20] *The Letters of Pelagius and His Followers*, 164–70. There is another string to Pelagius' bow: Told that sin is inevitable, habitual sinners will take comfort in their condition, believing that nothing else can be expected of them.

[21] Martin Luther, *The Bondage of the Will*, section 52. It is noteworthy that Maimonides (*MT* 1, Repentance, 5.4) takes the opposite view, arguing that the exhortation in the Bible would make no sense if God predisposed people to be righteous or wicked.

is possible, from which it follows that it is possible, albeit exceedingly difficult, for a human being to obey and thus rise above sin.

Consider a child who voluntarily offers her allowance to a homeless person on the street. As Kant tells us (R 6:48), even children are capable of detecting "the slightest taint of admixture of spurious incentives." There is no argument against the claim that even if the child acts on pure motives this time, making obedience to the moral law the sole motive for her action, she will have to strive to meet other obligations in the future – that is, the demands of morality are never ending. Thus Levinas compares ethical responsibility to insomnia in the sense that it has no termination and can never slumber.[22]

To use another metaphor, doing one's duty is not like winning a prize, or, to return to Sisyphus, like pushing a rock up a hill. There is no moment of finality and no cause for celebration. Still, the never-ending character of moral responsibility does not show that we are subject to a perversity of the heart in everything we do. To see this, let us assume for the moment that Kant is right: The child detects in herself a trace of self-interest when she gives her money and feels guilty about it. How can we ask her to strive for a higher level of purity if the propensity to evil in her is both radical and inextirpable by human power? She can, of course, ask to be forgiven for the impurity of her motives. Yet it will be a strange sort of apology, given that acting on impure motives is a universal phenomenon.

Kant has several answers he can give. The first is that when he says that that humanity is evil by nature, he is talking about the species as a whole, not individual members of it (R 6:25–6). Yet the species as a whole does not make moral decisions – only individuals do. If it is possible for an individual to act for morally pure motives, and more importantly, if such acts have in fact occurred, why should we conclude that the propensity to evil is universal?[23] Alternatively, why should we conclude that the human race is incapable of overcoming this propensity on its own power?

---

[22] *Face to Face with Levinas*, 30. Note that Levinas interprets the *eschaton* as the end of morality and thus as implying fusion with God. If I am right, Maimonides' view of the Messiah offers a powerful alternative.

[23] For an attempt to justify Kant's looking at the species *humanity* and attributing moral attributes to it, see Firestone and Jacobs, *In Defense*, 141–51.

The second answer is that the moral law *can* be fulfilled – at infinity. If fulfillment were never possible, Pelagius would be right. Recall, however, that Kant's position is only that the moral law cannot be fulfilled *in this life*. The third answer is that God will close the gap between disposition and deed if we make a concerted effort to turn ourselves around. On the basis of an intuition only he can have, God will see in us the person we were trying to be rather than the person we are. In this way, the disposition to act in a virtuous manner takes the place of the actual deed (R 6:74). However, it is important to remember that divine grace does not compensate for every failing. On the contrary, Kant insists (R 6:67) that it "makes up only for the deficiency which is in principle inseparable from the existence of a temporal being, [namely] never to be able to become quite fully what he has in mind." In effect, God will overlook the fact that we are only human if we make a real effort to be something more.

Fulfillment at infinity raises the question of how it is possible to make moral progress in a timeless realm, where considerations like motion and rest, or fast and slow, have no application.[24] On the second point, Henry Allison protests – as Pelagius would – that if we have done all that can reasonably be expected of us, no gap between disposition and deed remains to be closed.[25] Why seek repentance for a failing no amount of human effort can correct? This raises the central question of Kant's approach to morality. Is it fair to use a divine standard in evaluating the worth of human action?[26] Or, to put the question a different way, can reason command moral perfection if moral perfection can only be achieved by God? It is to that question that we now turn.

HOW CAN A FINITE BEING SERVE AN INFINITE GOD?

If divine norms are, by definition, infinite, Kant is right to say that the gap between what we do and what morality demands of us will also

---

[24] This criticism is made by Beck, *Commentary*, 270–1. For an attempt to make sense of Kant's view of the afterlife, see Wood, *Kant's Moral Religion*, 122–4.

[25] Henry E. Allison, *Kant's Theory of Freedom*, 175. Allison is here responding to an attempt by Allen Wood to defend Kant in *Kant's Moral Religion*, 236–48.

[26] This question, which is central to my argument, was suggested by Martin Kavka, *Jewish Messianism*, 123.

be infinite. The grounds for holding this view of divine norms are not hard to state. A monotheistic God is limited by nothing and therefore manifests infinite goodness. As the supreme archetype of goodness, God provides a standard for humans to emulate. Because the standard is perfect and we are fallible, the distance separating them cannot be traversed.

The appeal of this argument is so powerful that one can find traces of it not only in Kant but also in his arch rival, Kierkegaard. For Kierkegaard, God is infinite and incomprehensible. That is why if someone wants to demonstrate fealty to God, her actions must be infinite and incomprehensible as well. Anything less fails to understand the full extent of the challenge. For Kant, God is infinite *and* comprehensible – at least to the degree that he stands as the archetype of morality. Like Kierkegaard, however, Kant asserts that the challenge God puts before us is also infinite.

However great their differences, the views of both thinkers hearken back to the claim that the Law, although divine, is more than a finite being can hope to fulfill. Perhaps this should now be rephrased to say the Law, *because* divine, is more than a finite being can hope to fulfill. The original purpose of the Law (Exodus 19:6) was to create "a kingdom of priests and a holy nation." Does this mean it was supposed to create a nation whose holiness could approach that of God – even asymptotically? I think not.

We saw that in Maimonides' view, unlike that given to Abraham, the revelation given to Moses was intended specifically to take human fallibility into account. In addition to abstract principles about the existence and unity of God, it contained a priesthood, festivals, dietary laws, and other practices designed to appeal to a people who had forgotten monotheism and needed to learn it all over again. Not surprisingly, the Torah ends with what appears to be a strong statement of the *ought* implies *can* principle. The full text, which was referred to earlier, reads as follows (Deuteronomy 30:11–14):

What I am commanding you today is not too difficult for you or beyond your reach. It is not up in heaven, so that you have to ask: "Who will ascend into heaven to get it and proclaim it to us so we may obey it?" Nor is it beyond the sea, so that you have to ask: "Who will cross the sea to get it and proclaim it to us so we may obey it?" No, the word is very near you; it is in your mouth and in your heart so you may do it.

These words come from Moses' last oration and are generally regarded as the rhetorical climax of his prophecy. No doubt, they are thoroughly Pelagian in spirit.

Although Paul cites this passage at Romans 10:8, note two points: (1) He takes it to be talking about "the word of faith that we profess" rather than body of Jewish Law, and (2) he omits the phrase "so you may do it." Kant, too, seems to refer to the passage – or Paul's rendering of it – but takes it as a reference to the internalization of the moral law rather than a statement of the *ought* implies *can* principle.[27] Yet the sense of the passage is clear. As Goodman puts it, "The Torah does not require superhuman effort for comprehension or effectuation."[28] It is as if the Torah is saying that no metaphysical principle, no inherited transgression, no natural propensity stands in the way of our doing what God has asked – just effort. The same sentiment was expressed by Saadia, who argued that although the prospect of a person's fulfilling the Law may be low, it must be possible or else God would not have commanded it.[29]

Some have detected a reference to original sin in Psalm 51:5 ("I was born guilty, a sinner when my mother conceived me"), but the standard Jewish position on this matter is that stated at *Berachot* 60b and repeated by observant Jews every day: "My God, the soul which You have placed in me is pure. You have fashioned it in me, You breathed it into me, and You preserve it within me." From the standpoint of ritual, there is no ceremony in Judaism designed to cleanse one of the stain of original sin, because no such sin is recognized.

In defense of Paul and the idea of original sin, it may be said that if we look at Israel as a whole, there is no scriptural evidence that the Law was ever fulfilled. What kind of Law is it that has generation after generation falling short? Although the inference from "not fulfilled *yet*" to "not *fulfillable*" is not airtight, it does leave one with a presumption of skepticism. Either way, the precise nature of original sin is open to interpretation. Is it a *propensity* to evil in Kant's sense, a form of inherited guilt, or a state of total depravity? Jesus never mentions it. By the time of Augustine and Pelagius, it was still controversial

---

[27] R 6:104, 181.
[28] *On Justice*, 161.
[29] Saadia Gaon, *Beliefs and Opinions*, 217–8. Note that according to Saadia, Ecclesiastes 7:29 refers only to the universal *capacity* for evil.

enough to spark a major controversy. The Roman Catholic Church sided with Augustine and proclaimed Pelagianism heretical. If human effort is all that is needed to live a sin-free life, what need is there of the gift of grace?

At this point, it would be helpful to separate a number of claims. It is one thing to say, as with Goodman, that fulfillment of the Law lies beyond all past achievements of humanity, thus humanity would have to undergo a moral awakening to reach such a goal.[30] It is another thing to say that it exceeds human potential. By the same token, it is one thing to say that the Law aims at the perfection of the human race, another to say that the Law seeks to create a situation where people lead sin-free lives.

Unlike Kant, Maimonides claims that human nature will *not* undergo any change during the days of the Messiah. I take this to mean that although humanity will reach its full potential, it will not transform itself into a community of angels or return to the innocence Adam and Eve enjoyed before the fall. People will still have shortcomings and still need to apologize for them. His point is that the shortcomings they have will not prevent them from devoting themselves to perfection of the intellect. In any event, the fact that human nature will not change is what allows Maimonides to believe that the Messiah will come in finite time.

We can understand this better by looking at the lives of biblical heroes. Neither Abraham, Moses, nor David is perfect in the sense of living a sin-free life. Yet it could be said that all three sought and obtained a significant degree of human perfection. Repeating a rabbinic legend, Maimonides claims at the end of the *Guide* (3.51, 628) that Moses, Aaron, and Miriam were "kissed into heaven" because their love for God was so strong that they did not direct their thought to anything else. But as any reader knows, Moses was impatient when he struck the rock, and Aaron and Miriam incurred God's anger by challenging Moses' authority. Another rabbinic legend has it that four people, Benjamin the son of Jacob, Amram the father of Moses, Jesse the father of David, and Chileab the son of David, died because of the serpent (i.e., without sin).[31] Note, however, that in every case, their

---

[30] *On Justice*, 161.
[31] *Shabbat* 55b.

accomplishments pale into insignificance compared to their father or son, who did sin.

This takes us back to Maimonides' view of Rabbi Akiba. There is no question here of striving for something that outstrips human capacity. The issue is rather that of recognizing the limits of human capacity and doing the best one can within them. Although Cohen argues otherwise, his Jewish sources are few in number and not nearly strong enough to support such a sweeping conclusion. The idea that divine norms are by definition infinite and therefore cannot be fulfilled in finite time derives from Kant, who stressed that the chief virtue of Christianity is that it gave us a moral law that is "pure and uncompromising." Why is this necessary? Why could a just and gracious God not give us a law that takes into account the capacity of the recipients?

Kant's answer is that such a law would lower the standards of morality to suit our purposes and thus not be valid a priori. To this, Maimonides would reply that the first two commandments, which enjoin monotheism and the rejection of idolatry, are valid a priori. Although they cannot be fulfilled by repeating a few well-worn formulas, he would insist that Moses, the patriarchs, the prophets, Aristotle, and possibly Alfarabi did fulfill them. It is the other commandments, which deal with behavior, that take into consideration the circumstances in which people find themselves.[32] According to Kellner, if the first person to discover the truth of monotheism had been a Navajo rather than Abraham, then, from Maimonides' perspective, the Navajo would have been the chosen people, the Torah would have been written in their language, its narratives would reflect their history, and many of its commandments would reflect the social structure of their society.[33] On that scenario, even Jesus might have been Navajo.

Mindful of the need for a historical basis for religion, Kant (R 6:103) concedes that "due to a peculiar weakness of human nature, pure faith can never be relied on as much as it deserves, that is, to found a Church on it alone." This is exactly the point Maimonides makes

[32] For a detailed discussion of this aspect of Maimonides in regard to the Sabians, see Sarah Stroumsa, *Maimonides in His World*, 103: "One might say that in this way Maimonides developed the first systematic Jewish attempt to carry out a comparative study of the history of religion, an attempt to understand the laws of the Torah within their cultural context."

[33] Menachem Kellner, *Maimonides' Confrontation with Mysticism*, 81.

when he argues for the superiority of Mosaic religion to Abrahamic. Mosaic religion contained compromises whose purpose was to make it easier to fulfill the first and second commandments; Abrahamic religion contained little, if anything, of this sort, which is why Abrahamic religion failed. So whereas the Torah does contain compromises, it also contains laws that are truly commanding in Kant's sense of the term.

Allow me to construct two versions of what religion might look like. On the first, everything God commands can be fulfilled if we put forth sufficient effort. This assumes that God takes our capacities into account before issuing the commandments. Complete fulfillment of the commandments, either for an individual or for humanity as a whole, is unlikely but still possible. In the event that we fail to fulfill the commandments, there is always the possibility of repentance. But repentance is also a commandment. To fulfill it, one must admit what one has done wrong, suffer some sort of penalty or discomfort, and vow not to repeat the same mistake. Provided these conditions are met, a gracious God will forgive sin and grant atonement. But if they are not met, if repentance is perfunctory or insincere, no forgiveness is given. Like respect, forgiveness must be earned. So it is possible for a person to sin but still be in God's good graces. Overall, sin does not prevent the human race from reaching its full potential provided it has devoted itself to a life of holiness and is honest and remorseful about its shortcomings.

On the second, the commandments cannot be fulfilled in finite time, from which it follows that failure is inevitable. To cope with failure, we must turn to the grace of God. Whether we must develop a firm disposition to correct our behavior to be worthy of grace, or whether the gift of grace *precedes* any decision we make, grace always gives us more than we deserve. In that sense it is a rejection of the category of desert in favor of that of love. All that is asked of us is that we acknowledge the gift and display the humility that accompanies the recognition that it is God, not us, who is responsible for our salvation.

Although the first version is, broadly speaking, Jewish and the second, broadly speaking, Christian, we have encountered too many exceptions to put much confidence in labels. Were it not for his Christian upbringing, Kant, I suspect, would have been more comfortable with the first version because of its insistence on the category of desert. It is true that neither version says anything about the Messiah, but the first allows for the possibility that the human race can achieve salvation by natural means; the second allows for salvation only if the category of merit is superseded. By arguing that salvation can be achieved by rational means but only at infinity, Kant is in some sense a hybrid figure. My objection to the use of infinity in this context is that from our standpoint as finite agents undertaking one action at a time, it never comes and therefore leaves us precious little to hope for.[34]

INFINITY AND COMPLACENCY

An old saying has it that one should be careful what she wishes for because she may actually get it. Perhaps the same is true of the Messiah. For example, Derrida argues that insofar as it is open ended and future oriented, waiting for the Messiah is preferable to arriving at an inevitable and predetermined end of history.[35] From a religious standpoint, the idea that one could calculate the exact point at which the Messiah would arrive had great appeal. Before the days of Marxism, on which Derrida is commenting, people used astrology, numerology, questionable Bible interpretation – in short, anything they could get their hands on – to predict the day when God would see to it that every vestige of injustice is finally corrected.

Maimonides (*MT* 14, Kings and Wars, 12.2) warns people not to do this and, like Derrida, suggests that waiting with a hopeful attitude is preferable to attempting to identify a fixed endpoint. There is simply no way one can predict when a religiously inspired leader will succeed in bringing humanity to its senses. According to *Perek Helek*, even if such a leader did emerge and succeeded in doing what is required of the Messiah, there is no guarantee that the conditions he helped create will last forever. For all we know, humanity could slide back into an age of violence, superstition, and greed. So Maimonides did not conceive of the days of the Messiah as the end of history in some ultimate sense.

---

[34] Cf. Stéphane Mosès (commenting on Franz Rosenzweig), *The Angel of History*, 51: "At its most profound, human hoping will never be satisfied with the idea of an unlimited progress, an 'infinite task' that never succeeds."

[35] See Chapter 1, n. 37.

Yet unlike Derrida, Maimonides' messianism does have discernible content: As Isaiah (11:9) foretells, the earth shall be full of the knowledge of the Lord as the waters cover the sea. From a modern standpoint, his messianism is still tinged with dogmatism.[36] All of humanity will accept the true God, which is to say God as conceived by medieval rationalism. The idea that there might be other legitimate conceptions of God or that people might live worthwhile lives without believing in God at all is not a possibility.[37] In the final chapter, I will try to amend Maimonides' position by addressing this point.

For the present, I want to return to the question of whether the arrival of the Messiah will be an occasion for self-congratulation in the way that Francis Fukuyama's account of the end of history is an attempt to congratulate liberal democracy and free-market capitalism. We have seen, however, that bringing *is* into conformity with *ought* does not mean that we can rest on our laurels. This is true whether we look at it from the perspective of an individual or that of an entire society. Even if the child in my previous example manages to giver her allowance to a homeless person with a pure heart, she still has a lifetime of other decisions to make. Beyond the homeless person she has helped, there are other homeless people, and beyond homeless people, there are cancer victims, battered women, earthquake survivors, and falsely accused prisoners.

As Kant himself recognized, not all moral decisions are clear-cut. Some, for example giving to charity, involve wide or imperfect obligations and allow for a range of judgment and legitimate differences of opinion. Is it better to operate a soup kitchen or a public library? Is it better to run a public clinic or to devote one's life to finding a cure for some dreaded disease? Whatever the answers to these questions, limited resources will always stand in the way of accomplishing our goals.

Let us therefore admit that there will always be things a morally responsible person needs to do and decisions a morally responsible society needs to make. Let us also admit that the Messiah will not change this. The legislature will still meet, courts will still decide cases,

---

[36] See Chapter 2, section on life in the days of the Messiah, for the question of whether Maimonides thought everyone will have to embrace Judaism.

[37] It should be understood, however, that at no point does Maimonides consider, let alone recommend, forcible conversion.

and voices of dissent will still need to be heard. All the Messiah will do is get society to make its decisions in conformity with moral demands rather than a chorus of individual interests.

One of the reasons for saying that we can never do enough to fulfill our obligations is that if we were to agree that a person had acted on morally pure motives or that a society had devoted itself to doing the right thing, we would be encouraging a feeling of self-congratulation that would express itself in moral complacency. If I have done everything that can be asked of me, what more is there to do? I admit that complacency is the enemy of morality, and that there will always be things for me to do. Yet it does not follow from this that no matter what I do my actions are innately defective.

In fact, if there is a danger of complacency, it is with the opposite view. Suppose that evil is as ingrained in the human species as Kant thinks; suppose it is so ingrained in the human heart that even a simple act of charity by a small child is tainted by it; and suppose the possibility of eradicating evil would require infinite time to complete. Or, to follow Levinas, suppose that no matter what I do for the other person, it is never enough. Under these circumstances, a person might well conclude that her contribution to eradicating evil will never amount to anything and that the only sensible response is to make peace with it.

From an ethical perspective, any argument on behalf of complacency is bogus. We must strive to establish a just order no matter how small our contribution or how improbable such an order may seem. From a motivational standpoint, however, the idea of an infinite task cannot help but be demoralizing. Recall that for Kant, not only is the prevalence of evil universal, but it is also inextirpable by human power. Although his answer – accept God and eternal life as moral postulates – addresses the problem of evil at the level of what is possible in principle, it is hardly strong enough to overcome the dire picture of human behavior on which it is based. By his own admission, reason enjoins us to hope for something better.

To return to the issue of infinity, one can allow for the possibility that a morally perfect act has been performed in finite time and still hold that humanity is an end in itself. I cannot lie to a homeless person or use him solely as a means to achieve a greater good, because there *is* no greater good than recognizing his dignity as a human being. Even if taking his life would guarantee continued prosperity for a hundred other people, morality requires that I act to protect his life. Even that is not enough, because I must also act to promote his happiness as proportionate to his virtue. To go further still, it may be true, as Levinas argues, that the face of the other person signifies a transcendence so great that it calls my entire being into question. My claim is that none of this forces us to say that the child who gave her allowance to such a person failed to meet the demands of morality because she acted from impure motives.

It will be objected that if a homeless person is an end in himself and possesses infinite worth, whatever we do to help him will not be enough. How, exactly, can we act to promote his happiness in proportion to his virtue? Will this not require every resource at our disposal and every waking moment we have? I confess I do not know the exact degree of effort that would be needed to comply with the obligation to promote another person's happiness. Happiness for Kant is explained in terms of desire, but desire is anything but fixed. It can be altered by education, enculturation, or, in some cases, satiation. Regardless of where we draw the line for compliance with our obligation, the question is whether as human beings we are capable of reaching it. My claim is that if any effort we expend will not be enough, Pelagius' question comes back to haunt us: What sense does it make to criticize us for not doing more? Why, for example, should I feel shame in the face of the other person if my response is inadequate *by definition*?

To see this in another way, let us return to the supposition of widespread – even universal – evil. If it is evil and not just a case of necessity, then humanity bears responsibility for it. On that Kant would agree. If, as seems perfectly reasonable, this evil has come about in finite time, then why can it not be eradicated in finite time? Alternatively, if it cannot be eradicated by human effort in finite time, on what grounds can we say humanity bears responsibility for it rather than nature, God, or some other force over which we have no control?

"BE HOLY ..."

That brings us to holiness and the principle of *imitatio Dei*. God enjoins Israel to become a holy nation, and Jesus enjoins his followers to become like their Father in heaven. At a rudimentary level, no religious believer can deny this, because it goes to the very heart of spiritual aspiration. The problem occurs when we try to say what infinite means. If Cohen is right in saying that God can assign no labor of Sisyphus, there must be a respect in which "Be holy" can be fulfilled. If it can be fulfilled, we run the risk that a finite being will become Godlike. Neither of these is acceptable. The response – we can approach fulfillment asymptotically – tries to effect a compromise. On the one hand, we cannot rival God, because no matter how much progress we make, there will always be some distance between us and the holiness we seek. On the other hand, there is no labor of Sisyphus, because the distance we have to cover approaches zero. Thus holiness and, by implication, the Messiah are boundary conditions: They set the direction for moral striving without describing actual achievements.

The key word here is *approach*. Just as a curve does not touch the axis it approaches, so, as Wood suggests, is it wrong to view holiness as a term or member of the infinite series on which we are embarked.[38] If it were, then it would follow that evil is extirpable by human power provided we are given enough time to overcome it. This is clearly not Kant's view. In fact, Kant seems to recognize this when he says (*R* 6:48) that we can hope for constant progress from bad to better, but he does *not* say we can hope for progress from bad to best. Later he claims (*R* 6:51) that all we can hope to accomplish on our own power is that we attain the road that "leads in the direction" of holiness. To actually reach holiness, we need God's grace to do what we cannot do on our own.

We saw in an earlier chapter that for all its initial plausibility, the principle of *imitatio Dei* is problematic. God does not have to contend with emotion, inclination, exhaustion, or lack of resources, all things that impinge on the moral choices we face as human beings. God does not need festivals to raise his spirits, symbols to remind him of what happened in the past, or rules of mourning and repentance. Kant's response to this is to hope that, like the Marxist state, the statutory part of religion will whither away. That leaves us with a being that must contend with inclination and a being whose will is completely pure in that it has no need of imperatives or moral exertion.

[38] Wood, *Kant's Moral Religion*, 119. Note, however, as Wood does, that Kant's language is not always very precise.

Under these circumstances, the command "Be holy" becomes equivalent to "Make yourself into something more than human." The problem may not be as acute for a Christian as it is for a Jew given the status of Jesus as a moral intermediary. According to Kant (*R* 6:64), Jesus was afflicted with the same needs and inclinations as we and as a result felt the same temptation to transgress the moral law. If he did not transgress it, then, Kant reasons, he would be so far superior to us that he could not serve as an example. In other words, he would be divine rather than human. If, on the other hand, he were human, as Kant himself thinks, he could speak truly of himself "as if the ideal of goodness were displayed incarnate in him" because he would be speaking only of his disposition, not his actual achievement.

Needless to say, the passage is confusing and conflicts with traditional Christian doctrine. Insofar as holiness is the goal we are obliged to seek, we are asked to bring our will into conformity with the moral law. This is compatible with saying that, unlike God, we will still need imperatives; in fact, from our standpoint, the moral law *is* an imperative. Given the place from which we start – that we are evil by nature – the task before us is so daunting that even infinite time will not carry us to the end unless we rely on God's help. More specifically, the goal is to turn us into creatures that are more than human, which is to say creatures who feel temptation but manage to overcome it. On the traditional view, this is what Jesus did. He was tempted by Satan in the desert but did not submit. We saw, however, that no significant character in the Hebrew Bible does this, because all are guilty of sin at some level. It follows that if we are commanded to be holy in Kant's sense, we are commanded to become something very different from what we now are.

It was precisely this idea that Maimonides rejected. If the command "Be holy" asks us to live a life of piety and devotion to God, to join together with others to build a society that not only establishes order but addresses spiritual needs as well, there is no problem. However, if it asks us to change our inherent nature, to become divine in some sense of the term, then it asks the impossible. The reply "Yes, but I'm talking about infinite time" creates more problems than it solves. In this life, we have to contend with a conflict between practical reason on the one hand, and inclination and the desire for happiness on the other. It would seem, however, that if the soul survives death, it would enter a purely intellectual realm in which inclination and the desire for happiness are no longer present. Why, then, would we need to make infinite progress to reach the goal of holiness? If all we have is our rational nature, why would holiness not be available to us at the moment of death?

The moral consequences of such a view would be disastrous, because they would allow a person to do whatever he pleases in this life knowing that when inclination and the desire for happiness are removed, he will suddenly be transformed from a human creature to an angelic one.[39] So Kant must maintain that, whether in this life or the next, overcoming inclination requires effort on our part – effort and assistance from God. The question is how such effort is to be understood.

The usual defense of Kant is to say that we are well beyond the limits of reason and into the realm of hope. Yet hope still has to make rational sense. If, at bottom, the command "Be holy" amounts to nothing more than "Strive for holiness and trust in God to do what you cannot," Kant owes us an account of what such striving is like. On this point, Yovel objects that Kant's view of immortality makes sense only if the body is immortal as well as the soul.[40] The argument is that only if we are still conjoined with a body that possesses inclinations can the idea of moral progress in the next life be made coherent. Is this what Kant wants – a body that persists through endless reaches of time and presents us with constant moral challenges? It is hard to answer yes given, once again, that we are working with religion *within the limits of reason alone.* Moreover, even if we could make sense of moral progress in a disembodied state, Kant would still face the question of what it would mean for people in such a state to experience happiness in proportion to their virtue.

The alternative is to say that whatever the next life has in store, the moral challenges we face as human beings – or at least the ones we are capable of understanding – are limited to this life. But then Maimonides' question is valid: Can we be obliged to seek holiness as Kant understands it, to make ourselves into divine beings in the time we are allotted? The only way to give a positive answer is to abandon the *ought* implies *can* principle or deny that humans are evil by nature. The

---

[39] On this point, see Wood, *Kant's Moral Religion*, 118.
[40] Yovel, *Kant*, 113.

first option would do serious damage to Kant's moral theory because it would mean that reason culminates in an *absurdum practicum*. As he puts it (C2 5:114), if the highest good is impossible to achieve, then the moral law that commands it "must be fantastic and directed to empty imaginary ends and must therefore in itself be false."

The second option would offend Kant's Christian sensibilities by putting him squarely in the camp of Pelagius. Recall that for Kant Christianity destroyed man's confidence of being wholly adequate to the demands of morality in this life. A Pelagian Kant could still believe in an afterlife, but his belief would not have to carry the heavy weight it now does. For if the command "Be holy" did not exceed human capacity, we would not need infinite time or the gift of divine grace to explain the possibility of its fulfillment. For a Jew, the Pelagian view of *ought* implies *can* does not present a problem. As indicated earlier, it seems like a reasonable interpretation of Deuteronomy 30. If so, there is no reason why the Messiah needs infinite time or a miracle to make his appearance. If the rabbinic legend about two weeks of Sabbath observance is true, the Messiah is never more than thirteen days away.

5

History and Rationality

This chapter marks a transition from what has gone before, because it shifts the focus of the discussion from theological approaches to messianism to the historical record that underlies it. At bottom, messianism is a claim about history: the conviction that as events unfold, the will of God will become apparent and justice will be done. Thus the familiar refrain of the prophets: "The day is coming when ...." We have already encountered Cohen's claim (*RR*, 261) that the concept of history is a creation of the Hebrew prophets. In this sense, history is not just the record of how one event follows another but, as the prophets see it, the moral progress of the human race. It is clear, then, that how we understand history has a direct bearing on the theme of this book. Does history have a direction? What would it mean for there to be an end of history? Does the course of history really reflect the will of God?

Before we try to answer these questions, we should keep in mind that *history* is a greatly disputed term. In fact, the study of history is itself something that has a history. For the prophets, it is the gradual, and at some times mysterious, working of divine providence. For Thucydides, it is the recurrence of universal features of human nature. For Aristotle, on the contrary, it deals with individuals rather than universals and thus takes a backseat to poetry. For Maimonides, it is the recovery of an ideal condition from which humanity has turned its back. As late as the eighteenth century, Hume wrote, in the spirit of Thucydides,[1]

Mankind are so much the same, in all times and places, that history informs us of nothing new or strange in this particular. Its chief use is only to discover the constant and universal principles of human nature, by showing men in all varieties of circumstances and situations, and furnishing us with materials from which we may form our observations and become acquainted with the regular springs of human action and behavior.

Hume concludes that the actions of his contemporaries are just as close to the actions described by Polybius and Tacitus as the earth, water, and other elements investigated by modern scientists are to the earth, water, and elements investigated by Aristotle and Hippocrates; in other words, nothing of substance has changed.

By the time we get to Kant, the picture becomes more complicated. We need to believe that history will make progress if we are to have any chance of improving the moral quality of our actions. In regard to religion, Kant argues (R 6:111) that a basic moral predisposition has long been hidden in human reason, thus we can find traces of it even in ancient texts. This allows him to view the history of religion as a gradual progression from contingent or ecclesiastical factors to a purely rational religion in which all such factors are removed. That is why, in his opinion, Protestantism represents a higher form of religion than Judaism. That is not to say that he was completely happy with the Protestantism of his day – he departed from it in several ways – but that he saw Protestantism as closer to the moral core of religion than the Judaism of the Hebrew Bible.[2] Beyond Kant's treatment of the history of religion, there is his proclivity to view nature as a force pushing the human race toward greater civility over time.

What is for Kant a suggestion that history brings increasing clarity to an idea that lay dormant in human reason becomes for Hegel the basis of an entire philosophy. Rather than a mere collection of facts from which empirical generalizations can be drawn, history is the realm in which new and ever-changing conceptions of human life are realized

---

[1] David Hume, *An Enquiry Concerning Human Understanding*, 83.
[2] For more on Kant's dissatisfaction with Protestantism, see Wood, *Kant's Moral Religion*, 197–9.

and eventually superseded. To take an obvious example, the principles needed to explain the rise and fall of the Roman Empire are quite different from those needed to explain, say, the French Revolution and the origin of the modern state. In one respect, this view is in keeping with the future orientation of the biblical narrative, which presents us with unique events like the fall from Eden or the revelation at Sinai – events that change our entire conception of what it is to be human. To better understand Hegel's contribution to this discussion, we need to look at his thought in greater detail.

HEGEL AND THE IDEA OF REASON IN HISTORY

One way to understand Hegel is to see him as carrying Kant's critical philosophy a step further.[3] Although Kant questioned the ability of reason to demonstrate the truths of metaphysics, he continued to think that in its practical capacity, reason could establish the necessity of the moral law a priori. From Hegel's perspective, this is the same mistake all over again: that is, thinking that the principles that reason establishes represent truths valid for all time and not just expressions of the time and place in which it operates. His claim is that freedom in Kant's sense – self-appropriation of the moral law – cannot be understood apart from the ideals and social institutions of the Enlightenment culture from which it emerged. To suppose that it would be valid for a fifth-century Athenian, for whom the idea of the self as a moral subject was still in its infancy, is folly. Note, for example, that when the chorus tells Antigone she is acting autonomously (Antigone 1.821), it is not saying that she has appropriated the moral law in a rational fashion, but rather that she is acting as if she were a law unto herself. Similar considerations apply to virtue, happiness, punishment, rights, and the other issues to which practical reason addresses itself.

To make his point, Hegel argues that if we consider Kant's formulation of the Categorical Imperative apart from considerations of time and place – act only in accordance with that maxim through which you can at the same time will that it become a universal law – we will

---

[3] For an interpretation of Hegel along these lines, see Beiser, "Hegel's Historicism," in *The Cambridge Companion to Hegel*, 270–300.

find that it is empty.[4] In effect, all it says is that a person must will something in such a way that she avoids contradicting herself and can will that everyone do likewise. Hegel's point is that from such an abstract conception of morality, there is no way to determine the specific content of our obligations. Worse, one can justify any type of behavior, including the most immoral actions imaginable by saying that everyone should do likewise. Where, for example, is there a contradiction in willing that everyone commit murder? Granted, the human race would soon perish, but, again, where is the contradiction in willing this?

If we look at the way Kant tries to derive specific duties from the Categorical Imperative, Hegel continues, we cannot fail to notice that he brings in content that goes far beyond the absence of contradiction, such as human flourishing, the continued existence of the human race, and the institution of private property. The point is not that this content is objectionable in itself but that its validity depends on social norms that have evolved over time and cannot be known a priori. Just as reason has no access to a separate realm of metaphysical entities, Hegel argues, it has no access to moral principles that stand outside of history.

The Kantian response would be to point out that there are several formulations of the Categorical Imperative, and that the universal law formula is only one of them. We are also obliged to treat humanity as an end in itself, to view every rational agent as a will giving universal law, and to strive for the kingdom of ends. In addition, we are obliged to strive for the highest good, which involves promoting the happiness of other people. So it is a mistake to think that Kant believed that all duties can be deduced from a single principle. To say that my actions must be compatible with a principle is not to say they follow from it in the way that having interior angles equal to 180 degrees follows from the definition of a triangle. We have already seen that Kant allows for wide or imperfect obligations that leave considerable room for judgments of prudence or appropriateness.

In any case, Hegel's alternative is to recognize that reason has a history and can be understood only in connection with the norms and practices of which it is a part and from which it emerged. Seen in this

---

[4] Hegel, *PR*, 89–90 (135).

light, Maimonides was ahead of his time in suggesting that most of the commandments of the Torah were designed with the historical experience of the Jewish people in mind. As we saw, history might have taken a different path, making the Navajo the first nation to recognize the truth of monotheism. Had this been the case, the Torah would have contained different commandments, and Israel would have been just another nation that emerged in the ancient Near East and fell into obscurity when a stronger nation conquered it.

To us, the need to take historical circumstances into account may seem like a trivial point. Of course one has to consider history when examining a philosophic argument. Who would have thought otherwise? The answer is: just about every philosopher prior to Hegel. Historical change is so much a part of our conceptual apparatus that it is easy to forget that, with the exception of the Greek and Roman classics, history did not become part of the normal college curriculum until the late nineteenth century.[5] Hegel, then, was one of the first people to view history as more than a collection of facts, but as the development of the way we make sense of the world. "To him who looks at the world rationally," Hegel tells us (*RH*, 13), "the world looks rationally back." Kant's Copernican Revolution consisted in showing that this is true of nature. If we find necessity, it is because we have put it there. Hegel took the unprecedented step of arguing that this is also true of history.

In keeping with Kant's claim that the mind must order experience for experience to be intelligible, Hegel argued that the emergence of new categories means there is a sense in which people see the world in entirely new ways. Thus the world of Newton was fundamentally different from that of Aristotle, and the world of Einstein fundamentally different from that of Newton. In a moral sense, the world of Moses was fundamentally different from that of the Patriarchs, that of Socrates fundamentally different from that of Moses, and that of Jesus fundamentally different from that of Socrates. To suppose that there is a single account of truth, virtue, divinity, or authority to which all these people would adhere is folly.

---

[5] By the same token, Jewish history, as an academic discipline apart from the study of sacred literature, did not come into its own until the mid-nineteenth century in Germany. For an account of its development, see David N. Myers, *Resisting History*, 18–34.

Although it is true that great leaders give us new ways to see the world, it does not follow that they were fully aware of what they were doing. If great philosophers do not see all the implications of what they said, there is no reason to suppose that the people who were responsible for the overthrow of the *ancien régime* in France acted on purely noble motives or possessed extraordinary powers of comprehension. In all likelihood, their ability to see into the future was no greater than ours, which is to say that they saw next to nothing. In Hegel's terms (*RH*, 35),[6]

This connection [the universal must be actualized through the particular] implies that human actions in history produce additional results, beyond their immediate purpose and attainment, beyond their immediate knowledge and desire. They gratify their own interests; but something more is thereby accomplished, which is latent in the action though not present in their consciousness and not included in their design.

From this insight, Hegel develops the notion of *world historical figures*, people whose individual purposes contain or imply universal ideas that they help to actualize even though they are not aware of what they are doing (*RH*, 39–40). The justification for what they do cannot be derived from the laws and customs of the old order, because their place in history is that of showing that the old order is no longer valid. In this respect, they stand outside the normal distinction people make between right and wrong. What makes them heroic is that they act according to "a secret source whose content is still hidden and has not yet broken through into experience." Alexander the Great, Julius Caesar, and Napoleon are Hegel's chief examples of such individuals.

Behind Hegel's conception of world historical figures is a thorough rejection of the kind of Platonism that motivated Kant. If reason is to actualize itself, it can do so, as it were, only on the backs of individual agents guided by their own passions and proclivities. But for the activities of such agents, even the most appealing of principles would be imaginary and therefore worthless. Only what is present and actual has a claim to legitimacy. In Hegel's eyes, even Plato's *Republic*

---

[6] According to Shlomo Avineri, *Hegel's Theory of the Modern State*, 231–4, Hegel is not always consistent on the question of how much the actors are aware of the larger implications of what they are doing. Also see *RH*, 39–40.

is nothing but an interpretation of the nature of Greek ethical life at the time.[7]

The process by which principles are realized by individuals who may be unaware of the significance of what they are doing is what Hegel terms *the cunning of reason*. We saw that Kant, too, introduced an analogous process by which nature sees to it that art and science prevail over rudeness and violence. To this, Hegel objects (*RH*, 68) that no matter how varied, nature "shows only a cycle of constant repetition." No matter what we do, the sun rises in the east, unsupported objects fall to earth, and water freezes into ice in the winter. If the only thing that history offered us were nature, then, Hegel protests, we would die of boredom. The only things that produce genuine changes are events that take place in the realm of Spirit, which is to say human history and self-understanding.

The goal of self-understanding is the attainment of freedom. Freedom is the highest expression of human achievement and an end in itself. "World history," as Hegel proclaims (*RH*, 24), "is the progress of the consciousness of freedom." Because true freedom can be realized only in the context of the modern state, history is measured by the degree to which the modern state has been realized.[8] Obviously, the role of the modern state has evolved since Hegel's day. On the one hand, many people would object to the institution of a monarchy; on the other hand, almost all people would insist on universal suffrage rather than a society organized according to estates. Yet on a sympathetic reading of Hegel, these issues involve modifications rather than changes in principle. Like Hegel, we are still working within the context of a constitutional democracy.

It follows that there can be events – even major events such as wars or the production of great art – that do not count as history in the Hegelian sense of the term. Along these lines, Hegel claims (*RH*, 76) that the China of his day has a history whereas the India of his day, for all its spiritual and artistic splendor, does not. Yet we do not have to turn to Asia to make this point. As Terry Pinkard remarks, "The criterion for what counts as a world-historical event consists in its

---

[7] Hegel, *PR*, Preface (10).
[8] I say *true* freedom because, like Kant, Hegel does not define freedom as the ability to do whatever one wants.

playing a decisive role in the *story* of the rise of freedom."[9] So, says Pinkard, conflicts between the Hapsburgs and the Bourbons are important for understanding early modern Europe, but from Hegel's perspective, they are only a sideshow. The same might be said of nations or forms of social organization whose time, in Hegel's opinion, has come and gone. In the *Philosophy of Right*, for example, he claims that once a nation's hour has struck, it no longer counts in world history.[10]

Whether we view history in Hegel's sense as guided by the cunning of nature or the cunning of reason, we face the question of what is providing the guidance. For Kant, the answer is God as the benevolent author of nature. God, it will be recalled, is the only force capable of guaranteeing the possibility of bringing nature into harmony with freedom, the *is* with the *ought*. It will also be recalled that Kant's view of God, assumes that the union of *is* with *ought* is not a given, but something that needs to be accomplished. This is another way of saying that Kant's position begins with moral discontent: The way things are is unacceptable and has to be corrected. Belief in God is what motivates us to work for something better.

We will see in the next section that in his own way, Hegel, too, is theological. For the present, we need to recognize he is skeptical, almost to the point of being disdainful, of the idea that human existence should be understood as an attempt to strive for ideals that can never be actualized. As he sees it, the task of philosophy is to comprehend the present and the actual rather than have recourse to a "beyond, supposed to exist, God knows where."[11] By setting a standard of behavior *beyond* the world, Kant, in Hegel's opinion, devalues the importance of action that takes place *in* it. His response is to challenge the entire foundation on which Kantian philosophy is based. Accordingly, "*What is rational is actual; and what is actual is rational.*"[12]

On the surface, it might appear that Hegel is endorsing a form of conservatism according to which we should be satisfied with conditions as they now obtain. Yet this criticism misses an important point. For Hegel, actuality (*Wirklichkeit*) does not necessarily refer to current conditions, but rather to what has adequately fulfilled its essence.

[9] Terry Pinkard, *Hegel's Phenomenology*, 335–6.
[10] *PR*, 340 (218).
[11] *PR*, Preface (10).
[12] Ibid.

To borrow an example from T. M. Knox, we could say that a states-man who fails to accomplish anything during his term in office is not a real or actual statesman because effectiveness is a quality statesmen are supposed to have.[13] By the same token, Knox continues, if no exist-ing statesmen had ever been effective, it would be foolish to establish effectiveness as an ideal to which statesmen are supposed to strive.

To return to the quote, Hegel is making two points. The first is that reason is not what Knox terms "a mere ideal or aspiration," but is rather something that can effect change by becoming actualized in the course of history. The second is that what is effective in the world is the process by which this actualization occurs. In either case, Hegel is not so simple-minded as to think that no institution or person in authority can be criticized.[14] If one of the purposes of a modern state is to guarantee equal protection under the law, then a state that does not do so – and there are many that do not – is defective. Hegel's point is that the goal of establishing equal protection was not deduced by reason a priori but realized by real people acting on their own inter-ests. Once people became aware of the need for equal protection, it was the job of philosophy to do what the people who realized it could not: explain its meaning and provide a rationale. As he puts it, "To comprehend what is, this is the task of philosophy, because what is, is reason."[15] This led Shlomo Avineri to reflect that those who make history do not understand it, and those who understand it do not make it.[16]

In the case of the French Revolution, philosophy's job was to explain the principles that lay behind the destruction of the *ancien régime*. Yet though reason demanded the destruction of the old order, and philosophy can tell us why such destruction was necessary, Hegel was critical of the French Revolution for what he saw as its total reli-ance on abstract principles and consequent degeneration into a reign

---

[13] *PR*, vi, 302.

[14] For Hegel's relation to the Prussian state of his day, see Avineri, *Hegel's Theory*, 115–19, and note in particular his claim (116) that "the Prussia with which Hegel became associated in 1818 was not the Prussia of 1848, let alone 1914." For more on Hegel's mixed response to the Prussia of his day, see Charles Taylor, *Hegel*, 425–6, 452–61.

[15] Hegel, *PR*, Preface (11). Cf. Taylor, *Hegel*, 423: "To uncover reason is to uncover the force, the plan, already at work."

[16] Avineri, *Hegel's Theory*, 234.

of terror. Moreover, there is nothing in Hegel's thought that suggests we should resurrect the past or think that we are treading on thin ice if we attempt to change it. On the contrary, change is what brings reason closer to fulfillment.

Hegel is a conservative to the degree that the job of philosophy is to provide the rationale for principles after they have been realized, not to tell us where we ought to go in the future. His famous quote that "The owl of Minerva spreads its wings only with the falling of the dusk" means that philosophy cannot dictate to history the path that it is supposed to take. Given a particular social structure, even an astute philosopher is in no position to predict how it will end or what will take its place. All he can do is explain the logic behind the course that history has taken up to that point. This still leaves us with the question of what is behind the progress of humanity toward increasing levels of self-awareness. Is *reason* just another name for divine Providence, so that Hegel is still working in the prophetic tradition? Is such Providence inevitable, and if so, where is it taking us? It is to those questions that I now turn.

HISTORY AS A STORY

According to the traditional interpretation, Hegel viewed history as a necessary process culminating in the formation of the modern state, and he endowed the process with theological overtones. To cite one case, Hegel tells us (*RH*, 47) the following:

The insight to which … philosophy should lead us is that the actual world is as it ought to be, that the truly good, the universal divine Reason is the power capable of realizing itself. This good, this Reason, in its most concrete representation, is God. God governs the world. The actual working of His government, the carrying out of His plan is the history of the world.

In another passage (*RH*, 18), he goes so far as to say that history is the realm in which divine Providence manifests itself, and that by engaging in the philosophy of history, he is doing theodicy in a manner reminiscent of Leibniz.[17] This is all the more true if, as Hegel suggests

---

[17] For the religious overtones of Hegel's philosophy of history and the problems it posed for his followers, see Karl Löwith, *From Hegel to Nietzsche*, 212–19.

(*RH*, 23), the germ contains the entire nature of the tree down to the taste and shape of its fruit, so the first traces of spirit virtually contain all of history.[18]

Such passages raise the question of whether Hegel's view of history represents a return to the kind of dogmatic metaphysics Kant thought he had disposed of. Note, for example, that if Hegel is right about the cunning of nature, then, as Charles Taylor notes, there is an important sense in which the agency for historical events is not fully ours.[19] It is as if history in the form of what Hegel calls "an unconscious inner sense" overthrew France's *ancien régime* and devised the blueprint for the modern state.

As any reader can see, Hegel often speaks in colorful ways. The question is how much in the way of metaphysics we should ascribe to him. According to Pinkard, the answer is not much. We can begin by noting that unlike Maimonides, Hegel did not think that history would culminate when humanity fulfills the essential nature with which it was originally endowed. The goal toward which history moves is not something that nature has assigned it or that reason can articulate a priori. Nor is the goal of history fated in the sense that events could not have turned out any other way. It would be foolish to deny that history contains contingent events. Themistocles may have failed to convince the Athenians that the Persians could be defeated at sea, Caesar may have been unable to rally his troops at Gaulle, Napoleon may have had better weather at Waterloo.

In the twentieth century, both Hitler and Lenin survived numerous assassination attempts, many of which would have succeeded if events had been only slightly different. If we accept historical contingency, then the unconscious inner sense that Hegel speaks of cannot be a causal force moving people into situations that, left to their own devices, they would have avoided. Rather, it is how events fit together as seen from our vantage point. In Kantian terms, it might be better to express this by saying that it is *as if* an unconscious inner sense was at work given the direction that history took.

[18] Cf. *PR*, 342 (216): "[W]orld history is the necessary development, out of the concept of mind's freedom alone, of the moments of reason and so of the self-consciousness and freedom of mind. This development is the interpretation and actualization of the universal mind."

[19] Taylor, *Hegel*, 420.

This takes us back to Pinkard's claim that for Hegel, history is a story – more specifically, a story that we tell.[20] To continue with Pinkard, forms of life do not construct themselves to play the role that later generations will assign them.[21] To repeat, people act according to their own passions and proclivities. No metaphysical force is needed to explain what they do. "If they play crucial roles in world history," Pinkard argues, "it is because their contingently acquired attributes enabled them to play a role that we, living much later, can reconstruct so that their roles can be understood as having completed a certain conceptual development."

Such is the crux of the "non-metaphysical" reading of Hegel that Pinkard and Robert Pippin have done much to promote.[22] To a proponent of the traditional reading, history is more than just a story but the unfolding of the internal logic of universal reason. Yet if this is so, if there is a filament of necessity in the transition from one stage of history to another, and the germ contains the details of what will follow, why are even the best philosophers unable to interpret it and tell us where history is moving? Why does Hegel maintain that philosophers are only able to shed light on historical progress after the fact? We would reject as inadequate a scientific theory that had no predictive power. If all philosophy can do is look backward, what sense does it make to argue for a metaphysical force pushing it forward?

---

[20] Cf. Hayden White, *Tropics of Discourse: Essays in Cultural Criticism*, 84: "[N]o given set of causally recorded historical events can in itself constitute a story; the most it might offer to the historian are story *elements*. The events are *made* into a story by the suppression or subordination of certain of them and the highlighting of others, by characterization, motific repetition, variation of tone and point of view ... in short, all of the techniques that we would normally expect to find in the employment of a novel or play." I owe this reference to my colleague Barry Wimpfheimer, *Narrating the Law*, 65–6.

[21] Pinkard, *Phenomenology*, 336.

[22] In addition to Pinkard's work on the *Phenomenology*, in particular his discussion of Kojève, 436, n. 110, see Klaus Hartmann, "Hegel: A Non-metaphysical View," in *Hegel: A Collection of Critical Essays*, 101–24, as well as Robert Pippin, *Hegel's Idealism: The Satisfactions of Self-consciousness*, 167, 292. Pippin concedes that although Hegel appears to speak as if his theory commits him to historical determinism, all he is really committed to is the belief that his theory does a better job of explaining the facts than its rivals. See, however, Beiser, "Introduction: Hegel and the Problem of Metaphysics," in *The Cambridge Companion to Hegel*, 3, who criticizes the non-metaphysical approach as "anachronistic."

This is hardly the place to settle the question of whether the non-metaphysical reading of Hegel is valid except to say that the advantage of downplaying Hegel's metaphysical commitments is that it allows us to hold that the lessons of Kant's critique of metaphysics were not lost on him. Again, to use Kantian terms, we can *regard* history as a progressive development from one stage to the next, and much will be learned by doing so, but looking at history this way does not mean that we are ascribing superhuman insight to the actors or viewing them as players in a game whose outcome was decided before anyone came on the scene.[23]

We arrive at the same conclusion if we look at Hegel's understanding of Providence. According to traditional theology, God's Providence is hidden from us. Thus God will send the Messiah when it suits him. To ask "Why then?" or "Why there?" is to presume knowledge no one has. All we can do is wait. From Hegel's perspective, the problem with this view is that it makes Providence completely external to the actions it is supposed to direct. The hidden nature of divine Providence opens the way for imagination or superstition to supply the content that reason cannot – or, as Hegel puts it (*RH*, 16), "we gain the convenient license of indulging in our own fancies." His response is to say that Providence is nothing but the process by which humanity becomes conscious of its freedom. This happens when freedom is realized as a historical reality and is no longer just the germ of an idea. However, the endpoint is not predetermined in heaven or forced on an unsuspecting audience by miraculous incursions into human affairs. It is simply the point to which our actions have taken us, the point where the story we have been telling reaches closure.

Beiser explains this by invoking the Aristotelian distinction (*Posterior Analytics* 2.1) between that which is first or better known in the order of being and that which is first or better known to us.[24] The particular objects of sense are better known to us because of their immediacy, whereas the most universal truths are prior and better

---

[23] There are passages where Hegel speaks as if individual agents are just instruments of a higher force, for example, *PR*, 344 (217), but I do not think this represents his considered view.

[24] Beiser, "Hegel's Historicism," 291–3, does not cite a passage from Aristotle, which may account for the difference in terminology between my account of Aristotle's distinction and his. But I do not see any philosophic difference in what we are saying.

known in the order of being. We can see this by recognizing that for Aristotle the particular is unknowable as such; it can be known only to the degree that it embodies a universal. That is Aristotle's concession to Platonism. His rejection of Platonism consists in the claim that universals exist only to the degree that they are instantiated by a particular. For Hegel, too, individual actions are intelligible to the degree that they manifest or bring about the realization of freedom. Unlike God in traditional theology, however, freedom does not exist as a separate entity or controlling force.

What, then, is the point of closure? Here, too, we have to be careful not to be taken in by rhetoric. To say that history has reached its final stage is not to say that battles will cease, newspapers will run out of things to print, or people will be in a constant state of euphoria. To say any of this would be to abandon philosophy and return to mythology. The end of history is simply the point at which we understand what it means to be free and the social structures needed to realize such freedom have been put in place. It is still possible that conflicts may occur; the question is whether the outcome of these conflicts forces us to alter our conception of what it means to be free or leave it as it was. In particular, do they cause us to distrust the institutions of constitutional democracy and look for alternative forms of political organization? If the answer is no, then for all intents and purposes, the story of how freedom came to be realized is over.

One consequence of the end of the story is that the day of world historical figures is also over. The nineteenth century was greatly enamored of knights of faith, supermen, and others who acted as if they were above the law. In fact, part of the appeal of messianism as originally conceived was the lure of a hero who would do what we cannot do on our own. From a Hegelian perspective, however, such people, although necessary at one stage of history, no longer have a role to play. Once the modern state is realized, the only role left is to articulate and safeguard the principles that have already been established.

To say that a modern state promises equal protection to all its citizens is not, of course, to say that Germany, France, or the United States does an acceptable job of making good on their promise. So a leader could emerge who claimed that modern states are hypocritical, preaching one thing and practicing another. To the degree that she made the state live up to its promises, she would be making a significant contribution – perhaps a contribution that assumes messianic proportions. However, she would not be a world-historical figure, because she would be working with existing principles rather than pointing the way to new ones. To the degree that this story is messianic, it represents a modern attempt at deflation in the sense that there are no miracles, no new revelation, and no unrealizable goals to strive for.

From a Jewish perspective, Hegel will always be viewed with skepticism, not just because he had a low opinion of Judaism – so did Kant – but because his view of history has little to say to people whose fortunes do not put them front and center in humanity's march toward freedom. No matter how many times they may be told that "What is actual is rational" does not mean what it appears to say, they could hardly take it up as a rallying cry. Nor could they rest content with the claim that "The history of the world is the world's court of judgment" (*Die Weltgeschichte ist das Weltgericht*).[25] Ernst Bloch expressed the typical Jewish response to this by accusing Hegel of concluding a "premature and total truce with the world."[26]

To people on the margins of society, the Kantian separation of *is* from *ought* makes better sense. As Levinas tells us, "Not to submit the Law of justice to the implacable course of events, to denounce them if necessary as counter-sense [*contre-sens*] or madness, is to be a Jew."[27] Similar considerations apply to Hegel's relation to the Prussian State. It is seriously misleading to say that he regarded the Prussian State as the be-all and end-all of human development. At the end of *Lectures on the Philosophy of History*, he claims almost prophetically that America is the land of the future, where the burden of the world's history will reveal itself. Still, Hegel's lectures on history were given at the bequest of the state in order to dampen revolutionary sentiment. How ironic that two generations later, Hegel was invoked to do exactly the opposite.

At a deeper level, though, the problem with Hegel's view of history is that it attempts to reconstruct the past from the standpoint of a

---

[25] *PR*, 340 (216).

[26] Bloch, *Spirit*, 178.

[27] Levinas, *DF*, 227, also see 235–8 for more specific comments on Hegel. On the same theme, see Levinas's criticism of Hegel for denying the rupture between the ontological and the ethical in *Face to Face with Levinas*, 30.

privileged position in the present. Given this view, it is almost inevitable that past cultures or forms of social organization will seem like miniature or imperfect versions of what we now have. Hegel would no doubt respond that this is not so. If a previous form of social organization like the Greek city-state collapsed, it is not because it failed to live up to contemporary standards of how a society should be organized, but because it could not resolve the contradictions that emerged within it and therefore lost its claim to legitimacy.

Although Hegel is not committed to the view that mere passage of time results in progress, it is hard to see how he can avoid the claim that progress means supercession. As Christianity superceded Judaism, so Rome superceded Greece, and the French Revolution superceded feudalism. There are obviously cases where supercession occurs. But why could a person not say that although the rise of Christianity was a formative event in world history, it does not follow that it represents a more authentic conception of religion than Judaism any more than eighteenth-century sculpture represents a more pleasing or more refined form of art than sculpture from the age of Pericles? Why, in short, can historical progress not present us with a range of alternatives rather than a constantly ascending staircase where only one legitimate alternative remains?

We will see in the next section that history did not turn out the way a committed follower of Hegel might have expected. This fact led people to do to Hegel what he was accused of doing to others: argue that historical events had refuted him because he was unable to foresee the evil that modern European states were capable of inflicting on one another. I will try to show that this line of argument is seriously flawed. No philosophy of history can be judged on how well it predicts the future, because its job is not to make predictions but to interpret what has already happened. By the same token, the mere citing of historical evidence cannot refute a philosophic argument, because whatever evidence history may offer, we are always in a position to decide how to pass judgment on that evidence.

Did the destruction of the Second Temple refute ancient Judaism? Many people thought so at the time. How could an all-powerful God permit this to happen? From another perspective, however, so far from refuting ancient Judaism, the destruction of the Temple gave it a chance to transform itself. We can raise the same sort of question about any historical event. Did the French Revolution "refute" the *ancien régime*, or did it reveal the brutality of what took its place? Did the concentration camps refute the idea that humanity is an end in itself, or did they show us the horror of what happens when that idea is abandoned?

It is only when history is interpreted that we are in a position to say what ideas should be kept and what ideas no longer make sense. We saw that even Hegel had mixed reactions to the French Revolution and the Prussian State. To think that historical events carry their interpretations on their sleeves so that it is obvious what lesson we are supposed to learn is to misrepresent what historical reasoning is really about. As Cohen put it (*RR*, 3), "history in itself does not determine the concept of reason."

THE STORY TURNS SOUR

Although Hegel witnessed the rise of the modern state, he was not in a position to see the effect that industrialization, globalization, or massive population growth would have on it. No one was. Nor was he in a position to see that as such forces took hold, the nature of warfare would undergo fundamental changes. Armies would get much larger, would be mobilized much faster, and would possess weapons too terrible for anyone in his day to imagine: rifled artillery, the machine gun, high explosives, poison gas, the airplane, enormous iron-hulled warships. In addition to vast sums of money, the armies that employed these weapons would require constant training and outfitting. Increasingly, war would not be limited to specific times or regions but would involve much of the inhabitable area of the planet much of the time. As with many social problems, preparation for war would become a self-fulfilling prophecy. The enemy has introduced a new line of weaponry, has increased the size of its army, has mobilized its troops. Under such circumstances, a reasonable person might conclude that his own country needs to do the same – or more. If more, then the process of escalation starts all over again.

In August of 1914, Europe's states went to war on a scale unlike anything seen before. Even by contemporary standards, the casualties suffered boggle the mind. Verdun, 700,000; Gallipoli, 275,000; the Somme, 1,100,000; the Marne, 500,000. By contrast, the French lost 5,000 men at the Battle of Jena, whose gunshots Hegel may have heard, whereas the Prussians lost 25,000, a shocking number for the time. Appalling as the numbers for World War I are, they do not mention the millions of civilians who were killed, maimed, raped, displaced, or forced to suffer the horrors of "ethnic cleansing." No stranger to the human propensity for evil, Hegel (*RH*, 27) mentions the slaughter-bench of history, "at which the happiness of peoples, the wisdom of states, and the virtue of individuals have been sacrificed." So it is not as if he was looking at history through rose-colored glasses. Nonetheless, we can agree with Charles Taylor that after reading *Reason in History*, a contemporary of Hegel might have concluded that much of the horror and cruelty that people inflict on one another was behind them and had given way to an age of reason and freedom.[28] Even war, Hegel argued, had become rationalized and was now being waged in a humane fashion that avoids civilian casualties.[29]

Unfortunately history – in this case European history – took a bloody and brutal turn. The war ended not in triumph but in exhaustion and devastation. Germany lay in ruins. No question of principle was resolved. Hegel was well aware of the evil humanity inflicts on itself. After introducing the image of the slaughter-bench, he asks, "What was all this for?" In this case, the answer was nothing. In the words of Ernst Bloch, there was "no breadth, no outlook, no ends, no inner threshold, presently crossed, no kernel, and at the center no gathering conscience of the Absolute."[30] One could say, perhaps, that if no question of principle was resolved, there is a sense in which the original principles articulated by Hegel in the previous century, chiefly freedom and self-consciousness, were still intact. However, for a generation who had come to believe with Hegel that it is wrong to devalue the importance of action that takes place *in* history, this answer proved unsatisfactory.

Cohen had little patience for Hegel. Although he died before the war ended, from our perspective, Cohen's account of the conflict is so anomalous that it merits comment. Faced with growing anti-Semitism in Germany even among intellectuals, he had tried to argue that the

---

[28] Taylor, *Hegel*, 545.
[29] *PR*, 338 (215) and in addition 193 (297).
[30] Ernst Bloch, *Spirit*, 3. Note that *The Spirit* was written between 1914–16 and was first published in 1918 and again in 1923.

German ethos, understood as the liberal Germany that fostered the Enlightenment and made Germany a world center of science, philosophy, music, and scholarship during his lifetime (*Deutschtum*), and the Jewish ethos, understood as ethical monotheism (*Judentum*), were identical. So convinced was Cohen of this identity that he prayed for a victory of the Fatherland on the grounds that it would bring us closer to realizing the goal of universal humanity and would lay the foundation for world peace.[31] Needless to say, both of the terms in Cohen's equation were idealizations – in effect, the Platonic form of German culture and the Platonic form of Jewish culture. He rejected Zionism in favor of an ethical universalism and, as we saw, portrayed Israel as the suffering servant of humanity. Although the outcome of the war and the rise of the Nazi Party afterward made Cohen's equation look grotesque, dissatisfaction with his rational optimism emerged even earlier.

Beginning with Buber and continuing with Scholem and Benjamin, many Jewish intellectuals turned away from the Enlightenment and sought inspiration in Hasidism and Mysticism. The Kantian idea of steady progress toward an infinite and unrealizable goal was seen as a romantic delusion, and Hegel's attempt at a theodicy of world history, one of the many casualties of World War I. Before long, rationality became synonymous abstraction and sterility. Conversely, what was once rejected as mythology was now thought to reveal the fertility of the religious imagination and thus to provide a vitality that reason lacked. Zionism and Jewish cultural particularity became fashionable in intellectual circles. More importantly for present purposes, people began to think in apocalyptic terms. The German upper class will never accept Jews as full citizens, and attempting to reform it by providing a vision of a more inclusive society is a waste of time. Along these lines, Anson Rabinbach described the messianism that swept Jewish intellectuals of this generation as "apocalyptic, catastrophic, utopian and pessimistic."[32]

---

[31] Cohen, "Deutschtum und Judentum I" and "Deutschtum und Judentum II" in *Jüdische Schriften*, Vol. 2, 237–318.

[32] Anson Rabinbach, "Between Enlightenment and Apocalypse: Benjamin, Bloch and Modern German Jewish Messianism," *New German Critique* 34 (1985): 81. For other discussions of this period, see Jürgen Moltmann, *The Coming of God*, 29–41, and Pierre Bouretz, "Messianism and Modern Jewish Philosophy," in *The Cambridge Companion to Modern Jewish Philosophy*, 170–91.

Unlike the messianism of Maimonides or Cohen, which rejected cosmic upheavals, this messianism longed for one. Like the ancient prophets, it saw oppression and injustice everywhere. To suggest that we can correct them by making steady progress toward a better society is to cooperate with the very forces one is trying to overthrow, the forces of appeasement. The only hope we have is for a Messiah to burst onto the scene and free us from the tedium of living through an endless series of days, each like the one before it, without any possibility of definitive action or final resolution of humanity's ills. In short, hope for a Messiah made life worth living. For some thinkers, the nature of the "Messiah" was largely undetermined and meant only a radical disruption of the present order; for others, it came to be a synonym for revolutionary socialism.

The thinker who set the stage for this group was Ernst Bloch. His first book, *Spirit of Utopia*, was written during the war, while he lived in Switzerland, and revised afterward. Rather than wait for an apocalypse to occur, Bloch often writes as if the World War I *is* the apocalypse: "There has never been a more dismal military objective than Imperial Germany's: a suffocating coercion imposed by mediocrities and tolerated by mediocrities; a triumph of stupidity, guarded by the gendarme, acclaimed by the intellectuals who did not have enough brains to provide slogans."[33] In reading Bloch, one cannot help but be reminded of the rabbinic view that the Messiah will come when things have reached the lowest ebb. However, Bloch assures us, all is not lost: "Only in us does this light still burn, and we are beginning a fantastic journey toward it, a journey toward the interpretation of our waking dream, toward the implementation of the central concept of utopia ... *incipit vita nova*."[34] Such are the words of someone who has seen his country vanquished because of its own arrogance and stupidity.

The implementation of the utopia that will follow the apocalypse will require nothing short of a full-blown Marxist revolution. If there is any good that has come out of the war, for Bloch it is that the German ruling classes were devastated. Unfortunately, the window of opportunity created by the war's destruction soon closed. According to Bloch, profiteers moved in, the mighty *grand bourgeois* put out the

[33] Bloch, *Spirit*, 1.
[34] *Spirit*, 3.

fires, and the universities became corrupt and preached a return to German nationalism.[35] The state, which Hegel regarded as a precondition for the realization of freedom, thus became a military monopoly based on a "heathenish, satanic coercion."[36]

And yet one has to persist. There is the possibility of revolution, not just against capitalism, but against "the ceaseless, primordial locus of all enslavement, brutality and exploitation: against militarism, feudalism, a world from the top down."[37] In the end, the soul, the Messiah, and the apocalypse form what Bloch calls "the *a priori* of all politics and culture." To us, Bloch's rhetoric seems overheated; but to his contemporaries, it inspired a vision of the world that went from apocalypse to utopia. To the extent that Bloch was right, or even on the right track, one did not have to excuse oneself for invoking categories that previous generations of rationalist philosophers had tried so hard to discredit.

There is no question that Bloch had a lasting impact on the thought of his friend Walter Benjamin. Like Bloch, Benjamin's connection with traditional Judaism was tenuous. Both represent what Rabinbach called "Jewishness without Judaism."[38] In any case, the air of pessimism so prevalent in Bloch is also evident in Benjamin's "On the Concept of History," published in May of 1940, shortly before Benjamin, fleeing Nazi persecution, committed suicide. History, Benjamin tells us (*CH*, 9), is "one single catastrophe, which keeps piling wreckage upon wreckage" until the pile of debris grows toward the sky. Progress, in the sense of gradual improvement, is like a storm that blows us steadily into the future, rendering it impossible for us to "make whole what has been smashed."

Against the reform platform of Germany's Social Democratic Party, Benjamin (*CH*, 11) protests that nothing has corrupted the German working class as much as the notion that it was moving ahead with the current of history, a current being driven by technological advancement. The Social Democrats tried to sell the working classes on the idea that their labor and their sacrifices would be the redeemer of *future*

---

[35] *Spirit*, 235.
[36] *Spirit*, 239.
[37] *Spirit*, 244.
[38] Rabinbach, "Enlightenment and Apocalypse," 82.

generations (*CH*, 12). True, they might suffer now; but their suffering is not for naught, because their children and grandchildren will live better lives as a result. From Benjamin's perspective, the truth is the opposite: The working classes need to be motivated by the realization that their ancestors suffered as well. Behind the Social Democratic view of history is "the concept of its progression through a homogeneous, empty time," which is to say a time in which every moment resembles the one that came before it and the one that will come after it, so that nothing of any real consequence happens (*CH*, 13).

It is not just the Social Democrats that Benjamin is opposing. If history is "one single catastrophe," it cannot be the gradual unfolding of reason. The same is true of progress by secular or material means. Although it promises the realization of human freedom, all that such progress delivers is an endless progression through homogeneous time. Against this view, the purpose of revolution is to "blast open the continuum of history" (*CH*, 16). The Messiah, as Benjamin informs us (*CH*, 6), comes not only as a redeemer but also as the victor over the Antichrist.

Thus far, "On the Concept of History" sounds like a typical Marxist rejection of liberalism. It is noteworthy, however, that in addition to the idea of victory over the Antichrist, it begins and ends with obvious references to theology. In the beginning, Benjamin describes a puppet dressed in Turkish attire that used to play people in chess matches and beat them every time. In fact, a dwarf who was a chess master sat inside the puppet and pulled strings to allow it to make its moves. Benjamin claims that the puppet corresponds to "historical materialism," which is intended to win all the time. Yet the only way it can win is to enlist the services of the dwarf, who corresponds to theology, and has to be kept out of sight. So historical materialism has to hide the fact that it is at bottom a form of messianism.

In the end, Benjamin is more explicit. He tells us that the Jews were prohibited from inquiring into the future. This may be a reference to the fact that they were prohibited from trying to calculate the arrival of the Messiah or that, as the Talmud says, after the destruction of the Second Temple in the year 70, the job of prophecy was given over to children and fools.[39] According to Benjamin, the

---

[39] *Babba Batra* 12b.

Torah and the prayer books ask them to remember what happened in the past. However, unlike the Social Democratic view of history, the Jewish one does not culminate in a future that becomes "homogeneous, empty time." Why not? Because "every second was the small gateway in time through which the Messiah might enter." Simply put, it is only the expectation that at any minute history might explode that kept the Jews alive.

Finally there is Scholem, whose observations about messianism constitute the framework for much of this work. Recall that for Scholem Jewish messianism in its origin and its nature is a theory of catastrophe. As he sees it, the crux of apocalypticism is its pessimistic view of the world, what one might call anachronistically its rejection of the idea of reason in history. If apocalyptic writers display hope for a better future, it is not because history will take us there, but because history as we know it will perish and be replaced by something vastly different. More specifically, history will be destroyed or upended by a force that comes from outside history.

Scholem (*MIJ*, 9) therefore attacks those thinkers, rabbinic or philosophic, who sought to "suppress exceedingly vital elements in the realm of Judaism, elements filled with historical dynamism even if they combined destructive with constructive forces." By the same token, the escapist and extravagant character of utopianism subjects the idea of redemption to the wild indulgence of fantasy. "But," Scholem (*MIJ*, 14) continues, "it always retains that fascinating vitality to which no historical reality can do justice." Asked to choose between such vitality and what Scholem saw as a life lived in deferment, he had no hesitation picking the former.

Scholem's concept of vitality flies directly in the face of the Hegelian conception of the end of history. Although Hegel envisioned further development of constitutional democracy in America, he closed off the possibility that history would be upended by an outside force that would establish an entirely new order. From his perspective, there is no such force. The revolutions that have occurred were brought about by human agents, and at this point in the world's history, the age of revolution is over. In fact, Hegel was suspicious of anything that allowed people to indulge their fantasies of utopia. For Scholem, this way of thinking takes away one of the most important features of human life: the expectation and contemplation of the radically new.

WAS HEGEL VINDICATED?

From a global perspective, it was not the apocalyptic, catastrophic, utopian, and pessimistic messianism of Jewish intellectuals that mattered, but that of communism and fascism. In an odd way, the rise of apocalypticism after World War I, much of which was founded on the collapse of the Hegelian view of history, may have shown that in one respect Hegel was right – not that rationality had been realized in the establishment of the modern state, but that messianic fervor with its embrace of catastrophe and utopia can and often does lead to disaster.

Both Judaism and Christianity have rich apocalyptic traditions. The difference, according Scholem, is that Jewish apocalypticism is inherently nationalistic. He argues, "The national antithesis between Israel and the heathens is broadened into a cosmic antithesis in which the realms of the holy and of sin, of purity and impurity, of life and death, of light and darkness, God and the anti-divine powers, stand opposed." Few would deny that such thinking strikes a responsive chord in the human psyche. The battles that one fights are not over differences of opinion but cosmic struggles between good and evil. In such a struggle, compromise is out of the question. Either the enemy is destroyed or everything of value in the world will be destroyed first.

Whether in the ancient world or the modern, the problem of the religious imagination is that by bringing an element of transcendence to human experience, it runs the risk of bringing a transcendent element to human destructive capacity as well. Confronted with the horrible devastation of World War I, both communism and fascism took on apocalyptic overtones and indulged their fantasies to the utmost. In their case, history as we know it would perish not from divine incursion into human affairs, but from human beings taking it upon themselves to save civilization from its enemies. Both envisioned a final struggle against their enemies and preached that the hour of decision was at hand.

Norman Cohn is right to say that given our liberal sensibilities, not only the rhetoric but also the actions of these movements are barely comprehensible.[40] In the next chapter, I will raise the question of whether this is understated: Perhaps they are not comprehensible at

[40] Norman Cohn, *Pursuit*, 288.

all. For the present, the important point is that according to Cohn, the strangeness of communist and fascist worldviews derives from the fact that we tend to look at them in a historical vacuum, not recognizing that this kind of apocalyptic urgency has deep roots in European history – roots that take us all the way back to ancient times.

Take a defeated or dispossessed people who have lost faith in existing social structures and who have lost patience with the uncertain course of historical progress. Tell them that their problems are not their fault but the fault of outsiders or impersonal historical forces. that pay no attention to right and wrong. Tell them that unless they act quickly, the chances of overcoming these forces will vanish. Arm them, organize them, and march them off to war. The story has been told a thousand times. A large part of the motivation for Hegel's finding reason in history was to argue that however familiar the story may be, it no longer makes sense, because history has reached a point where apocalypse and utopia have become the stuff of mythology.

One can always argue that rationality does not capture every aspect of human experience, but this only invites the reply that when you depart from it in such a dramatic fashion, you run the risk of taking us back to *tohu vavohu*, a world that is unformed and void. In fact, the brief but terrible histories of fascism and communism in Europe only show that in the end, constitutional democracy had to be defended or restored.

Considerations like these led Francis Fukuyama to argue in 1989 that with the collapse of the Soviet Union, the end of history had been reached, and no serious alternatives to liberal democracy now exist.[41] To his credit, Fukuyama does not think the end of history is a time to rejoice. On the contrary, he thinks it will mean the end of art and philosophy as well as the beginning of an era when all conflicts will be driven by economic and technological considerations. He even suggests that out of boredom, people may want to invent history all over again. Far from constituting a resolution of the issue, Fukuyama's claims re-raise the same old questions.

For all its triumphs, liberal democracy does not work in every part of the world, including Iraq, Afghanistan, and many of the inner cities of

---

[41] Francis Fukuyama, "The End of History?" *The National Interest* 16 (Summer 1989): 3–18. Also see the follow-up essays in *The End of History and the Last Man.*

the United States. Even in places where it does seem to work, it has led to boom-and-bust cycles in the economy with the human misery that results from the latter, massive amounts of debt, a permanent under-class, and a life devoted to endless accumulation and consumption – exactly as its Marxist critics predicted. Can liberal democracy solve these problems, or will it give way to alternative forms of social organ-ization, possibly a superior form?

The jury is out. The owl of Minerva spreads its wings only with the falling of the dusk. All we can say is that whatever happens, it will not be historical facts alone that validate or refute a philosophic theory. If a new form of social organization develops, we will have to decide whether it represents an improvement on what it replaced or whether it overlooks lessons history has already taught. If a new form of social organization does not develop, we will still have to consider what the alternatives are. All this boils down to the claim that the story of history is more than an enumeration of facts, or what Benjamin (III) called a chronicle. If the idea that there is reason in history is to make sense, we need to be clear what facts are important and what use we intend to make of them.

RATIONALITY IN DEFIANCE OF HISTORY

In many ways, the most radical Jewish thinker to emerge from the experience of World War I was Franz Rosenzweig. I say *radical* not because his pessimism was greater than that of Bloch or Benjamin, but because instead of viewing redemption as a force breaking *into* history, he saw it as liberation *from* history. Rosenzweig's disillusion-ment with World War I is evident in the foreword attached to his first major work, *Hegel and the State*. Although the book was not published until 1920, Rosenzweig tells us that work on it was essen-tially finished before the war broke out.[42] During the time the book was being written, "hope was that the Bismarckian state ... would expand itself into a free empire breathing the air of the world." The purpose of the book was to enable Rosenzweig to take the reader beyond the "hard and limited" Hegelian conception of the state and open it to the possibility of a new German future. However, as

---

[42] Franz Rosenzweig, *Philosophical and Theological Writings*, 74–5.

Rosenzweig admits, "A field of ruins marks the spot where the empire previously stood."

Rather than the horrors of the war, the *Star of Redemption* begins with a rejection of absolute idealism. From Parmenides to Hegel, the goal of philosophy was to assert a unity between thought and being. This led to the idea that all reality could be encompassed within a philosophic system. The problem with such a system is the assumption that thought can overcome all opposition, so that in the end, nothing can maintain an identity outside the system. Rosenzweig begins by asking a simple question: Where in all of this do *I* fit in? We saw that according to traditional philosophy, the individual is unknowable in its individuality. We can know it only to the degree that it embodies a universal quality, which means that we can put it in a category and make it transparent to reason. However, Rosenzweig protests, this view of philosophy overlooks the fact that human experience takes place at a pre-theoretical level where rational transparency is not available.

The crux of Rosenzweig's "New Thinking" is therefore an attempt to recapture this level of experience and to focus on the individual in her finitude, an individual who must confront irreducible facts like the inevitability of her death. As Rosenzweig tells us in the first two sentences of the *Star*, "All cognition of the All originates in death, in the fear of death. Philosophy takes it upon itself to throw off the fear of things earthly, to rob death of its poisonous sting." Unfortunately, as Rosenzweig remarks a few pages later, our terror as we tremble before this sting condemns traditional philosophy to the status of a cruel lie.

In terms later made famous by Levinas, Rosenzweig rejected a totalizing vision of the world in which the elimination of oppositions means that everything is rendered homogeneous.[43] In that respect, Rosenzweig's break with Hegel is more profound than that of Bloch or Benjamin. We do not need an apocalypse or the arrival of a Messiah to have alterity. Our own sense of ourselves as human beings is enough to make us see that absolute idealism does not capture every aspect

---

[43] For Levinas's relation to and deep respect for Rosenzweig, see "Between Two Worlds," in *DF*, 181–201, as well as his Foreword to Stéphane Mosès, *System and Revelation*, 13–22. For further commentary, see Richard A. Cohen, *Elevations: The Height of the Good in Rosenzweig and Levinas*, and Robert Gibbs, *Correlations in Rosenzweig and Levinas*. See, however, Peter Eli Gordon, "Franz Rosenzweig and the Philosophy of Jewish Existence," in *Modern Jewish Philosophy*, 132–5, for important reservations.

of reality. Nor, as we will see, does it capture the need for spiritual fulfillment. In the case of Judaism, an important part of the fulfillment is the sense of being part of a people whose destiny is to stand over and against the course of history as Hegel understood it.

To understand Rosenzweig's conception of Judaism, we have to turn to his conception of eternity, which in turn is based on his view of temporal asymmetry. The past presents itself to us with what Rosenzweig calls (*SR*, 226–7) "the endless indifference of a sequence," where each moment resembles another, and the sum of all moments forms an interminable series. The greatest mistake we can make is to think that the future stretches out before us in the same way. Thus the "pure historian" comes up with the idea that all eras, past and present, are equally immediate to God. Rosenzweig's point is that this is not the way time is actually experienced. The future is defined by anticipation, or what Stéphane Mosès terms "a tensing toward the not-yet."[44] The future is messianic in the sense that it is infused by the impatience of wanting to bring the Messiah, even if it is before his appointed time. Against Cohen's suggestion that the Messiah only comes at infinity, Rosenzweig maintains that every moment of time is lived with the expectation that he *will* come. Absent messianic expectation, the future would be nothing more than "a past distended endlessly and projected forward." Put otherwise, there is no point in striving for something that does not have an identifiable, that is, achievable, end – exactly the point made by Pelagius centuries earlier. Without such an end, the result would be quietism.

Rosenzweig's asymmetry enables him to distinguish between eternity in a strong sense and endless duration. Because each moment of the future brings the expectation of the end, Rosenzweig asserts somewhat paradoxically, eternity is always already in existence but at the same time still to come. More fully (*SR*, 224), "It is not yet in existence once and for all. It is eternally coming. Eternity is not a very long time; it is a Tomorrow that could as well be Today. Eternity is a future which, without ceasing to be future, is nonetheless present." The idea of living in anticipation of the Messiah, a future that is nonetheless present, allows us to see that the Jewish understanding of redemption differs from the Christian.

---

44 Moses, *System and Revelation*, 136.

For Christianity, redemption is on the way; in Hegelian terms, it is something whose progressive unfolding we await and work for. By contrast, Judaism, says Rosenzweig, experiences redemption in the present, which is to say an eternal present that begins anew at the very moment that it vanishes.[45] If Christianity asks us to come to the Father through the Son, then Rosenzweig famously adds that Judaism is already with the Father. As evidence of this, he cites the yearly cycle of holidays, a cycle that, if understood correctly, has no beginning and no end – in effect, an eternity.

This means that Judaism takes up a place that is outside history. Where Hegel saw Judaism as an oppressive and outmoded religion, Rosenzweig sees it as the *telos* of all religion. In symbolic terms that derive from the image of a star, Judaism is the fire, Christianity the rays. In Rosenzweig's view, both are needed. There is no possibility of asking the nations of the world to stop what they are doing and take up a posture that removes them from the flow of history and the possibility of progress. Rosenzweig is simply saying that whereas the possibility of progress is one way to understand redemption, it is not the only way. Redemption can also be experienced as present.

What does it mean to take up a place *outside* history? For Rosenzweig, it means that Jewish existence is not justified by the things most people regard as important: land, language, custom, military victory, in short all the things that are situated *in* history. In his view (*SR*, 305), Judaism "was robbed" of these things long ago. What he really means, of course, is that Judaism was *liberated* from these things. The Jewish sense of belonging is self-reflective, and that is what explains its status as eternal: It does not take root in anything external, anything but "ourselves." Thus Jewish existence constitutes an anomaly because it looks upon the rise and fall of empires with indifference.

In its own way, Rosenzweig's account of Judaism was as much an idealization as Cohen's, which goes to show that even at the level of lived experience, idealization has a role to play.[46] To a more realistic observer, the reason Jews did not define themselves in terms of land, language, custom, and military victory is that the harsh reality of exile

[45] *SR*, 289.

[46] According to Mosès, *The Angel*, 44, the idea of the metahistorical vocation of the Jewish people, as presented in the *Star*, should not be understood as a theory of political practice but as "a guiding idea, that of 'the limit imposed on all politics.'"

prevented them from doing so. Rather than living in an ever-present eternity, most Jews had adopted the passivity that comes from a life lived in deferral. The difference between Rosenzweig and Cohen is that rather than putting the ideal at an infinite distance from the present, Rosenzweig melded it *into* the present.

As with any idealization, problems arise. Yosef Yerushalmi objected that understanding of the past is critical to Judaism, as shown by the fact that to remember is a divine commandment.[47] Rosenzweig addresses this point in the *Star* by saying that Judaism does not look upon its history as a point receding into the past but as a spiritual moment lived in the present.[48] In his defense, it could be said that although every Jew is asked to recall the experience of the Exodus, she is asked to recall it in such a way that she views it as if she herself had been liberated from Egypt. Not surprisingly, Zionists objected that, far from a virtue, statelessness was a curse that had to be corrected.

From my standpoint, the most serious objection is the historical one raised by Emil Fackenheim. Commenting on Rosenzweig's near conversion to Christianity at an early age, Fackenheim writes,[49]

Events since Rosenzweig have shown, for all with eyes to see, that the price for his return to Judaism can no longer be paid. Rosenzweig was able to carry out his postmodern return to the premodern Jewish faith only by making *all* Jewish existence ahistorical or, which is the same thing, by sacralizing it. ... Yet, less than four years after Rosenzweig's death events began to unfold – events still far from over and done with – which, for better or worse, have cast the Jewish people back firmly, inescapably, irrevocably, back into history: not into sacred history, but rather into the flesh-and-blood history of men, women, and children – as Rosenzweig himself well put it, the history of *Mord und Totschlag.*

I have already indicated that I am suspicious of events that show anything for all with eyes to see. It is, moreover, a gross oversimplification to imply that Jewish history prior to Rosenzweig's death knew nothing of *Mord und Totschlag.* In fact, that is Rosenzweig's point. Jews were no strangers to catastrophe, but unlike other peoples, they did not

[47] Yosef Yerushalmi, *Zakhor, Jewish History and Jewish Memory*, 8. For further discussion of this issue, see Myriam Bienenstock, "Recalling the Past in Rosenzweig's *Star of Redemption*," *Modern Judaism* 23 (2003): 226–39.

[48] *SR*, 304.

[49] Fackenheim, *MW*, 33.

view them as decisive. As we saw with the destruction of the Second Temple, the faith endured. But let us dig deeper.

The events Fackenheim is talking about are the Holocaust and the formation of the State of Israel. Because the next chapter is devoted to the former, I will not discuss it at length here except to say that for Fackenheim, it represents a kind of evil unlike anything any people had experienced before, a historical *novum*. In regard to the formation of the State of Israel, it is undeniable that Rosenzweig would have expressed himself differently if he had known what few in his generation could foresee. For him, Jewish existence in the diaspora is both final and essential. Like Cohen, Rosenzweig thought that the destiny of the Jewish people is to remain in a stateless condition in order to teach the rest of humanity that there are values that transcend history and politics. By contrast, some of the early Zionists argued that Jewish existence in the diaspora is untenable, so that the only way the Jewish people can survive is if, like other nations, they have a homeland.

From our perspective today, it is possible to live an authentic Jewish life either inside or outside a Jewish homeland. Here, I submit, is a clear case in which history offers us alternatives from which to choose rather than a clear-cut winner and loser. Still, the question remains whether the Holocaust and the formation of the State of Israel would force Rosenzweig to abandon his understanding of Jewish spirituality. The answer is not as simple as it might first appear.

We can think of existence outside history in static, quasi-Platonic terms, but I follow Levinas, who was no stranger to the horrors of World War II, by saying that to do so is to misrepresent Rosenzweig's central insight. To be outside history means, in addition, to live *in defiance* of history. Commenting on Rosenzweig's view of Judaism, Levinas maintains (*DF*, 199), "This most ancient of claims is its [Judaism's] claim to a separate existence in the political history of the world. It is the claim to judge history – that is to say, to remain free with regard to events, whatever the internal logic binding them. It is the claim to be an eternal people." In other words, the idea of an eternal people is based on the premise that there are ideals that no historical outcome can refute. That is what the Jews in the Warsaw Ghetto who made Maimonides' twelfth principle (the coming of the Messiah) their anthem before being led to their death must have known. It trivializes their memory to think that they expected the Messiah to appear as a deus ex machina. Rather, they were affirming a timeless commitment to the idea that history does not have to be brutal, death does not have to be the only way to settle disputes, and in the end, evil will not triumph. As Fackenheim himself comes to see, it is this sense of defiance in the face of history that gave many of the victims of the Holocaust their only hold on human dignity.[50]

Hegel is undoubtedly right to say that such ideals are historically conditioned in the sense that our understanding of human dignity may not be the same as that of someone living in the first century A.D. Every ideal is subject to rational scrutiny, and every age brings a new generation of scrutinizers. My point is that none of this forces us to say that such ideals stand or fall on the outcome of historical events. To return to Levinas, Rosenzweig's analysis of Jewish spirituality is an attempt to reject the idea of historical necessity (*DF*, 201): "What Rosenzweig teaches us is the notion that the ritual year and the awareness of the way its circularity anticipates Eternity is not only an experience that is valuable as the time of history and universal history, but 'anterior' in *truth* to that time, and that the defiance shown to history can be as real as that of history." As we have seen, defiance is another name for the right to judge. Unless we hold on to this right, we run the risk of letting armies and political campaigns do our thinking for us. So far from rationality, the outcome of that would be the most egregious form of dogmatism.

---

[50] See Fackenheim's account of the Polish woman Pelagia Lewinska's final realization in *MW*, 217–8. This issue will be discussed in greater detail in the next chapter.

6

History and Irrationality

As it happens, the twentieth century did provide an event that seemed to come from outside of history and to shatter everything that went before it. It was not the arrival of a Messiah; rather, it was the occurrence of evil so monstrous that one cannot help but raise the question of whether we can really understand it. Even if we can, we face the obvious question of how evil on this scale can be reconciled with belief in the coming of a Messiah. As Bouretz puts it, "Our imagination of the best, even divested of its former giddiness, still remains imprisoned by our experience of the worst."[1] As a result, we cannot help but ask whether the occurrence of monstrous evil is not the ultimate refutation of the future orientation of Jewish thought and practice. Remember that some rabbis speculated that the Messiah would come when humanity reached such a low ebb that God would have no choice but to intervene to prevent disaster. Where, then, was the Messiah, or, more broadly, where was the helping hand of God as millions of people were led to their deaths?

EVIL WRIT LARGE

World history contains no shortage of man-made catastrophes, many of them directed at Jews. A person who read *Mein Kampf* might have been able to predict that if Hitler came to power, there would be an

[1] Bouretz, *Witnesses*, 1.

outbreak of anti-Semitism along the lines of *Kristallnacht* – in effect, a pogrom – and a return to ghetto existence. Although Hitler does say that German sacrifices made on the Western Front in World War I would not have been in vain if twelve or fifteen thousand Jews who were corrupting the nation had been forced to submit to poison gas, it is a long way from a pogrom to the Wannsee conference convened in January of 1942, when the plans were laid for the Final Solution to the Jewish Problem.[2]

What exactly was that problem? In Hitler's eyes, the Jews were not just an enemy of the Reich but a unique and insidious enemy. It was not just that the Jews were foreign in the sense of not being of Aryan stock, but they were stateless, homeless, cerebral, and demonic – parasites who, instead of raising an army and engaging in a fair fight, sought to destroy European culture from within. As Moishe Postone sees it, the Jews were not so much an inferior race as an *anti-race*.[3] By draining the energy of legitimate races, in particular the Aryan one, and by draining their material resources as well, the unannounced plan of the Jews was to create a Bolshevik society in which everyone else would be enslaved. They may pose as bankers, shopkeepers, civil servants, and other professionals, but in the end, their hearts were set on Bolshevism.

At first, Nazi Germany did everything it could to expel its Jews. Himmler even proposed shipping them to Madagascar. The problem was that no matter how many Jews left Germany, the conquest of foreign territories, particularly on the Eastern front, meant that the number of Jews living within the domain of the Reich continued to increase. The Final Solution to this problem was the extermination of all Jews no matter where they might be. There were other enemies of the Reich who were killed as well: Gypsies, Poles, homosexuals, political dissidents, the mentally ill, and the physically handicapped. However, as far as we know, Hitler did not see the need to eliminate them *wherever they might be*.[4] In his eyes, it was the Jews who started

---

[2] Hitler's *Mein Kampf*, 620.
[3] Moishe Postpone, "The Holocaust and the Trajectory of the Twentieth Century," in *Catastrophe and Meaning*, 89.
[4] In *Rethinking the Holocaust*, 48–53, Yehuda Bauer uses the totalizing nature of the Holocaust to distinguish it from other genocides. On the issue of moral comparisons among instances of mass murder, see the second section of this chapter.

World War I, who stabbed Germany in the back, and who, left to their own devices, were intent on starting another war. For Germany to regain its honor and prevent economic and cultural disaster, the Jews had to be eliminated.[5] Among his last words in the bunker in Berlin was the hope that the German people would continue their fight against Judaism and Bolshevism.

It is in this sense that Hitler's vision counts as apocalyptic, even redemptive, to use a term introduced by Saul Friedländer.[6] We have seen that genuine apocalypses do not promise an improvement in the status quo but a radical transformation: to eliminate evil once and for all. In Leni Riefenstahl's immortal film *The Triumph of the Will*, Hitler descends from above, church bells ring, and Germany exults in the arrival of its savior. His mission is not to destroy European culture but to defend it against its natural enemies. The battle might be costly, but in his mind, the outcome was so important that any level of sacrifice would be justified. If the chief contribution of Judaism to world culture was the idea of humanity as a moral universal, or if, at its spiritual core, it cared nothing about land, language, or military victory, then there is a perverse sense in which Hitler was right: The Jew was the ultimate enemy of the Reich. Ironically, the Jew was also the enemy of the Soviet Union. Although anti-Semitism was never as central to Soviet policy as it was to the Nazis, Richard Overy writes that it differed only by degree.[7]

The culmination of such hatred in Germany was the Holocaust, evil so vast that it strains human capacity to come to grips with it. From a philosophic standpoint, the Holocaust raises a number of questions. In the first place, God was silent. No voice was heard, no Messiah appeared, and no disruption of the natural order occurred, despite sincere and repeated pleas from people in distress. In fact, one of the most remarkable things about this period was Hitler's ability to *avoid* assassination.

In the second place, there was no clear way in which the overwhelming horror of the event could be seen as advancing the cause of human

[5] For the centrality of anti-Semitism to Hitler's view of the world, see I. Kershaw, *Hitler, the Germans and the Final Solution*, chap. 4. Notice Kershaw's repeated use of the word "salvation" in describing Hitler's viewpoint.

[6] Saul Friedländer, *Nazi Germany and the Jews*, 72, 87.

[7] Richard Overy, *Russia's War*, 309.

progress. The result is that both religious and secular theodicies were left with nothing significant to say. Standard responses to evil – such as (1) we need it to be able to recognize goodness, (2) we need it to have the opportunity to strive for goodness, and (3) a certain amount of evil is needed if goodness is to triumph in the end – run aground against the cruel facts of mass murder. The events in question are not just evil but irredeemably so. I will have more to say about redemption at the end of this chapter and into the next; for the present let me simply say that by *irredeemable* I mean that no other event, past or present, neither the death and resurrection of Jesus nor the coming of a future Messiah, can offset the extent of the tragedy or atone for the sins of the perpetrators.

This raises the question of whether our normal ways of thinking about evil are adequate to account for something this terrible. From a philosophic perspective, the traditional view of evil begins with Socrates, becomes a staple of medieval Neo-Platonism, and survives in slightly altered fashion in Kant.[8] We saw that for Kant, evil occurs when an agent subordinates the maxim incorporating obedience to the moral law to a maxim that incorporates selfishness. This is another way of saying that when we act in an evil fashion, we are promoting our own self-interest over the interests of humanity. Because reason is the source of morality, and morality contains its own incentive to obey – duty for duty's sake – evil by its very nature is *irrational*. That does not mean that a criminal cannot display cunning in figuring out how to rob a bank, but that in doing so he violates his own sense of fairness. We can see this by realizing that unless the criminal knew that stealing is wrong, his action, although obviously harmful, would not be evil. In short, evil occurs when a moral agent chooses to do it in the knowledge that it is wrong.

Why does the agent make this choice? Although historical or psychological factors might help us to understand the causes operating on the criminal's mind, according to Kant, causes of this sort could at best explain what the criminal did, not why what he did is wrong. To get at the latter, we would have to refer to his decision to reject morality in favor of self-interest. If the decision is free, it must be spontaneous

---

[8] On this point, see Maimonides' claim at *GP* 3.10–11, 439–40, that all evils are privations and derive from ignorance.

in the sense that no external cause determines its outcome. This means that to be responsible for what he has done, the criminal must be able to follow the dictates of morality or not. If no causal explanation will work, then the criminal's decision, although understandable in the sense of being normal or predictable, is at bottom inscrutable. Commenting on this aspect of Kant's position, Allen Wood describes the criminal's decision as *rationally motivated unreason* and likens it to *akrasia*.[9] This leaves us with the claim that, prevalent as it is, evil is always something of a mystery. Our situation resembles that of Othello at the end of the play when he asks Iago why all this tragedy happened. Yet all Iago says is "Demand me nothing: what you know, you know."

Another consequence of Kant's view, as Card points out, is that there is no systematic way to distinguish between the evil involved in telling a lie and the evil involved in operating a death camp.[10] Although Kant introduced the idea of *radical* evil, he did not mean a particularly loathsome or widespread form of it, but rather the fact that the subordination of morality to self-interest corrupts everything we do. Unlike Socrates, Kant takes up the idea that human behavior may be demonic, which is to say that people might do evil not out of self-interest but for its own sake. We saw that Kant was thoroughly convinced of human depravity. Yet he firmly resists the suggestion that human behavior can be diabolical in this sense (*R* 6:36):

The human being (even the most wicked) does not repudiate the moral law whatever his maxims, in rebellious attitude (by revoking obedience to it). The law rather imposes itself on him irresistibly, because of his moral predisposition; and if no other incentive were at work against it, he would also incorporate it into his supreme maxim as sufficient determination of his power of choice, i.e. he would be morally good.

If we do evil, it is not because there is something intrinsically appealing about it, but because we want to satisfy our own desire for happiness.

---

[9] Wood, "Kant and the Intelligibility of Evil," unpublished manuscript.

[10] Claudia Card, *The Atrocity Paradigm*, 73–95. For a similar attempt to introduce a category of atrocious as opposed to ordinary evil, see Marilyn McCord Adams, *Horrendous Evils and the Goodness of God*, 26–7. Both thinkers follow the lead of Hannah Arendt, whose thought is discussed in greater detail in the following section.

Is this credible? The way we answer this question will have a direct bearing on how we understand the events of the twentieth century and what it means to say that history has an end.

EVIL AND SELF-INTEREST

Simply put, the Kantian view of evil is that we allow self-interest to trump morality. That this is true in a myriad of cases no one would deny. Most normal cases of evil, such as theft, murder, or lying, do involve a person putting his own interests above those of others. To this, we may add crimes motivated by jealousy or revenge. Kant is right to think that such emotions derive from the feeling that we are in competition with others for limited resources. In looking at a phenomenon as massive as the Holocaust, it is undeniable that politicians, scientists, shop owners, business executives, and perhaps millions of others acted in exactly this way. The question is whether all evil should be understood as the pursuit of self-interest, and the obvious answer is that a great deal depends on what one means by self-interest.

If self-interest is understood broadly as anything that satisfies one's desire, then Kant's account of evil would be true in the sense that even the most self-destructive behavior can be explained by saying that the agent regarded it as pleasant or experienced some sort of morbid satisfaction in contributing to his own downfall. In stretching self-interest to include anything the agent desires, however, Kant opens himself to a classic objection raised by Bishop Butler: Although it might be formally correct to say that all actions are motivated by self-interest, we would still want to distinguish actions that proceed from "cool consideration that it will be to my own advantage" from actions in which a person courts certain ruin to do good or evil.[11] Consider someone who risks his own life or well-being to save the lives of others. Although we could describe such action as self-interested on the grounds that the person's image of himself requires heroic action, unless we adopt a strong view of human depravity, it would be misleading to do so. By the same token, consider someone who risks his life or well-being to

---

[11] Bishop John Butler, *Fifteen Sermons Preached at Rolls Chapel*, 168–9, cited by Card, *Atrocity*, 85.

torture or kill others. Again, we would be inclined to say that something other than self-interest is involved. The cost of identifying self-interest with anything that satisfies one's desire is that the claim that someone acted in self-interest becomes tautologous.

I will have more to say about self-interest later in this chapter. At present, I want to turn to the reluctance of most philosophers to discuss evil in depth. The first problem is that in addition to being a difficult subject, it is a highly emotional one. In the case of the Holocaust, there is the claim that by trying to understand evil this massive, we are in effect taming it and doing its victims a profound injustice. The only authentic response is to abandon rationality and recoil in horror. Along these lines, Arthur Cohen wrote, "There is something in the nature of thought – its patient deliberateness and care for logical order – that is alien to the enormity of the death camps."[12] And according to Emil Fackenheim, "We cannot comprehend it but only comprehend its incomprehensibility."[13] Even one of the perpetrators wrote, after witnessing the killing of Jews on the Eastern Front, "I can't begin to give you the details, it is simply unthinkable that such things exist…. The war here in the East leads to things so terrible I would never have thought them possible."[14]

Against this view, I want to argue that although recoiling in horror is *an understandable* response, it cannot be the final one. To return to the example of Iago, we cannot let evil proclaim its unintelligibility and simply walk off stage. In the words of Amos Funkenstein, "We cannot excuse ourselves from the obligation to understand the Nazi mentality if we want to condemn it, let alone if we want to prevent similar crimes from being committed again."[15]

---

[12] Arthur A. Cohen, *The Tremendom*, 1.

[13] MW, 238. According to Benjamin Pollock, "Thought Going to School with Life? Fackenheim's Last Philosophical Testament," *AJS Review* 31:1 (2007): 145–6, Fackenheim expresses ambivalence on this point and sometimes suggests (e.g., MW, 217–18) that those who resisted the evil of Nazi oppression *did* grasp the totality of its horror and could not have done what they did unless this were true. See the account of Pelagia Lewinska that follows.

[14] Cited in John K. Roth, "On Losing Trust in the World," in *Echoes from the Holocaust*, 164.

[15] Amos Funkenstein, "Theological Interpretations of the Holocaust: A Balance," in *A Holocaust Reader*, 182. On this point, also see Berel Lang, "The Humanities," *The Oxford Handbook of Holocaust Studies*, 684.

A second problem has to do with the connotations of terms describing evil behavior. Consider the word *diabolical*. On one meaning, it refers to evil or cruelty so awful that it is worthy of the devil. In this sense, no one would deny that Hitler's actions were diabolical. We have seen, however, that for Kant it meant the pursuit of evil for its own sake. As I have presented Hitler thus far, his actions do not count as diabolical in Kant's sense of the term. As I see it, Hitler did not view the killing of Jews as evil at all, but on the contrary, a great good. Anti-Semitism was for him more than just propaganda; it was a principled position for which he was willing to pay enormous costs. The crux of his position was correctly expressed by Himmler in a speech to the SS in Poznan, Poland, in October of 1943: "We have the moral right, we had the duty to our people to do it, to kill this people who wanted to kill us."[16]

Needless to say, there was no desire on behalf of world Jewry to threaten the German people or any other people. That is why Hitler's attack on the Jews now seems like the ravings of a madman. However, at the level of generality at which we are operating, the fact remains that he thought he was embarked on a heroic endeavor. Rather than diabolical, the evil involved is better described as *ideological*, the acceptance of a worldview that deprives a portion of the human race of any trace of dignity. Strictly speaking, *ideology* refers to a system of thought rather than a mode of behavior. To say that Nazi ideology is evil is therefore to say that a person can be held morally responsible not only for what she does but also for what she believes. To assent to a morally repugnant doctrine is itself a moral act. In Kantian

---

[16] If identifying the intentions of a moral agent is a difficult process when dealing with a single individual, it is all the more difficult, perhaps impossible, when dealing with nations or authors of national policy. For further discussion of these difficulties in connection with the Final Solution, see Berel Lang, *Act and Idea in the Nazi Genocide*, especially chaps. 1 and 2. Against Lang, my position is not an outgrowth of the Platonic view that no one does evil willingly. Nor do I think that my view lessens the guilt of the perpetrators. In defense of an alternative view – that the Nazis *did* know that the Final Solution was morally wrong – one could point, as Lang does, to systematic attempts to disguise it. Be that as it may, Hitler and Himmler made numerous attempts to justify the extermination of the Jews and to silence resistance, opposition, even reservation. One of the problems we run into here is the use of a term as broad as "the Nazis." If it is unrealistic to think that all Nazis, even all Nazis involved in the act of genocide, had a single intention, it is equally unrealistic to think that national propaganda is always consistent.

terms, it is to uphold a maxim that says one should deny that humanity is an end in itself. Once this is denied, normal virtues like loyalty, fidelity, or willingness to serve one's country lose whatever value they may have had.

We can see this in another way by recognizing that although loyalty, fidelity, or willingness to serve one's country are often good, they are not good without qualification. If loyalty to a just cause is virtuous, loyalty to criminals is not. In order to pursue virtue, a person must first ask, What am I being loyal *to*? In many cases, that is a difficult step to take because it carries the risk that one might have to disassociate himself from his peer group or even his country. One can, of course, ignore the question and just assume that loyalty is a virtue in itself. Although that choice can be regarded as cowardly, it is not diabolical.

The final problem is that discussions of evil often contain a strong measure of homiletics – as if the purpose of the discussion is more to condemn evil than to try to understand it. I want to resist this tendency by assuming that we do not understand evil unless we can see why it is appealing and why, if circumstances were different, we could imagine ourselves doing it. My purpose in making this assumption is not to excuse evil, but to understand why it is so common and how it is that millions of people could be entranced by it.

To see why evil cannot be identified as the pursuit of self-interest, let us first look at a form that I will term *brutality*. A memorable description of it can be found in Thucydides' account of the Massacre at Mycalessus[17]:

The night he [Diitrephes] passed unobserved near the temple of Hermes, not quite two miles from Mycalessus, and at daybreak assaulted and took the town, which is not a large one; the inhabitants being off their guard and not expecting that any one would ever come up so far from the sea to molest them, the wall too being weak, and in some places having tumbled down, while in others it had not been built to any height, and the gates also being left open through their feeling of security. The Thracians bursting into Mycalessus scaled the houses and temples, and butchered the inhabitants, sparing neither youth nor age, but killing all they fell in with, one after the other, children and women, and even beasts of burden, and whatever other living creatures they saw…. Everywhere confusion reigned and death in all its shapes; and in particular they attacked a boys' school, the largest that there was in the place,

---

[17] Thucydides, *The Peloponnesian War*, 416.

into which children had just gone, and massacred them all. In short, the disaster falling upon the whole town was unsurpassed in magnitude, and unapproached by any in suddenness and horror.

The taking of the town and the massacre of its inhabitants served no strategic purpose. It was nothing more than an orgy of killing undertaken by soldiers who had nothing to fear from their victims.

If pursuit of self-interest is too simple an explanation for something like this, so is evil for evil's sake.[18] To do evil for evil's sake, a person would have to recognize the categories of good and evil and pursue the latter in a clear-minded way, making sure that no trace of goodness intervened. Thus Satan in *Paradise Lost* is perfectly lucid about his intentions. Thucydides attempts to explain the massacre at Mycalessus in racial terms, comparing the Thracian to barbarians; but this explanation overlooks the fact that indiscriminate killing of this sort is well nigh universal – as Joshua's conquest of Jericho, the Japanese conquest of Manchuria, and the American massacre at My Lai clearly show.

In the *Nicomachean Ethics* (7.5), Aristotle claims that there is a class of actions, which he terms wildness or brutishness (*theriotes*), that lies beyond the realm of vice, but does not say much more. Earlier in the same book (7.3), when discussing moral weakness, Aristotle points out that there are conditions such as sleep, madness, or drunkenness when it is fair to say that a person both does and does not have knowledge, that is, he can repeat certain phrases as an actor repeats his lines without the meaning of those phrases being part of them.

Following on this insight, we might say that there are conditions in which a person both does and does not hear the voice of reason. To be sure, a person who puts himself or others in such a condition is responsible for the outcome; but when he is in that condition, it is as if reason speaks to him with little or no authority. The hardship and deprivation imposed by war may therefore induce a state similar to madness or drunkenness, a state where the constraints imposed by society or even by one's own conscience have little or no effect.

It may be that part of the appeal of moral drunkenness is just that: It provides a temporary respite from the demands of reason. If Kant

---

[18] Cf. Card, *Atrocity*, 94: "Still, doing wrong for its own sake is a very simple and not the most interesting account of diabolical evil. Nor is it the only conception, if that term is intended to capture evil's most extreme forms."

is right, reason speaks to us in every waking moment and, for all intents and purposes, says the same thing: that the demands of morality take precedence over everything else. Furthermore, if Kant is right about depravity, we will always fall short of what reason asks us to do, with the inevitable result that we have to contend with feelings of guilt and remorse. One could therefore say, as with Kierkegaard, that the moral law demands, and in making a demand – by its demand – only condemns.

Because condemnation is all too frequent, who has not wished she could escape it once in a while? Put otherwise, who has not wished for times when she could turn off the commands of reason, which, in Kant's words, always speaks in a stern and unyielding voice? This is exactly what happens when one becomes a member of a mob. Additional examples can be found in mass political rallies, rock concerts, or victory celebrations after an athletic event. Not only is there no regard for self-interest in such moments; on the contrary, it is also the *loss* of self that gives such moments their appeal. It is, after all, the self that imposes rules and feels remorse when they are broken. Once the self is surrendered, all that matters is the irresistible inertia that drives the group forward and blocks out the thought of anything else.

With the loss of self comes the feeling of being part of something *greater* than the self. Gustave le Bon, a proponent of racial superiority whose work on mass psychology may have influenced Hitler and Mussolini, wrote, "Whatever be the ideas suggested to crowds they can only exercise effective influence on condition that they assume a very absolute, uncompromising, and simple shape."[19] He goes on to say that in their moment of excitement, crowds enter "a purely automatic and unconscious state." In philosophic terms, they make a decision to embark on a moral holiday.

The intensity of mob behavior is part and parcel of its appeal – as is shown by Bill Buford's frightening book, *Among the Thugs*.[20] A journalist who set out to investigate British soccer hoodlums, Buford comes to see that the usual explanation for their behavior – that is, the perpetrators are just lower-class trash – will not work. As the story unfolds, he begins to discover that his status as a neutral observer is no

[19] Gustave le Bon, *The Crowd*, 34.
[20] Bill Buford, *Among the Thugs*.

longer valid, because he has crossed over and become one of the thugs himself. The intensity he describes rivals that of orgasm or religious ecstasy, experiences that can also be compared to madness or drunkenness. To allow oneself to be taken over by this sort of intensity with no regard for health, physical safety, or monetary security is in fact to leave all considerations of self-interest aside. Once self-interest enters the picture, and with it the familiar pattern of means–end reasoning, the intensity of the moment is compromised.

The other side of madness is normalcy, the comfort of knowing that one is safe, that the future holds no great surprises, and that one is part of a social network that offers meaning and purpose. Instead of brutality, we could follow Hannah Arendt in calling this kind of evil *banality*, although I prefer to call it *moral indifference*. It is the evil that results when people do what they are told without regard for its consequences. In an early essay, Arendt suggests that Himmler, a one-time chicken farmer and devoted family man who looked forward to collecting his pension, was such a man.[21] This gave rise to the concept of "desk killer," whose day-to-day motivations are out of all proportion to the enormity of the evil they produce.

This is not the place to delve into the psychologies of particular people, but rather to point out that Arendt originated a trend in historical scholarship that argues that much of the responsibility for the killing did not belong to demons or ideological fanatics but to ordinary people. Although some people object to the use of "ordinary" in this context on the grounds that it excuses the behavior that results, this objection is groundless. The terrifying truth behind this type of evil is that it shows how thin the line is that separates normalcy from atrocity.

In 1992, Christopher Browning published a study of Reserve Police Battalion 101, one of the *einsatzgruppen* assigned to implement the mass murder of Jews on the Eastern Front. He describes their activity, which consisted of rounding up and shooting unarmed men, women, and children, as follows[22]:

When the first truckload of thirty-five to forty Jews arrived, an equal number of policemen came forward and, *face to face*, were paired off with their

---

[21] "Organized Guilt," in *The Jew as Pariah*, 232.
[22] Browning, *Ordinary Men*, 61. Browning's account was challenged by Daniel Goldhagen in *Hitler's Willing Executioners*, 203–62. Goldhagen does not dispute

victims. Led by Kammer [a first sergeant], the policeman and Jews marched down the forest path. They turned off into the woods at a point indicated by Captain Wohlauf, who busied himself throughout the day selecting execution sites. Kammer then ordered the Jews to lie down in a row. The policemen stepped behind them, placed their bayonets on the backbone above the shoulder blades as earlier instructed, and on Kammer's orders fired in unison.... Thereafter, the "pendulum traffic" of the two firing squads in and out of the woods continued throughout the day. Except for a midday break, the shooting proceeded without interruption until nightfall. At some point in the afternoon, someone "organized" a supply of alcohol for the shooters. By the end of the day of nearly continuous shooting, the men had completely lost track of how many Jews they had each killed.

As the title of the book suggests, the men who did the killing were ordinary, middle-aged, mostly working-class, from Hamburg, who on the basis of social background and ideological temperament were ill suited to the task at hand. Although they were exposed to anti-Semitic propaganda before the mission, Browning points out that they were too old to have been exposed at a formative period in their lives and came from a part of Germany that was generally unreceptive to the Nazi cause.[23]

Unlike the Thracian soldiers in Thucydides' example, the men of Reserve Police Battalion 101 were not battle-hardened troops who formed a mob and began to kill indiscriminately; in fact, they were not really "troops" at all, but police sent specifically to kill unarmed civilians so that the real troops could be assigned more important duties.

Although those who refused to participate were allowed to step aside without fear of reprisal, most of the men did exactly as they were told. The killing that resulted was both organized and systematic. Even if one cannot imagine the horror of executing innocent people in

the claim that the men of Police Battalion 101 were ordinary. I am hardly the first to point out that his central thesis is that the principal motivating factor behind such behavior was German anti-Semitism going back to the nineteenth century. This raises a number of questions. (1) Was anti-Semitism before Hitler more pronounced than in other countries? Note, for example, that before 1932, overtly anti-Semitic political parties in Germany received a relatively small percentage of the vote. (2) How does one account for the mass murder of other groups like Gypsies or Poles? (3) How does one account for the active participation of non-Germans in mass murder? For more on the concept of the "desk killer," see Alan Rosenberg and Paul Marcus, "The Holocaust as a Test of Philosophy," in *Echoes from the Holocaust*, 201–22.

[23] Browning, *Ordinary Men*, 182.

this fashion, it is important to remember that their action required the assistance of scores of other people who organized the battalion; provided it with equipment; transported it to the Eastern Front; supplied it with food, cigarettes, and alcohol; and deported those Jews who were not shot to death camps. In the words of the theologian Richard Rubenstein, "It was when the bureaucrats took over from the bullies that mass murder became possible."[24]

My claim is that as awful as this action was, it was more the result of not caring about the moral consequences of one's behavior than of anything described as diabolical. Granted that the results of indifference can be just as heinous as anything concocted by Satan, we have to ask what is behind the decision to suspend morality in favor of a pure instrumentality. Again, it is hard to see how the pursuit of self-interest is the motivating factor. If the men of Reserve Police Battalion 101 did not fear for their lives, neither is it clear that they acted as they did in order to further their careers or receive a monetary reward. It is rather that they too decided to take a moral holiday.

Following Christine Korsgaard, Card suggests that the motivating factor is not self-interest but self-esteem, or better yet, one's conception of oneself. This is based on the fact that people often sacrifice their own interests in order to serve the interests of a larger group. In Korsgaard's words, "People who care only for what they get and not at all for what they *are* are surely uncommon."[25] Even the worst of us, Korsgaard adds, "seem to want others to like and admire us." In fact, one could go so far as to say, as with Korsgaard, that in most circumstances, the wholehearted endorsement of our identities *based on the opinions of others* is a determining factor in what makes life worth living. However one views one's self-esteem, there is no denying that it is a complicated idea that usually undergoes revision and in some cases is never fully worked out. One cannot even begin to form such an idea with learning from and responding to outside influences. There is no way we can determine a priori what kinds of behavior earn the respect of others and what kinds earn contempt.

---

[24] Richard Rubenstein, *The Cunning of History*, 27. Cf. Raul Hilberg, *The Destruction of the European Jews*, 649: "No moral problem proved insurmountable. When all participating personnel were put to the test, there were very few lingerers and almost no deserters."

[25] Christine Korsgaard, *The Sources of Normativity*, 250–1.

The same is true for how to define success or failure, love or hate, civilization or anarchy.

We saw that although loyalty, fidelity, or willingness to serve one's country are often good, they are not good without qualification. In the case of Reserve Police Battalion 101, the group was given a job to do that many regarded as distasteful. Although refusing to participate may not have meant death, it surely would have meant that the burden of killing fell to others and that one was likely to be seen as "soft" or "uncooperative." We can only speculate on whether the men bothered to ask the question "What am I being loyal *to*?" The results suggest that, like most of us, they neglected to raise it. At the end of his book, Browning confirms that within almost every social organization, the peer group exerts enormous pressure on how one views behavior and establishes norms.[26] He then states the terrifying conclusion: "If the men of Reserve Police Battalion 101 could become killers under such circumstances, what group of men cannot?"

Card takes this to mean that Kant's denial of a diabolical will is partially wrong and partially right.[27] It is wrong mainly because it fails to recognize that people can and do sacrifice their own self-interest to achieve other ends. It is right to the degree that the forms of behavior we have examined thus far are not motivated by evil for its own sake, but rather that morality is something we can turn on or off when it suits us. If Kant could widen his conception of the things that stand as rivals to morality, he would still be in a position to say that evil is the result of subordination – not the simple case in which a person hears the voice of reason but pursues self-interest instead, but what we might call a second-order case of subordination in which a person puts himself in a condition where the voice of reason is muffled and others do one's thinking for him. In doing so, a person runs the risk of crossing the line that separates normalcy from atrocity and becoming a monster. Worse, he runs the risk of crossing the line and not even realizing it.

According to Kant, the Enlightenment was supposed to release us from the immaturity of letting other people think for us.[28] Realizing

---

[26] Browning, *Ordinary Men*, 189.
[27] Card, *Atrocity*, 92.
[28] Kant, "And Answer to the Question: What is Enlightenment," in *PP*, 41.

that such immaturity was still widespread, he denied that his was an enlightened age and proclaimed that it was instead an age of enlightenment. The point of the distinction is that whereas much remains to be done, "we do have clear indications that the way is now being opened for men to proceed freely in this direction and that the obstacles to general enlightenment – to their release from their self-imposed immaturity – are gradually diminishing.[29] Unfortunately, Kant's faith in human progress was too optimistic and his estimate of the allure of self-imposed immaturity too low. We will see, however, that whether the ideals of the Enlightenment as expressed by Kant are still valid remains an open question.

FROM EVIL TO RADICAL EVIL

In *The Origins of Totalitarianism*, Arendt, reflecting on accounts of Nazi and Soviet death camps, suggested that we understand *radical* evil in a new way: not the perversity of the heart that Kant thought lies at the bottom of everything we do, but as *total* or *absolute* evil, a form of that outstrips normal categories like punishment, restitution, or forgiveness[30]:

When the impossible was made possible it became unpunishable, unforgivable absolute evil which could no longer be understood and explained by the evil motives of self-interest, greed, covetousness, resentment, lust for power, and cowardice; and which therefore anger could not revenge, love could not endure, friendship could not forgive.

Just as the victims in the death factories or the holes of oblivion are no longer "human" in the eyes of their executioners, so this newest species of criminals is beyond the pale even of solidarity in human sinfulness … we have nothing to fall back on in order to understand a phenomenon that nevertheless confronts us with its overpowering reality and breaks down all standards we know.

Unlike murder, in which the criminal seeks merely to eliminate the victim, this kind of evil introduces a crime in which the criminal seeks total domination of the victim: the elimination of all vestiges of dignity, spontaneity, or individuality – hence the lines of anonymous, apathetic

---

[29] Ibid. 44–5.
[30] Arendt, *The Origins of Totalitarianism*, 459. For a general discussion of Arendt's position and the criticism it raised, see Michael Morgan, *Beyond Auschwitz*, 9–27.

victims walking passively to their death, what later came to be called the *Muselmänner*.[31]

At the bottom of Arendt's view of radical evil is the desire of the totalitarian state to show that everything is possible, that there are no limits to its need to assert complete control over everything. Again from Arendt: "Suddenly it became evident that things which for thousands of years the human imagination had banished to a realm beyond human competence can be manufactured right here on earth."[32] The view that everything is possible is usually offered as a way of understanding omnipotence. In this way, the totalitarian state claimed to usurp the special prerogative of God, whose power is so great that the human mind cannot comprehend it. That is why the quotation just cited continues by referring to a man-made purgatory and hell.

Although Arendt credits Kant with a premonition that evil could be radical in this sense, there is nothing to indicate that Kant was thinking of anything so extreme. Again we face the question of what counts as self-interest. Both individuals and states have always been willing to eliminate people who stood in their way. Yet Arendt and those who follow here in using the term *radical* evil are talking about something beyond the mass killing of innocents: that is, the systematic degradation of the victim, so that in the end she is robbed of anything

---

[31] Note that in Adams's attempt to define a particularly egregious form of evil in *Horrendous Evils*, 26–7, in most cases, the destructive force of such evil goes beyond concrete disvalue such as the infliction of pain and includes an attempt to "defeat the individual's value as a person, to degrade him/her to subhuman status." Also note, as Adams does, that some of her instances of horrendous evil do not involve injustice but cases of extreme negligence, for example, a father running over his child in a car accident. One problem with Adams's account is her contention (36, 174) that because we cannot adequately conceive what we cannot adequately experience, "our power to cause horrors outweighs our powers of conception." If this means that only the victims of horrendous evils really understand how bad they are, I must part company. What about the perpetrators who commit them precisely because they are horrendous? What about victims whose perspective is limited or whose power of understanding is impaired? Behind Adams's view is Christology: God in the person of Christ has suffered pain, torment, and humiliation and knows exactly what they are like.

[32] Ibid. Cf. Steven T. Katz, "Technology and Genocide: Technology as a 'Form of Life,'" in *Echoes from the Holocaust*, 284: "In every case we experience that mentality called by German technocrats *Machbarkeit*, the fluid possibility that nothing is given, all is open to novel forms of arrangement, original constellations of relationships, unprecedented usages. Nothing, including Jewish bodies living or dead, has innate worth, only instrumental, extrinsic value."

of value and becomes completely superfluous. I submit that whereas killing another person can be understood in terms of self-interest, systematic degradation cannot. By the same token, torture to get valuable information, although objectionable in its own right, can be understood in terms of self-interest, but torture for the sake of mere amusement cannot. To enjoy torture, a person would have to recognize the value of human dignity, or else the act of inflicting pain and humiliation would have no appeal. Insofar as they have appeal, there is no question of the criminal's acting in a state of madness or drunkenness. In this case, the horror of the motivation is fully proportionate to the horror of the act.

Consider the following passage from *The Brothers Karamazov*[33]:

"By the way, a Bulgarian I met lately in Moscow," Ivan went on, seeming not to hear his brother's words, "told me about the crimes committed by Turks and Circassians in all parts of Bulgaria through fear of a general uprising of the Slavs. They burn villages, murder, outrage women and children, they nail their prisoners by the ears to the fences, leave them until morning, and in the morning they hand them all – all sorts of things you can't imagine. People talk sometimes of bestial cruelty, but that's a great injustice and insult to the beasts; a beast can never be so cruel as a man, so artistically cruel. The tiger only tears and gnaws, that's all he can do. He would never think of nailing people by the ears; even if he were able to do so. These Turks took pleasure in torturing children too, cutting the unborn child from the mother's womb, and tossing babies up in the air and catching them on the points of their bayonets before their mothers' eyes. Doing it before the mother's eyes was what gave zest to the amusement. Here is another case that I thought very interesting. Imagine a trembling mother with her baby in her arms, a circle of invading Turks around her. They've planned a diversion; they pet the baby, laugh to make it laugh. They succeed, the baby laughs. At that moment, a Turk points a pistol four inches from the baby's face. The baby laughs with glee, holds out its little hands to the pistol, and he pulls the trigger in the baby's face and blows out its brains. Artistic, wasn't it? By the way, Turks are particularly fond of sweet things, they say."

The fictional nature of the story should not mislead us. Murder victims are often tortured before they are killed, and for no apparent reason. It is here that we encounter the demonic, or what I will call *sadism*. To pursue torture for the sake of amusement is to pursue it not only in

---

[33] Fyodor Dostoevsky, *The Brothers Karamazov*, 283.

the full knowledge that it is evil, but also *because* it is evil. The problem here is not that a person embarks on a moral holiday, but that he keeps the demands of morality firmly in mind and rebels against them, seeking to explore a realm in which all boundaries have disappeared and everything is permitted.

But let us go deeper. What kind of amusement is involved in torturing another person? At an elementary level, people have always been fascinated with horror. In the Middle Ages and even into the early modern period, people waited in line for hours to see convicted criminals drawn and quartered. Even today, when sensibilities are more squeamish, people find dark, sadistic, or self-destructive characters in novels or on television more interesting than characters who routinely do the right thing. Movies about underworld figures are fascinating because they reveal the inner workings of a part of society with which few people have any direct contact. Horror movies constitute a genre all their own. In large, tourist-oriented cities, people line up and pay money to visit torture museums – not out of interest in the history of punishment but, I suspect, out of a morbid fascination with the possibility of totally dominating another human being. Perhaps there is the illusion that once everything is permitted, something important will be revealed, a form of experience previously denied us.

At a more abstract level, inflicting torture takes one outside the normal boundaries of what is or is not possible to do. Like sex, it creates a world all its own, a world in which what was previously unavailable is now available. Note, for example, the sheer glee with which torture, rape, and sodomy were depicted at Abu Ghraib and the degree to which the whole experience soon became pornographic. Along similar lines, some of the pictures of Reserve Police Battalion 101 show men laughing as Jews are tortured or humiliated.

Although this kind of behavior may overwhelm our moral sensibilities and leave us speechless, there is nothing about it that is unique. I see no reason to think that it is not found in prisons, mental hospitals, boarding schools, orphanages, or other places where victims are helpless and the watchful eye of society is temporarily shut. In totalitarian regimes, it not only occurs but also, if Arendt is right, occurs by design, because it is here that the last restrictions on the power of the state are lifted. Recall Winston Smith's experience in *1984*: His tormentor will hold up four fingers, say that they are five, and Winston will actually come to believe that they are five. From this, it is but a short step to the final result: He really *will* love Big Brother. The purpose of the concentration camps was to accomplish something similar: not just to kill, but to make the inmates so disgusted by their conditions, so sick of the smell of their own feces and vomit, that they saw themselves as the subhuman creatures that Nazi propaganda claimed they were and would therefore go to their deaths willingly. In Primo Levi's account of Auschwitz, there is yet another step: getting some victims to take part in the torture and death of other victims.

There is no obvious way Kant can account for this sort of evil except to fall back on depravity and perversity. But again, a slight modification in his theory would give us the wherewithal to say more. We saw that for Kant reason seeks the unconditioned. Give it a series of causal connections, and it will form the idea of a first cause. Give it something that is accounted good, and it will form the idea of the highest good. Give it the fact of moral obligation, and it will form the idea of a morally perfect being. Yet if reason provides access to the unconditioned, for Kant it is the only thing that does. This is another way of saying that the unconditioned cannot be an object of possible experience, and that is where we encounter a familiar problem. Give people a limit, and they will look for some way to circumvent it. From a religious perspective, anyone who claims to see or hear God in a literal sense is claiming to experience the unconditioned. Along these lines, Kant defines fanaticism as the belief that one can experience the supersensible through feelings or intuitions (2CR 5:136).

I want to suggest that the desire to reach the unconditioned goes far beyond religious extremism; correctly understood, it extends to any experience whose intensity is so great that it seems to take one beyond the distinction between possibility and impossibility. In this way, it may be understood as a protest against finitude. Although Kant is right to include religious ecstasy as such an experience, he also could have included orgasm, horror, torture, and the ideology of totalitarianism – all things in which there is a loss or a transcendence of categories like the self and other, good and evil, true and false. To return to *The Triumph of the Will*, the effect of Hitler's rallies was to produce a mass hysteria in which these very categories tend to break down. We could say, therefore, that totalitarianism is based on the assumption that the categories we use to form our most cherished intuitions about what it is to be a human being are malleable.

The way it justifies that assumption is to create situations where those categories cease to function. They are, then, putty in the hands of the leader. To the degree that they can be broken down or reshaped, it is true that anything is possible. If anything is possible, then the power of the leader will present itself as unconditioned, so that in the last analysis, the will has triumphed over everything else.

In the opening lines of Genesis, God wills that there be light, and suddenly there is light. The lure of totalitarianism on a grand scale, or the excitement that the sadist feels in torturing his victim, is that the power that once belonged to God now belongs to us. It is Satanic in precisely the sense that it represents a rebellion against God and an attempt to usurp the power of God.

Extending Kant in this way, what we get is not just a transcendental illusion, but an aspiration that reaches fulfillment in the worst behavior of which human beings are capable. Although the transcendence of limits may advertise itself as liberation, Arendt is right to say that the outcome of totalitarian domination in the form of concentration camps, constant purges of the political apparatus, and mass liquidations is that ultimately everyone becomes superfluous, which is to say that the idea of humanity becomes superfluous. Not only is it not an end in itself, but also, in the hands of totalitarian regimes, it may not even be a means to an end. As Elie Wiesel put it, "at Auschwitz not only humanity died but the *idea* of humanity as well."[34]

If history is a story that we tell, and the story is supposed to show how the power of reason asserts itself, then the story reached a low ebb in the twentieth century. Tyrants and dictators are hardly new. Nor are torture, mass murder, and racial prejudice. In some cases, the Hebrew Bible goes so far as to *command* mass murder.[35] From a moral perspective, the numbers do not matter. Once we admit that every human life is of infinite or inestimable worth, we lose the ability to say that x number of innocent deaths is worse than y because x is greater than y. With this, we lose the ability to say that one atrocity outstrips the

---

[34] Elie Wiesel, *Legends of Our Time*, 230.
[35] For example, Numbers 31; Deuteronomy 7:1–2; 20:16; 1 Samuel 15: 2–3.

other or is almost as bad as the other. When moral sensibilities are overwhelmed, and punishment and forgiveness no longer applicable, comparisons of this sort no longer make sense.[36] By suggesting that the violation of human dignity is quantifiable, they become offensive in their own right.

From a historical perspective, however, there was something new about the totalitarian regimes of the twentieth century: the technology at their disposal. At an abstract level, technology is neutral: It enables one to do his work faster or more efficiently *whatever that work may be*. It is hardly the case that all or even most victims of the Holocaust were killed in a high-tech fashion. Some were shot and pushed into unmarked graves, some were put in trucks and gassed with carbon monoxide, some were packed into cattle cars and left to freeze to death, some died of starvation or disease. The fact that the killing in Cambodia and Rwanda was low-tech does nothing to diminish the horror of what happened there.

Nonetheless, technology does make a difference, if not morally then ideologically. The fact that one can do one's work faster means that one can accomplish more in the same amount of time. With the prospect that ever more work can be done in ever shorter periods of time comes the aspiration to total control of either the environment or a civilian population. In the twentieth century, the ability to disseminate propaganda, subject every aspect of a person's life to some form of surveillance, or conduct war on a global scale all took enormous leaps forward. Again we have the phenomenon of going from the conditioned to the unconditioned without examining the consequences. Before long, world domination and with it the prospect of eliminating whole classes of people became a serious option for government planners. Without the railroad, for example, it is hard to see how a Final Solution to the Jewish Problem could have been discussed. With

---

[36] A bit more clarification is needed here: *Moral* comparisons no longer make sense. This does not prevent comparisons made on the basis of political, economic, or technological factors. In "The Unique Intentionality of the Holocaust," in *Post Holocaust Dialogues*, 287–317, and later in *The Holocaust and Mass Death Before the Modern Age*, Vol. I of *The Holocaust in Historical Context*, Steven T. Katz attempts to argue for the uniqueness of the Holocaust without making judgments of better or worse. I have expressed skepticism about whether this is possible, but see Katz's reply to my skepticism in *Historicism, the Holocaust, and Zionism: Critical Studies in Modern Jewish Thought and History*, 165–6.

it, what was for centuries a pipe dream became a matter of national policy. To some it must have seemed as if the dream of cosmic upheaval could now be realized by human means alone.

The world had seen mob violence and evil regimes before, and there was nothing novel in the idea that the torture of another human being could be thrilling. If philosophy has failed to account for the demonic, it may be, as Arendt suggests, that it was still committed to the idea that Satan had a divine origin and thus could not be completely evil. According to the usual mythology, he was once an angel in good standing. Yet one does not have to look to mythology to see that some forms of human behavior are both premeditated and irredeemable. Nor does one have to think on a cosmic scale. All one had to do is observe the intense satisfaction that people derived from inflicting pain on helpless victims. What was novel was the idea that all natural and human obstacles to evil could be eliminated so that mass murder could be an instrument of state policy as easily as building roads or cutting down trees.

It bears repeating that mass murder on the scale we are now considering is too vast a phenomenon to be explained by one type of evil. In addition to brutality, ideological fanaticism, moral indifference, and sadism, there was cowardice, betrayal, greed, self-denial, and numerous other vices. The challenge is to explain evil in such a way that we can distinguish normal cases, where punishment and forgiveness are appropriate, from horrific cases, where they are not. We have seen that although selfishness is one motivation for evil, it does not do justice to everything history puts before us. If, however, we admit that history offers cases of irredeemable evil, what sense does it make to speak of a messianic future? Must those who hold out the hope of a better future not ignore what is right before their eyes?

MENDING THE WORLD

Even the most casual student of the Holocaust will recognize in this subtitle a reference to Fackenheim's magnum opus. Fackenheim was the first and probably the most important philosopher to argue that the Holocaust constituted a unique event in world history and cannot be subsumed under normal categories supplied by philosophy or theology. What the Holocaust offers us is not just evil but evil for evil's sake, what Fackenheim terms a celebration of evil.[37] Getting right to the heart of the matter, he argued that if Hegel were alive today and could read the accounts of Auschwitz, he would abandon his theory of history.[38] It is not just that Nazism represents a relapse into barbarism but, to use Fackenheim's expression, that it is *radical anti-Spirit*, the total opposite of everything history is supposed to be. However, this does not mean that nihilism is the only authentic response. The challenge Fackenheim sets for himself is to find an adequate response to the Holocaust without minimizing its enormity and incomprehensibility. We have seen that the "evil for evil's sake" explanation, although valid for some cases, does not cover everything that needs to be covered. Moreover, there is no reason to think that it was unknown before Hitler came to power. So rather than examining Fackenheim's arguments for uniqueness and incomprehensibility, I want to look at his account of what constitutes an authentic response.

In large measure, Fackenheim's view of the Holocaust is informed by what one might call a metaphysics of immanence. In an essay critiquing Cohen, he concludes by saying that a modern Jew can put less trust in Cohen's God-idea than in the ancient God of Israel on the grounds that the latter acts *in* history while the former is "divorced from history and therefore impotent."[39] Fackeheim's criticism of Cohen mirrors Hegel's criticism of the Platonism of Kant. Laws and principles have no vitality on their own. Reason can actualize itself only on the backs of individual agents guided by their own passions and proclivities. Except for such agents, even the most appealing of principles would

---

[37] Emil Fackenheim, *The Jewish Return into History*, 1978.
[38] Fackenheim's dialogue with Hegel occupied much of his philosophic career. For openers, see *The Religious Dimension in Hegel's Thought*. For a parting shot, see "Hegel and the Jewish Problem," in *The Philosopher as Witness*, 15–25. For the argument that Hegel would no longer be a Hegelian, see *Encounters between Judaism and Modern Philosophy*, 153–69, and MW, 236–8, 319. According to the non-metaphysical reading of Hegel, there is nothing in his theory to prevent the emergence of a tyrant who completely ignores mankind's struggle to realize its own freedom. All Hegel is committed to is the claim that if such a tyrant were to arise, he would have no awareness of who he is or what he represents. For more on Fackenheim's claims about Hegel and Hegelianism, see Laurie McRobert, "Emil L. Fackenheim and Radical Evil," *Journal of the American Academy of Religion* 57 (1989): 325–40, and Pollock, "Thought Going to School," 136–43.
[39] Emil Fackenheim, "Hermann Cohen – After Fifty Years," *Leo Baeck Memorial Lecture* 12 (1969): 3–17.

be purely imaginary and therefore worthless. As Fackeheim puts it, "Authentication is possible only by a witness who *exists in* his particular situation, not by scientific observers, philosophers, or theologians who fancy themselves as transcending every all-too-particular situation." This does not mean that Fackenheim denies the possibility of transcendence, only that, as the foregoing passage continues, one can transcend his historical situation only from *within* it.

We can understand this claim by breaking it into two steps. The first step may be described as Aristotelian: The primary reality is the individual, not an abstract property or principle. Principles are valid only to the degree that individuals act on them. The second step is Hegelian: All individuals have a history that informs the principles they hold and the meaning they attach to them. As we saw, autonomy would mean something very different to a fifth-century Athenian than it would to an eighteenth-century European. In contemporary terms, all individuals are situated. Putting these two steps together, we arrive at the conclusion that, for Fackenheim, there is no possibility of an ethics that rests on judgments derived a priori, or what Thomas Nagel called a view from nowhere.

With these points in mind, let us say that history does not refute philosophic theories in the way that anomalous results refute a scientific theory or textual evidence refutes an interpretation. Rather, Fackenheim's point is that an idea is refuted when people no longer bear witness to it or care whether anyone else does. There was a time when people were willing to die to defend the idea that kings rule by divine right, but few people would go to war to defend this idea today. Without witnesses to validate it "in flesh and blood," the idea that kings rule by divine right no longer affects the course of history. For all intents and purposes, it is dead.

We can now understand why Fackenheim does not respond to the Holocaust by falling back on the idea that humanity is an end in itself. His method requires him to find someone who stood up for humanity when history presented the opportunity. He is disdainful of much of the philosophic tradition for turning its back on the whole issue, or, as in the case of Heidegger, for openly supporting Hitler. The only exception he can find is Kurt Huber, a relatively obscure Neo-Fichtean. Even if we were to return to greats like Kant and Hegel, Fackenheim would argue that the depravity of the human condition is insufficient to account for the likes of Hitler, Himmler, or Eichmann. In large measure, I agree.

What then is the fate of humanity as an end in itself? In what is clearly one horn of a dialectical argument, Fackenheim maintains,[40]

Perhaps it was so in Kant's time.... But is this belief warranted in the age of Auschwitz? Then and there, one kind of common Man – the *Muselmann* – was made into a uniquely uncommon victim, while the other, the manufacturer of the victim, was made – *let himself* be made – into a uniquely uncommon criminal. And "uniquely uncommon" in both cases was this, that personality was destroyed. It is true that Kant's belief in humanity could at no time be verified. However, not until the advent of the Holocaust world was this belief *refuted*, for here the *reality* that is object of the belief was *itself systematically annihilated*. The awful legacy for philosophy is that the annihilation of human personality robs the Idea of Humanity of its indispensable basis. And thus it could come to pass that Kant's categorical imperative, with its heart and soul destroyed, was invoked by its most dedicated enemies [Eichmann].

From a traditional perspective, this argument is seriously flawed. Although it is true that Eichmann invoked the Categorical Imperative at one point in connection with the idea of doing one's duty, this fact is no more relevant to its validity than the batting average of a professional baseball team. At Nuremburg, some Nazis invoked Zionism to argue that their view of Diaspora Jewry was not much different from what other Jews had said, but Fackenheim would have been the last person to argue that Zionism was thereby refuted.[41]

More importantly, the systematic deprivation of human dignity has no tendency to show that the idea of human dignity is invalid. Kant was not trying to tell us how we act but how we *ought* to act. Far from undermining the idea of human dignity, the fact that someone is denied it shows exactly how important the idea is. Suppose for a moment that the idea of human dignity is no longer applicable. On what basis will we condemn those who rounded up innocent people and sent them to their deaths? We could return to ideas like ignorance of the good, excess of emotion, or perversity of the heart, but none of these would have the same force or explanatory power as the claim that humanity is an end in itself. As I once argued, Fackenheim has

---

[40] *MW*, 273.
[41] Cf. Lang, *Act and Idea*, 209–11.

confused the validity of the moral law with the conditions necessary for realizing it.[42]

To be sure, the idea of humanity has a history. It began with the claim that humanity was made in the image of God and continued with the claim that God abhors the shedding of innocent blood. From there it came to mean that even the stranger, the non-Israelite, has to be accorded certain rights. Granted, it is a long way from biblical literature to Kant's ethical writings. Still, the traditional philosopher will object, the fact that the idea of human dignity took centuries to develop does not show that the validity of the insight it encapsulates rests on historical contingencies. For Kant, no historical event could possibly refute it, because nothing that we do to a person can take away her status as an end in herself.

The obvious answer to these concerns is that Fackenheim has given up on traditional philosophy and taken a hermeneutical turn. However, this presents him with a problem.[43] If he were to end his discussion of the Holocaust with the *Muselmänner* walking to their death and the idea of human dignity refuted by the death camps, any idea suggestive of hope or decency would have been refuted, and all that would be left is what Fackenheim calls "paralyzing impotence."[44] Such impotence would lead to atheism and take away any possibility of transcendence in the form of a commanding voice from above. Anyone familiar with Fackenheim's work will see that this result would nullify his 614th Commandment: that Jews may not give Hitler a posthumous victory so that the continued survival of the Jewish people after Hitler takes on the status of a sacred obligation. If thought cannot comprehend the enormity of the Holocaust, then at least it can resist it.[45] But resistance cannot be vindicated a priori. To remain true to his own method, Fackenheim must defend the idea of resistance by finding an actual *resister*.

---

[42] Kenneth Seeskin, *Jewish Philosophy in a Secular Age*, 205–6.

[43] The best single account of Fackenheim's hermeneutical predicament is that of Michael Morgan, "Emil Fackenheim: Fidelity and Recovery in the Post-Holocaust Epic," in *Beyond Auschwitz*, 155–95. Note, in particular, Morgan's claim that Fackenheim denies the possibility of transcending history by assuming an impersonal, detached point of view. I have no quarrel with the attribution of this claim to Fackenheim. From my point of view, however, the Holocaust shows that just such a point of view is necessary.

[44] MW, 239.

[45] Ibid.

He does so by turning to Pelagia Lewinska, a Polish woman (not Jewish) who died at Auschwitz[46]:

At the outset the living places, the ditches, the mud, the piles of excrement behind the blocks, had appalled me with their horrible filth.... And then I saw the light! I saw that it was not a question of disorder or lack of organization but that, on the contrary, a very thoroughly considered conscious idea was in the back of the camp's existence. They had condemned us to die in our own filth, to drown in mud, in our own excrement. They wished to abase us, to destroy our human dignity, to efface every vestige of humanity, to return us to the level of wild animals, to fill us with horror and contempt toward ourselves and our fellows. But from the instant that I grasped the motivating principle ... it was as if I had been awakened from a dream ... I felt under orders to live ... and if I did die at Auschwitz, it would be as a human being, I would hold on to my dignity.

From this Fackenheim goes on to argue that resistance to evil is an ontological category, a defining feature of human existence.

Yet remember the dilemma he has constructed for himself: Pelagia Lewinska's remarks are but one horn of a dialectical argument. If we affirm solidarity with the *muselmänner*, we are left with paralysis. All we can do is recoil in horror. If we affirm solidarity with the likes of Pelagia Lewinska, paralysis is unacceptable, and active resistance is the only legitimate response. Fackenheim concludes by reiterating a familiar existentialist theme: "[P]ost-Holocaust thought ... must dwell, however painfully and precariously, between the extremes, and seek a *Tikkun* [mending] as it endures the tension."[47]

Why is there any tension? Fackenheim wants to avoid criticizing the victims from the comfort of hindsight and thus to avoid asking why the *Muselmänner* did not come to the same conclusion as Pelagia Lewinska and resist, if not physically, then at least morally. If they despaired of their situation and walked silently to their deaths, there is a sense in which we must despair as well. This is true if it means that the human spirit can be broken by torture or systematic deprivation. The generation of the Exodus was broken by slavery. Winston Smith is broken by the horrors of Room 101. There is ample reason to despair if one wants to hold on to the idea that the human will is indomitable.

---

46 *MW*, 217.
47 *MW*, 310.

The sad truth is that in one respect, totalitarian regimes are right: Anything is possible if we take that to mean that anyone's will can be broken. To the victim of torture, death is often a blessing.

The appropriate reply is that totalitarian regimes are wrong if they think they can create conditions that delegitimate or "refute" the idea that humanity is an end in itself. That is Pelagia Lewinska's point: The filth and the piles of excrement cannot destroy her dignity as a human being. Nothing can – not even the breaking of her will if that is what her captors set out to do. There is simply no connection between the desperate nature of her physical circumstances and her moral status as a human being. To give her captors the power to take away her moral status is to give them a power no one – especially them – can possibly have.

Unfortunately, this reply is denied to Fackenheim as long as he holds on to a metaphysics of immanence. If history can refute an idea like human dignity, then those who control history are right to think that they can do what they set out to do. By contrast, a metaphysics of transcendence denies this. Those who control historical forces can kill and destroy in massive proportions, but they cannot turn wrong into right. Even God must yield to the demands of morality as Abraham and Moses demonstrate when they call God to account.

The conviction that there are things history cannot refute is precisely what is behind resistance – or, as I called it in the previous chapter, defiance. If my reading of Rosenzweig is correct, it is what sustained the Jewish people for thousands of years despite everything history threw at them, what enabled them to see themselves as an *eternal* people. In this context, *eternal* is another name for *transcendent*. From a historical standpoint, Christianity has always had a significant advantage over Judaism: It was not just the dominant religion in Europe, but according to its narrative, the redeemer has already come. Rather than a vague abstraction whose arrival at a future date is open to question, Jesus was an actual person who existed "in flesh and blood." It is the fact that Christianity is grounded in history that allowed Hegel to attempt a historical theodicy. For Judaism a theodicy of this type is impossible. Whether we understand the redeemer as a person or an age, Judaism holds that to date redemption is ungrounded – a hope or aspiration rather than a historical fact. To talk about redemption, then, is therefore to look beyond history rather than within it.

Even if Hitler had succeeded in killing all the enemies of the Reich, if Pelagia Lewinska had not come to realize that she was under orders to live, and no one had put up any resistance, from a Jewish perspective, it would still be true that humanity was made in the image of God and that the taking of innocent human blood is abhorrent. History shows how often these convictions have been ignored. But to ignore something is not to refute it. To refute them, conditions would have to arise in which it is a good thing that innocent human blood is shed. My claim is that whatever direction history has or will take, this can never happen.

I am not arguing that every moral judgment can or should have such an absolute character. Part of the motivation for acquiring moral sensitivity is being able to decide when historical circumstances are relevant and when they are not. In this case, they are not. As moral agents, we are sometimes able to see beyond the circumstances in which we find ourselves and legislate for all humanity. As we saw in the previous chapter, we have the freedom not just to study history but to defy it. As Fackenheim himself came to see, sometimes defiance is the only authentic option.

THE PRECARIOUS FOOTHOLD OF MESSIANISM

"Ethics," as Steven Schwarzschild once wrote, "means to have an alternative to reality."[48] In this context, an alternative to reality means an alternative to history, a way of telling the story so that human degradation is no longer part of the narrative. I have argued throughout this book that there is no way we can assure ourselves this will happen. The historical record provides more than ample evidence that it probably will not. How, then, can one view the horrors of the Holocaust and still long for the days of the Messiah?

The answer is that to long for the days of the Messiah, one has to weaken one's commitment to the principle of induction: that what has happened in the past limits what is reasonable to expect from the future. More specifically, one has to say that whereas the principle of induction may be true for natural events like the motion of the planets, it is not necessarily true for human ones like the decision to go to war.

[48] *PI*, 73.

Again, from a Jewish perspective, the past is horrible, an unredeemed narrative in which human relations were decided more by power than by reason. That is why there has to be a way of saying that things could be different, so that rather than repeating itself, history could move to a new and better era. Without this belief, we would be forced to say that evil is inevitable, which would be tantamount to giving in to it. I submit that along with monotheism, belief in a better future is one of Judaism's two most valuable contributions to world culture. This is another way of saying that if generalizations from past experience are all we have, the religion would be seriously defective.

We have seen that evil is not just a miscalculation about what is in a person's self-interest. In extreme forms, the person who does evil does not care about self-interest as we normally understand it. Even if this is true, evil must be chosen or it is not evil at all.

I have argued that if our choice of evil is spontaneous, there is no reason why we could not choose goodness as well. No propensity or inborn disposition pushes us in one direction rather than another. To speak in a colloquial fashion, the good news is that however evil the human spirit has become, it is capable of becoming good to the same degree. If there was a Holocaust, there can also be a society totally dedicated to justice, mercy, and intellectual growth. The bad news is that there is nothing that can make people choose the latter, nothing that can provide assurance that another Holocaust will not occur. We have already witnessed the horrors of Cambodia and Rwanda. At this point, it is difficult for anyone to look at recent history and not come away thinking, like Ed Tom Bell, the local sheriff in the movie *No Country for Old Men*, that he is overmatched by the forces of evil.

How, then, is it possible to maintain a messianic vision of the future? Recall Mendelssohn's conviction that although individuals might make moral progress, there is no reason to think that humanity as a whole does. Had he lived to see the horrors of the twentieth century, he may well have concluded that humanity is moving backward. The answer is that a messianic view of the future does not rest on a cognitive judgment. To hope for a better future is not like predicting that there is a one-in-three chance it will rain tomorrow. There is simply no way we can assess the chances of overcoming evil, and even if we could, it goes without saying that they would be exceedingly small. It is here that theoretical reason and practical reason diverge: the former telling us that history contains one atrocity after another, the latter telling us that we have it within our power to act differently.

So our position with respect to a messianic future is not that of knower to object known but that of agent to aspiration. To paraphrase Kant, I *will* that history not repeat itself, that power is not the only way to resolve disputes, and finally that human beings no longer feel the need to take moral holidays; I stand by this … and I will not let this belief be taken from me. Although our situation is vastly different from Pelagia Lewinska's, we could even say that we are under orders to do so if that means that taking history in a different direction is a moral necessity.

If it is morally necessary to take history in a different direction, then it must be possible to do so. It is on that possibility, however precarious, that messianism gains its foothold. To the person who asks, "Is that all there is?" the answer is "Yes, that is all there is." Morality demands that we proceed on the assumption that the world can be perfected and that our contribution can make a difference. In the words of Rabbi Tarfon (*Avot* 2:16), it is not our responsibility to complete the task, but neither are we free to evade it. Yet there is no guarantee that our effort or anyone else's will succeed. Life does not come with guarantees. Anything more than acceptance of our duty, such as relying on the prospect of divine intervention or thinking one can predict the course of divine providence, presumes knowledge no one can have. Even if there were divine intervention, it would raise the inevitable question: Why now and not then? Why did God stand by as Police Battalion 101 and thousands of other killers did their work with impunity? There would be no answer and no hope of finding one. So the only legitimate response is to recognize that the future course is entirely in our hands, shaky though they are.

If the appeal of evil runs as deep as I have suggested, there are always likely to be people who succumb to it and a part of everyone that finds the idea of rebellion against the demands of morality enticing. We can admit this without having to admit that evil will always have the upper hand so that whole societies will be dedicated to it. To feel and, better yet, to understand the appeal of evil is not necessarily to succumb to it. It will be objected that all of this is beside the point if, as I have argued, history contains instances of *irredeemable* evil, that no future event can offset the extent of the tragedy or atone for the sins of the perpetrators.

Some evil, I think, can be redeemed. To take a simple case, a person who lies in order to save face can redeem herself if she seeks forgiveness from the victim, feels remorse or regret, and makes a genuine effort not to repeat her action. To take another case, Ernest Hemingway was a bully and an anti-Semite, but it is possible to argue that his contribution to literature offsets his character flaws. Even in the case of murder, it may be possible for a person to redeem himself if he makes a substantial effort to do so. This is the task that Dostoevsky puts before Raskolnikov in *Crime and Punishment*.

If, however, redemption means that we will be able to seek comfort in the idea that on balance the death and suffering of millions of people were worth it because they contribute to a greater good, then redemption is an illusion. No amount of happiness, even happiness in proportion to virtue, can offset the damage that people have inflicted on one another. Especially with events as awful as the Holocaust, there is no systematic way to determine what constitutes a means to an end and what constitutes the end itself, when God has acted and when not. All historical redemption means is that moral atrocities will cease and that people will be given the chance to live their lives free from want and terror. It is to that vision that we now turn.

7

Redemption

Shortly after World War II, history took another surprising turn when the United Nations voted to allow the formation of the modern State of Israel. Had the long-awaited redemption finally come? The prayer for the State of Israel read in synagogues around the world on the Sabbath and festivals strikes a cautious note: It is "the *beginning* of our redemption" (*reshit zemihat geulatenu*). Although centuries of exile had ended, a new set of problems arose.

From the moment of its birth, the State of Israel was attacked by its neighbors, who refused to recognize the legitimacy of a Jewish State. We can only wonder what course history would have taken if they had realized from the beginning that cooperation with Israel was in everyone's interest – or if Israel had realized after the Six-Day War that settlement building was not in anyone's interest. To this day, there are still powerful forces in the Middle East that deny Israel's right to exist. Although they may scoff at the idea of human rights in their own backyards, they are typically among the first to accuse Israel of human rights violations when events get out of control. Thus redemption, although a step closer, is still not a reality.

That raises the question of what full redemption would be and how it will arrive. We have seen that Jewish tradition never reached a single answer to this question. Would the arrival of the Messiah be preceded by painful birth pangs, a national mood of repentance, the coming of Elijah, or a cosmic event like the exploding of a supernova? Maimonides argued that no one is in a position to know the exact sequence of events because they are not explicitly stated by the prophets and therefore do not constitute official dogmas of the religion.[1] We saw earlier that he conceived of the coming of the Messiah as a gradual process consisting entirely of natural events.

For all the authority that his name conveys, Maimonides represents the opinion of only one person. Prior to World War II, the standard Orthodox position was that insofar as it called upon people to hasten redemption by secular means, Zionism amounted to heresy. Only God can determine when the right time will come. We can beseech God to bring redemption as soon as possible, but all we can do on our own is obey the commandments and wait for God to act.

In the words of Shlomo Avineri, this attitude led to a paradox.[2] On the one hand, there had always been a fundamental tie between the Jewish people and the Land of Israel. Although they may be scattered across different lands, speak different languages, and live in widely different conditions, all Jews could agree that Israel was the land of their ancestors. Not a day went by without the mention of Jerusalem and the hope that one day it would be restored to its former glory. On the other hand, few Jews availed themselves of the opportunity to settle there. Centuries of exile had created a mood of passivity fed by the conviction that the future of the Jewish people was entirely in the hands of God.

Against the mood of passivity, many of the early Zionists took a naturalistic approach to the question of Jewish settlement in Palestine. Waiting for God to act had led to centuries of oppression. According to Spinoza, the passivity that results from obedience to Jewish Law had robbed the Jews of their masculinity.[3] If they could overcome their loss of strength and nerve, they might be able to establish a homeland once again. At bottom, he suggested that they stop thinking in supernatural terms and take matters into their own hands.

Putting religious aspirations aside, the early Zionists argued that a state is needed to ensure the physical safety of the Jewish people and allow them to enjoy the same opportunities enjoyed by Germans, Frenchmen, Englishmen, or anyone else. To suppose that these

[1] *MT* 14, Kings and Wars, 12.2.
[2] Shlomo Avineri, *The Making of Modern Zionism*, 3.
[3] Spinoza, *Theological-Political Treatise*, 46.

opportunities would be offered to Jews currently living in Germany, France, or England is folly. Although the theory of the modern state might be liberal and open-minded, the ruling classes of such states were anything but. For the Zionists, the only way to solve the problem was to create a secular state of their own. Religious qualms would only confuse the issue and raise unrealistic expectations. Thus the saying, "We will know we have become a normal country when Jewish thieves and Jewish prostitutes conduct their business in Hebrew."

Between these two extremes arose Rabbi Abraham Isaac Kook, the father of religious Zionism. Born in Latvia in 1865, Kook emigrated to Palestine in 1904 and became Chief Rabbi in 1924. As he saw it, nothing in Judaism prevented one from working toward redemption in stages or from ending the harsh reality of exile. There is no reason why secular Jews cannot facilitate the process of redemption by returning to the homeland even if their intentions are simply to live an ordinary life. This conviction led to a sharp distinction between the subjective intentions of an agent and the objective results of the ensuing act, which Aviezer Ravitzky likened to Hegel's notion of the cunning of reason.[4] Once this distinction is made, we can say á la Hegel that people acting on the basis of their own motivations with no understanding of the significance of what they are doing can be agents in the grand scheme of divine Providence. Just returning to the homeland is, on Kook's view, an act of repentance.

As with Hegel, the mention of divine Providence raises the question of historical determinism. Not surprisingly, Kook allowed himself to speak as a prophet and foresaw a spiritual awakening of global proportions: "The light of penitence will be manifested first in Israel, and she will be the channel through which the life-giving force of the yearning for penitence will reach the whole world, to illuminate it and to raise its stature."[5] Although optimistic, this sentiment is not yet deterministic. For the latter, we must turn to Kook's son, Rabbi Zvi Yehudah Kook: "This special life necessity, following its one certain path with utmost fidelity ... toward its well-established destination and its perfect, immutable realization – this life necessity is none other than

---

[4] Aviezer Ravitzky, *Messianism, Zionism, and Jewish Religious Radicalism*, 110–11.
[5] Abraham Isaac Kook, *The Lights of Penitence, The Moral Principles, Lights of Holiness, Essays, Letters, and Poems*, 56.

the historical necessity and cosmic determination that come through the grace of the divine covenant with the Eternal One of Israel."[6] These words, written in 1951, take Zionism to a new level and raise the question of what happened to the covenant between God and Israel in the years from 1943 to 1945.

To that question, the Zvi Yehudah Kook replies,[7]

The blood of the six million represents a substantial excision from the body of the nation. Our whole people have undergone heavenly surgery at the hands of the destroyers.... God's people had clung so determinedly to the impurity of foreign lands that, when the End Time arrived, they had to be cut away, with a great shedding of blood.... This cruel excision reveals our real life, the rebirth of the nation and the land, the rebirth of the Torah and all that is holy. These historical, cosmological, divine facts must be seen as such.

Unlike Rabbi Joel Moshe Teitelbaum, the leader of the Satmar hasidim, who blamed the Holocaust on the sins of Zionism, he blamed it on the culture of exile. Each shows us the lengths to which people with a fixed conception of historical progress will go to maintain the consistency of a rigid and simple-minded position.

After the 1967 War, when Israel gained control of East Jerusalem and what are commonly referred to as "the occupied territories," Zvi Yehudah Kook went further. Military victory was further evidence of God's involvement in Jewish history. The next logical step is for Jews to take complete control of the land that God promised them in ancient times[8]:

The true Redemption, which is to be manifested in the complete resettlement in the land and the revival of Israel in it, is thus seen to be a continuation of renewed settlement in the Land, accompanied by the ingathering of the captive exiles within its boundaries ... Hence when this state of ours is in full control, both internally and externally, then the fulfillment of this mizvah of the inheritance can be truly revealed – the mizvah that is the basis and essence of all mizvot that, by means of our rule, can accomplish the act of Redemption.

The consequences of this view are well formulated by Kellner: Jewish rule over the whole Land of Israel and the ingathering of the exiles not

---

[6] Quoted in Ravitzky, *Messianism*, 125.
[7] Quoted in Ravitzky, *Messianism*, 127.
[8] Quoted in David J. Schnall, *Beyond the Green Line: Israeli Settlements West of the Jordan*, 19.

only make redemption possible but also guarantee it.[9] Anything that interferes with them is unacceptable. Thus the end of history is one in which Jews will rule over and dominate gentiles.

As Kellner notes, Zvi Yehudah Kook's position stands in marked contrast to Maimonides' claim that Jews did not long for the days of the Messiah so that Israel may exercise domination over other peoples. On the contrary, Maimonides held that the Messiah would restore sovereignty to Israel *and* make peace with the other nations of the world. Gradually, the whole world would come to recognize the truth of monotheism, a process in which Jesus and Mohammed could be seen as playing important roles. The reason Israel longed for the days of the Messiah was to devote itself to the Law and its wisdom. In effect, the days of the Messiah will be a time when the whole world will follow Israel's lead by turning itself into one grand research institute. This does not mean that everyone will be a philosopher, but there will be general agreement about the importance of study, so that many of the obstacles that now stand in its way will be eliminated. Although political institutions will still be needed, domination of foreign peoples is not part of the picture.

We saw in an earlier chapter that Maimonides envisioned a reconstructed Temple and the reinstitution of animal sacrifice. Again history intervened. The taking of East Jerusalem in 1967 brought the Temple Mount into Israeli hands and raised the question of whether Jews could pray there. At first the Temple Mount was closed to Jews on the grounds that it was too sacred for ordinary people to enter. But in 2003, it was opened, raising the question of whether rebuilding the Temple should be considered a serious possibility.

Aside from the political question of what to do with the Dome of the Rock and the Al-Aqsa Mosque, which occupy almost the same location, the idea of a rebuilt Temple raises religious issues. Traditional Jews pray for the speedy rebuilding of the Temple every day. In view of the fact that the priesthood had fallen into disfavor with the Pharisees and in some quarters was viewed as corrupt, it is not clear whether the rabbis who instituted these prayers really wanted to see the Temple rebuilt or whether they were simply paying lip service to an older tradition. Some passages portray the destruction of the

---

[9] Menachem Kellner, "Messianic Postures," 512.

Temple as a paradigm of everything that is wrong with the modern world.[10] Maimonides (*GP* 2.37) argued that the experience of exile was so traumatic that the Jewish people became depressed and could no longer produce prophets. The implication is that when sovereignty is restored and the Temple rebuilt, everything will go back to the way it was supposed to be.

Yet this is clearly a fantasy. By some accounts, the Second Temple was an inferior version of the First.[11] Even the First did not prevent civil strife, idolatry, and oppression of the poor. Fantasy or not, however, the desire to rebuild the Temple plays an important part in the traditional liturgy, and study of how to conduct the appropriate sacrifices has proceeded without interruption. For some Jews, neglecting the duty to rebuild the Temple can only incur the wrath of God; for some Christians, a rebuilt Temple in Jerusalem would facilitate the second coming of Jesus. But who will conduct the sacrifices, and how will they purify themselves?

The Temple Institute, an organization founded by Rabbi Israel Ariel, has attempted to supply answers and has produced over ninety of the implements needed to carry out the required rituals.[12] We have seen that Maimonides did not subscribe to the view that the Messiah would rebuild the Temple by supernatural means. Whether he would have allowed people who are not the Messiah to take the responsibility for rebuilding it is unclear. Although some may cringe at the idea of animals being sacrificed in a Third Temple, the rationale for doing so is straightforward: (1) God commanded that animal sacrifices be done

[10] On this theme, see Barry Wimpfheimer, *Narrating the Law*, 58–60. Note how according to some traditions, even the pleasure of sexual intercourse was taken away from Jews and given to sinners.

[11] See Ezra 3:12, where those who remembered the First Temple weep in disappointment at the sight of the Second, and *Yoma* 22b, which says that the Second Temple lacked five things the First one had: the Ark, the sacred fire, the Shekinah, the Holy Spirit, and the Urim and Thummim.

[12] The Temple Institute's activities are plainly visible on its Web site: http://www.templeinstitute.org/. In addition to preparing for the reintroduction of sacrificial worship, it conducts educational programs and welcomes thousands of visitors a year, including Jews and Evangelical Christians. For an account of its history and activities, see Motti Inbari, *Jewish Fundamentalism and the Temple Mount*, chap. 1. The Temple Institute is only one of several groups hoping for a rebuilt Temple. Also see the Temple Mount Faithful (http://www.templemountfaithful.org/) and the Movement for the Establishment of the Temple.

in a central location, and (2) the Torah is valid for all time. When the Romans destroyed the Temple, there was no way Israel could fulfill these commandments. However, now that a sovereign State of Israel has control of the Temple Mount, are Jews not obliged to return everything to its original, divinely ordained condition?

Admittedly, the positions I have discussed so far are those of the radical political and religious right and hardly reflect the views of Israeli society at large. Unlike many of its neighbors, Israel tolerates a wide range of opinions. In fact, much of Israeli society is defiantly secular.[13] I emphasize these views because they highlight the dilemma I have been discussing for much of this book. If we take a purely secular approach to history, the idea of a messianic future becomes suspect; if we retain the idea of a messianic future, we run the risk of embracing mythology. In addition to its theological shortcomings, mythology of the sort we are considering typically involves an "us versus them" worldview and claims of racial superiority. In one of his more expansive orations, the younger Kook proclaimed that the State of Israel is divine and stronger than either America or Russia because it occupies a cosmic position that they do not.[14]

Along these lines, Ravitzky notes three themes typically found in this kind of thinking: determinism, essentialism, and perfectionism.[15] The determinism is accounted for by the fact that God's will is all-powerful and cannot be resisted. Essentialism means that the day-to-day issues that normally concern governments are of little import. Perfectionism takes us back to the idea that a perfect God will never be satisfied with an imperfect response from us. Thus anything less than total obedience to the commands of God, anything that smacks of compromise or conciliation, is unacceptable. In the words of Yogi Berra, this is *déjà vu* all over again. Not only can no state fulfill the expectations this kind of messianism arouses, but it is also dangerous to try.

---

[13] Even among religious Israelis, Yeshayahu Leibowitz warned after 1967 that maintaining control of the occupied territories would turn Israel into an agent of repression and that Israel should give up the idea of dominating other peoples.

[14] Quoted in Ravitzky, *Messianism*, 132. It is views like this one that led David Hartman to downplay the significance of messianism. See *Israelis*, 144: "I argue that justifying our national existence by claiming that we are the instruments for realizing God's messianic redemptive plan is both unnecessary and morally and politically dangerous."

[15] Ibid, 138.

DEFLATION AND A DISENCHANTED WORLD

We have already seen how Maimonides attempted to deflate the idea of a messianic future: no miracles, no new revelation, no return to lost innocence, no entry into an earthly paradise. As Kellner shows in *Maimonides' Confrontation with Mysticism*, his analysis of the Messiah is but one aspect of a wider strategy, which Kellner characterizes as an attempt to disenchant the world.[16] We can understand this by seeing that Maimonides' overall goal is to deny that there is any essential or ontological difference between those things designated as holy and those designated as profane. To use Kellner's example, radioactivity existed before Geiger discovered a way to measure it. By the same token, many people have said or would say that holy places, persons, nations, times, or artifacts possess a special quality that cannot be measured by natural means but that gives them a unique status. According to what is widely regarded as the traditional view, the Messiah will be such a person, the Temple Mount is such a place, and the Jewish people are such a nation.

Maimonides will have none of this. To take the last example first, there is no biological trait that renders the Jewish people closer to God than anyone else. Although Maimonides considered it a historical fact that the Jews were the first people to discover the truth of monotheism, in his opinion, they are as susceptible to idolatry as anyone else. The same is true for the Land of Israel and its holy sites. They are and will always be important because of the events that took place there, and they should be protected and cherished for exactly that reason. Yet there is no inherent property that distinguishes the soil of Israel or the location of the Temple Mount from any other place on earth. Nor is there any reason to suppose that people who reside on the land will enjoy insights that others lack. Strictly speaking, God has no favorite places, no locations where prayers have a better chance of being answered or sins have a better chance of being forgiven.

Going further, the same analysis applies to the Hebrew language, sacred artifacts, magical names, magical numbers, and blessings or incantations. Whether we refer to Maimonides' view as nominalistic or naturalistic is immaterial; the important point is that for him holiness

---

[16] Menachem Keller, *Maimonides' Confrontation*, 294.

is conferred upon things for historical or institutional reasons; it is not a property they possess in their own right. In its own right, everything other than God is something created *by* God and therefore has nothing in common *with* God. So there is no way for a natural object to possess supernatural powers and no semidivine agents to which we can appeal for help or guidance. Unlike the world of mythology, where the line separating gods and humans is blurred, Maimonides offers us a world where the line separating the divine from the human is sacrosanct, which means that there is no possibility of crossing it – even in infinite time.

In a disenchanted world, the only way we can improve our lot is to improve our mind or the moral quality of our actions. As Maimonides understood the commandments of the Torah, their whole purpose is to bring us to a point where we recognize the importance of the intellect and devote ourselves to study and worship. Everything else is a means to that end. Not only do the commandments not reinforce a mythological worldview, according to him, but they are also designed specifically for the purpose of rejecting it. The job of the Messiah will be to help create an environment in which the commandments can be fulfilled with full knowledge of what we are doing and why. The Messiah will reestablish sovereignty *so that* Israel can lead the world away from ignorance and superstition.

We have seen that mythology is not just a religious matter; it exists in politics too, when a people claim that their nation has been blessed with special powers or endowed with special privileges. In its extreme form, it exists when a people come to believe that their nation is on the same footing as God or has usurped the power of God. That is what leads to the view that there are no limits to what the state can do. If, however, the line separating the divine from the human is sacrosanct, then, to repeat, there is no possibility of crossing it. Every human being and every human institution is finite. In that respect, the need to purge ourselves of the lure of mythology is as pressing today as it ever was.

The continued need for Maimonides' vision should not prevent us from recognizing that there are aspects of his thought that are anachronistic. The most obvious is the suggestion that the Messiah will be a descendent of David who rules over Israel as a king. We saw that kingship was not originally the preferred form of government in the Bible; and even in the days when Israel was ruled by a king, there were any number of social and religious problems. To modern ears, kingship is inferior to constitutional democracy, a form of government with which neither Maimonides nor his contemporaries would have had any experience.

The same can be said for the idea that all Israel will be reunited in one place. From our perspective, this is neither possible nor, for security reasons, desirable. Before the emergence of constitutional democracy, exile meant religious, political, and economic deprivation: being a stranger in a land not your own. But what sense does it make to say that people who enjoy the full rights of citizenship, who have taken on leadership positions in their host countries, who have offered their lives in defense of those countries, and who could emigrate to Israel but choose not to are living in exile? In the twentieth century, the best-known claimant to the title of Messiah, Menachem Mendel Schneerson, lived in Brooklyn.[17] Although it is true that the modern state has not always been able to protect its minorities, in a disenchanted world, where no state can claim it is under the special protection of God, there is no guarantee that any country can.

---

[17] Although Schneerson took up a right-wing position in regard to Israeli politics, forbidding any transfer of land to the Palestinians, and attributed special status to the Land of Israel, Elliot R. Wolfson, *Open Secret*, 132–3, argues that his position is more sophisticated if one takes into account that he often speaks of Israel or Jerusalem in mystical terms that go beyond "a strict cartographical demarcation." In fact, Wolfson's Schneerson is a master of esoteric concealment whose message is deeply paradoxical. Thus messianic expectation (124) is "fulfilled by bringing to light what is currently occluded, rendering manifest the presence presently absent in its absent presence by learning to hear and see." And (125–6), "In the return of what has always been what is yet-to-come, it is precisely the absent presence of the Messiah that imparts meaning to the pending advent of his present absence." It may be doubted whether this level of subtlety reached all or even most of Scheerson's followers, who were told that the birth pangs of the Messiah have already occurred, that the Messiah could come any day, any minute, and might already be here. Esoteric concealment may also account for the difference of opinion among Schneerson's followers on whether he himself was the Messiah. According to Wolfson (273), "[T]he image of the personal Messiah may have been utilized rhetorically to liberate one from the belief in the personal Messiah." Ditto for his view of the metaphysical status of the Jewish people, which, though it refers to Maimonides, is for the most part a reiteration of Judah Halevi. In the end, Wolfson ascribes a "postmessianic [i.e., impersonal] messianism" to Schneerson. It will soon become clear that for different reasons, I too subscribe to an impersonal form of messianism. For a much less sympathetic portrait of Schneerson, see David Berger, *The Rebbe, the Messiah, and the Scandal of Orthodox Indifference*. For Schneerson's theological determinism regarding world events, see Ravitzky, *Messianism*, 197–9.

That brings us to animal sacrifice in a rebuilt Temple. Maimonides was the first Jewish thinker to argue that the sacrificial cult was a concession to human fallibility necessitated by the historical circumstances in which the Jewish people found themselves. It was justified by the fact that everyone else in the ancient Near East was doing it, and that the original recipients of the Torah would not have understood how a religion could exist without it. That raises the question of what to do if circumstances change and we find ourselves in a world where practically no one is doing it. Maimonides remained consistent to the end: If the Torah commands sacrifice, and if the return of sovereignty permits us to reinstate it, then we are required to do it.[18] The truth is, however, that in our world, a rebuilt Temple presided over by a high priest would take on the character of a Disneyland-style theme park attracting thousands of people seeking cures for incurable ailments, divine revelation, and instant forgiveness of sin. In short, it would be a mockery of everything Judaism is supposed to stand for. Better the research institute than the theme park. Better yet adherence to the words of Hosea 6:6: "I desire mercy, not sacrifice; and knowledge of God rather than burnt-offerings."[19]

Finally, there is the idea that the whole world will become a research institute. Maimonides was an uncompromising intellectualist. For him, the way to salvation is through the pursuit of truth. Truth, in turn, is understood within the context of the Neo-Platonized Aristotelianism prevalent in Maimonides' time. Simply put, there is for him *a* truth that all human beings are supposed to grasp. Although he acknowledged that there are questions that may remain unresolved, he still thought they fell within the purview of a single worldview. He did not consider and would not have been comfortable with the idea of alternative conceptual schemes. By the same token, he thought that evil is always the result of ignorance and never considered the possibility that some people may do evil for its own sake.

For us it is different. Not only is our conceptual landscape more varied, but the unresolved questions we face are also indicative of much deeper disagreements than he would have recognized. Beyond

[18] Again Kreisel, "Maimonides on Divine Religion," argues that Maimonides' conservatism is based on the fact that Christianity and Islam had surpassed Judaism in popularity and threatened the claim that the Torah is valid for all time.

[19] Cf. Psalm 40:6: "Sacrifice and offering you do not desire ..."

that, we have seen that a one-size-fits-all analysis of evil is hard to square with the lessons of human experience. Even our concept of a research institute has changed to include such things as a theater, an art museum, a concert hall, a policy center, an industrial design center, and a management school. In addition to pursuing various kinds of truth, it attempts to raise moral and aesthetic sensitivity, promote cultural exchange, and address social policy questions. The upshot is that our view of human perfection admits of much greater diversity than Maimonides', and that is all to the good.

By the time we reach thinkers like Mendelssohn and Kant, the issue is not truth but purity of purpose. So let us simply say that in the days of the Messiah, human societies will enable people to redeem themselves in multiple ways, some academic, some not. We can still agree that to do this, societies will have to put an end to war, eliminate poverty, provide adequate medical care, and ensure the fairness of the justice system.

How to accomplish all of this takes us well beyond the scope of anything Maimonides had to say or of the issues discussed in this book. The question at issue is not what political or economic policies ought to be adopted to make this happen, but rather what ought to be the contribution of Judaism or religion in general. To that question Maimonides' answer is still valid. The most important contribution of religion is to insist on the inviolability of the line separating the divine from the human, or, to say the same thing, the *creator* from *creation*. On that score, the record of Judaism is clearly inadequate. As Kellner indicates, following in the footsteps of Graetz, Scholem, and Idel, Maimonides' attempt to demythologize Judaism boomeranged severely.[20] No sooner did he attempt to take away the magical component of ritual than Kabbalah, which may have been motivated by a reaction against Maimonides, reinstated it.[21]

Kabbalah is, of course, a subject unto itself. Even if it is fair to characterize it as a reaction against Maimonides' rationalism, Kabbalah is only one of several factors that need to be considered. There is also the thought of Judah Halevi, who argued that Jews have a special relationship with God not shared by other peoples, and that Jews in

[20] Kellner, *Maimonides' Confrontation*, 287.
[21] On the relation between Maimonides and Kabbalah, see Moshe Idel, "Maimonides and the Kabbalah," in *Studies in Maimonides*, 31–81, and "Maimonides' *Guide of the Perplexed* and the Kabbalah," *Jewish History* 18 (2004): 197–226.

the Holy Land experience a higher degree of intellectual perfection than Jews in the Diaspora.[22] Beyond that, there is the general trend of normative Judaism, which has been to bring back some version of enchantment in the form of either holy places, sacred implements, or a unique, metaphysical status for the Jewish people. According to Rabbi Abraham Isaac Kook, "A Jew cannot be as devoted and true to his own ideas, sentiments, and imagination in the Diaspora as he can in Eretz Israel. Revelations of the Holy, of whatever degree, are relatively pure in Eretz Israel; outside it, they are mixed with dross and much impurity."[23] The irony of this, of course, is that according to the Torah, the greatest revelation of all time occurred in the wilderness of Sinai, a place with neither walls nor fences.

As alluded to by Kellner, the reason for Maimonides' unpopularity is that the sobering nature of his thought made it difficult for most Jews to accept. Suppose that you are living in exile in a ghetto with no political rights to speak of and no hope of gaining a university education. Suppose that you are the victim of anti-Semitic violence or systematic discrimination. Or, to turn the clock forward, suppose that the next bus you board may contain a suicide bomber. The result of such conditions is likely to be an inward-looking philosophy founded on the distinction between "us and them," and holding out the prospect that divine intervention will correct what human effort cannot. How will we know when to expect such intervention? The answer is that we will need someone who is close to God and able to interpret the numbers or read the signs that hold the key to the future. Ironically, the number of people willing to fill this role has never been small, even though their success has never been great.

If exile is no longer a significant factor in people's lives, dissatisfaction with technological progress and the seemingly endless encroachment of science on every aspect of human life has provided enchantment with yet another rallying cry. By most accounts, religion is supposed to provide a respite from science. Told that Judaism does not empower one with anything beyond what can be detected by natural means, many people feel let down. What about God? What about God's love for Israel?

---

[22] *Kuzari*, 1.95, 5.23.
[23] Quoted in Arthur Hertzberg, *The Zionist Idea*, 420–1.

If, as I have argued elsewhere, Maimonides is committed to creation *ex nihilo*, then there is a power in the universe that resists explanation by natural means. Yet in his view, we have no direct access to such power. All we can do is recognize it and celebrate the fact that we are part of its creation. There is no way such power can be harnessed for specific human needs or directed to human ends. Rather than empowerment, what Maimonides wants from us is the opposite: a sense of our own limitation. That, at least, is the lesson he draws from the Book of Job. As for God's love, Hartman is right to claim that for Maimonides, God's love is manifest in his acceptance of human fallibility.[24] As we saw, most of the commandments are addressed to exactly this point and ask no more of people than what they are capable of doing.

This is a hard message to sell, especially in times when events in every part of the world seem to be careening out of control. Yet if Maimonides has taught us anything, it is that returning to an enchanted world will not solve our problems. From his perspective, enchantment *is* the problem. Not only does it offer false hopes and, in the present environment, stand in the way of peace, insofar as it posits intermediaries between God and us, it runs the risk that people will forget God and focus on the intermediaries instead. All such intermediaries are contingent, which means that their status as sacred implements or historical sites is contingent as well. As indicated in a previous chapter, it might have happened that the Navajo were the first people to discover monotheism. If so, the Temple Mount would be just another hill, and the vestments of the High Priest no different from any other ancient relic.

As with Maimonides, so with Levinas, who argued that Judaism sees religious enthusiasm and the idea of "charmed" or "sacred" objects as the essence of idolatry.[25] Faced with the objection that a Judaism devoid of miracles and enthusiasm runs the risk of being viewed as atheism, Levinas answers that it is a risk that must be run. The true place where the divine word comes into contact with the world is human existence, not only with but also *because* of its torment, unease, and self-criticism. This, Levinas tells us, is a religion for

[24] Hartman, *Israelis*, 75.
[25] Levinas, *DF*, 14.

adults. To ignore the true God is, of course, an evil. Levinas goes further, however, maintaining that for all its failings, atheism is superior to worship of a mythical god.

As we saw in the previous chapter, our hope for a better future rests on a narrow foothold. In this instance, that hope rests on whether Judaism will get to the point where it realizes the full implications of being a monotheistic religion. Again, miracles are of no help. The question is whether we are willing to approach the sacred literature of Judaism with the same critical attitude we apply to other subjects or be satisfied with mystification. If the latter, then history may take an ironic turn: The first people to discover the truth of monotheism will not be the people who bring the Messiah.

LIFE IN A REDEEMED WORLD

In the spirit of negative theology, I begin this section by characterizing redemption in terms of what it is not. A redeemed world is not a utopia in which all human problems have been resolved. In keeping with Levinas's theme of torment, unease, and self-criticism, there will always be questions to ask, competing answers to consider, and lack of certainty to deal with. The notion that there is only one right way to seek God will be abandoned in favor of a universalistic view according to which the God whose image is reflected in humanity loves and is equally available to all humanity.

In the ethical sphere, redemption will not enable us to reach such a high level of perfection that we will be able to say that all previous suffering was worth it. Although there are cases where compensation for a wrong is morally required, the evils discussed in the previous chapter do not fall into that category. The perpetration of genocide and, if Ivan Karamazov is right, the systematic degradation of a single human being are not the sort of things that can be balanced off by personal gain or social fulfillment.[26] So there will be no point at which

---

[26] In this respect, I am in agreement with Adams, *Horrendous Evils*, 189, that no package of merely created goods would suffice to balance off or defeat horrendous evils. The difference is that Adams goes further, arguing that God's goodness *is* sufficient to ensure that every participant in horrendous evils, whether victim or perpetrator, lives a full life of positive meaning. For my part, the latter claim, though possibly true, involves more speculation about the nature of God and the next life than I am

we can look back on human history and say that all previous suffering was redeemed. Nor will there be a reckoning in which sinners and nonbelievers are punished. To borrow Cohen's way of speaking, a reckoning of this sort is an idea of the imagination, a fantasy, not an idea of reason.

In the sphere of religion, there will be no attempt to cross the line that separates the divine from the human, only the humble recognition that it cannot be crossed – even with the blessings of a charismatic religious leader, even in moments of intense inspiration, even if we are granted infinite time. In simple terms, redemption implies the end of fanaticism. What it does not imply is the end of dissent. Instead of fanatics, we will have the opposite: skeptics, atheists, agnostics, and a range of other options to consider.

In political terms, redemption means liberation. God redeemed Israel from Egyptian bondage during the story of the Exodus. We saw, however, that the gift of freedom was not enough. Instead of establishing a just and holy order, the people used their freedom to bring about a whole new round of provocations against God. Then, as now, political sovereignty does not guarantee reconciliation between God and humans. Even if we think in purely secular terms, political sovereignty does not guarantee that a people will achieve everything that can be asked of it. That is where religion comes in. To do everything that can be asked of it, a people must also tend to the needs of the poor, establish peace with other nations, educate its citizens, and ensure that the stability it maintains is founded on just treatment of all citizens.

I have argued throughout this work that no obligation we face requires superhuman effort to fulfill. It does require that the disdain that religious traditions have shown to nonbelievers will be redirected to the real culprits: greed, superstition, violence, and injustice. That means religious traditions will have to undergo a fundamental change in orientation: Instead of pointing the finger at outsiders and asking why they cannot be more like us, religious traditions will have to take a long, hard look at insiders and ask whether they have set themselves on the right path. Are Jews really monotheistic? Do Christians really believe in turning the other cheek? Do Muslims really devote

comfortable with. Note how, like Kant, Adams assumes that the moral progress in the next life is possible.

themselves to a just and merciful God? The same can be said for the inferior status often assigned to women, gays, lesbians, and others who fall outside the model of a heterosexual male serving as the head of a household. If God is beyond the categories of gender, gender preference, or family, then we should be perceptive enough to realize that these things have nothing to do with intellectual or spiritual fulfillment.

Finally death. Every religious tradition has a teaching about death, and in the twentieth century, it became a preoccupation for existentialists like Rosenzweig and Heidegger. I suggest, however, that Cohen (*RR*, 134–5) is right to say that the Hebrew prophets did not indulge in speculation about the meaning of death but recognized that "the true riddle of human life is not death, but poverty." As he sees it, death is a riddle only the mystic can solve (if he can solve it at all). Poverty is different. The solution to the riddle of poverty requires a reassessment of the way human resources are allocated. Although difficult, this is an ethical endeavor rather than a speculative one. We are therefore in a position to see whether our efforts bear fruit. In Cohen's words (*RR*, 136),

I cannot be indifferent to poverty, because it is the sign of the distress of culture, and because it calls into question true morality. Poverty cannot be compared to physical suffering, because the latter is individual and subjective, whereas social suffering is not only the suffering of the majority but also the qualitative evidence of the low level of the culture.... Thus the poor man typifies man in general.

More than church or synagogue attendance, more than gross domestic product, the true measure of a culture for Cohen is the way it deals with its poor.

The issue of suffering leads directly to the paradigm of the suffering servant and the possibility of redemption through suffering. To understand Cohen's position on this issue, we need to return for a moment to Kant. In a passage that many of his critics ignore, Kant argued that we have a duty not to avoid places where the poor congregate, such as hospitals and debtors' prisons.[27] His rationale is that sympathy can

---

[27] *Metaphysics of Morals*, 250 (457).

sometimes accomplish what the mere recognition of duty cannot: spur the self toward action.

This theme takes center stage for Cohen, who argues (*RR*, 17) that it is through the observation of the other person's suffering that he is transformed in our eyes from a He to a Thou. Put otherwise, it is when I feel sympathy for the plight of the other that he ceases to be what Cohen calls *the next man* (*Nebenmensch*) and becomes *fellow man* (*Mitmensch*). As Cohen sees it, unlike the philosophic tradition, which has often been suspicious of pity as a moral emotion, the Hebrew prophets were obsessed with it. This, more than speculation on the afterlife, is what motivated them to say that the human condition is an outrage. For Cohen, pity is not just *an* emotion, but, from a moral perspective, the quintessential emotion. Pity is therefore the messenger (*Bote*) or the motor of the will (*RR*, 141–2). Rather than the person who recognizes the duties we owe to humanity in the abstract, it is the person who establishes fellowship with the poor who achieves correlation with God.

From the suffering we recognize in others, we turn to the suffering we inflict on ourselves through the recognition of our sins and the need to seek penance. If my fellow man suffers, I must take partial responsibility. Eventually suffering takes on a universal dimension, as a person suffers not only for his own sin but also for the sins of others (*RR*, 225). Put all this together, and we arrive at the conclusion – so congenial to Christians – that the ideal person suffers.

There is ample precedent in Judaism for a suffering Messiah as opposed to one who subdues enemies and rules in triumph over a rebuilt Jerusalem. Thus according to Isaiah 53:4, "Surely he has borne our infirmities and carried our diseases." We saw that according to *Sanhedrin* 98a, the Messiah will be a leper outside the gates of Rome bandaging his sores. The significance of this message could hardly be lost on a people in exile who were, in effect, bandaging their own wounds. Where is God in all of this? Where is divine justice? We saw that for Cohen, Israel's fate is to bear the suffering of humanity on itself. As the suffering Messiah is to Israel, so Israel is to the other nations of the earth. This is another way of saying that for Cohen, Israel's mission among the other nations is not to be a model of military prowess or economic efficiency but of piety and humility. By agreeing to suffer on behalf of others, Cohen argues, Israel has abandoned any sense of self-assertion or aggrandizement.

Although Maimonides agreed that domination of other nations is not part of Israel's destiny, he does not present the Messiah as a suffering servant. We may assume that piety and humility are features of the Messiah's persona and that he will be thoroughly familiar with the tragedies and indignities that go with exile. In the *Mishneh Torah* (1, Character Traits, 2.3), Maimonides points out that Numbers 12:3 says that Moses was not just humble, but *very* humble. Still, Maimonides does not picture the Messiah as a leper.

Against Cohen, I want to argue that suffering may be *a* way for a person to achieve redemption if it is connected with a noble motive like responsibility for sin or compassion for one's neighbor. Suffering can lead to humility and compassion in just the way Cohen supposes. However, it can also lead to a feeling of victimization, which results in self-pity and hostility toward others – exactly the opposite of what Cohen intended. One cannot achieve a superior level of piety merely because one suffers. Beyond these objections, there is the objection of Kant. Goodness does not entail happiness. Although a world in which everyone is good would be a significant improvement on this one, we can conceive of something better. If goodness is not joined with happiness, we are obliged to bring them into harmony with each other. By itself, suffering does not fulfill this obligation. Let us say, therefore, that it is only when suffering leads to a moral awakening that it is ennobling.

Surely there are other ways in which a person can experience a moral awakening. For Maimonides, it occurs when one feels awe and humility before God and translates this experience into acts of loving kindness. For Spinoza, it occurs when one accepts the necessity of God's decrees and recognizes the futility of trying to work against them. For Kant, it occurs when one makes the decision to join an ethical commonwealth. For Levinas, whose thought on this matter is close to Cohen's, it occurs when one looks into the face of another person. For some, it can occur when listening to a piece of religious music or viewing a work of religious art. There is even the possibility that it can occur when seeing the mutilated bodies of concentration camp victims. In the words of Ezekiel (11:19), all of these are ways of replacing the heart of stone with a heart of flesh.

In a redeemed world, every religion will take it upon itself to see that this occurs. This does not mean that specific practices such as prayer, festivals, dietary laws, or Sabbath observance will be forgotten, but only that they will be directed toward their true end. In the words of Amos 5:21–3,

> I hate, I despise your festivals, and I take no delight in your solemn assemblies. Even though you offer me your burnt offerings and grain offerings, I will not accept them; and the offerings of well-being of your fatted animals I will not look upon. Take away from me the noise of your songs; I will not listen to the melody of your harps.

Even if a Third Temple were built and animal sacrifice reinstated, it would likely fall victim to the same abuse that plagued the first two: the belief that all one has to do is kill animals and sing hymns to atone for sin. What Amos wants instead is a just and holy order. Nowhere does he say that festivals and sacrificial offerings have no role to play. His point is that unless they culminate in a moral transformation, they are wasted. To return to Maimonides, these activities have no inherent power to influence God or bring about atonement. They are designed to influence *us* by bringing about a reevaluation of the lives we live.

MORAL MAN/IMMORAL SOCIETY

Those familiar with Christian theology in the twentieth century will recognize at once that the title of this section is taken from a classic work by Reinhold Niebuhr. Broadly speaking, Niebuhr's claim is that there is a disconnect between the behavior of individuals and the behavior of states. This is based on more than the logical claim that a whole may possess properties not possessed by any of the parts but on the recognition that the very qualities that contribute to the morality of an individual may inhibit the morality of the group. We can see this in several ways. The same imagination and intelligence that enables people to provide for their needs also makes them long for things that go well beyond their needs. As Kant noted, this condition leads to jealousy, selfishness, and social discord.

Niebuhr goes on to argue that society will never be able to satisfy everyone and will always face the question of how to achieve an equitable distribution of resources.[28] The same loyalty that prevents anarchy in intragroup relations encourages it in intergroup relations.[29] Thus kings and tyrants demand the loyalty of their subjects so that they can follow their own whim or caprice when it comes to dealing with other states or groups. The same altruism that allows an individual to forego his own interests in favor of those of the group allows the group to exploit those who are powerless or disaffected.[30]

The result is that one cannot assume as Plato did in the *Republic* that the character of the state will reflect the character of its citizens. If so, one cannot hope that a moral awakening among the citizens will necessarily produce a similar awakening in national policy. According to Niebuhr, states are by nature complacent, egotistic, and proud. What state has not claimed that it is acting in the service of God, the general good of mankind, or the interests of world culture? Alternatively, what state really has acted in the service of these things rather than promote its own interests?

There is no shortage of examples to support Niebuhr's claim that states have acted and continue to act in an egotistical fashion and rarely exhibit the inclination to repent. Nor is there reason to think that a moral wakening among the citizenry is all that is needed to secure peace, eliminate poverty, and ensure equal protection under the law. Even the most well-meaning of states must deal with issues to which religion has no ready answer, such as when to go to war, how to balance the needs of the environment against the need for economic growth, or whether to devise an educational system designed to bring up the bottom or stimulate those at the top. The general thrust of Niebuhr's position is to warn against the dangers of a utopianism based on nothing more than sentiment and hope. States will always have to exercise coercion, and the only way to oppose one form of coercion is to devise another form that is stronger.

It is hard to read Niebuhr and not hear the echo of Augustine. The secular state is run by people and designed to serve their immediate interests. The basis of its authority is the threat of coercion. As such, it

---

[28] *Moral Man*, 1–2.
[29] Ibid., 16.
[30] Ibid., 89–91.

can never embody perfect justice. Although there can be better states and worse, we should not be surprised to learn that secular rulers are corrupt, hypocritical, self-serving, and faced with the task of trying to resolve irreconcilable conflicts. The most we can expect from them is that they make a tolerable attempt to steer clear of these things and punish the guilty parties. The reason for this sorry state of affairs can be found in original sin, which is so prevalent in political life that it hardly needs further justification. The only certain way out is to recognize the superiority of the church, which unlike the state eschews coercion and is founded on the grace of God. Once again, divine grace must do the work that human effort alone cannot.

Is the human situation this bleak? There is little question that Niebuhr has stacked the deck in favor of negativity. If secular states do not always reflect the character of their citizens, it is possible that the state may also accomplish more and better things than the citizens would, left to their own devices. As Thucydides tells us, the same state that started the Peloponnesian War and massacred the people of Melos also established itself as the schoolhouse of Greece. In biblical times, the same king who received the gift of wisdom and the privilege of building the First Temple also had a thousand wives and was viewed as a second Pharaoh by many of his subjects. More recently, the same state that went on a communist witch hunt during the Cold War and dropped napalm in Vietnam also helped to defeat fascism and passed the Civil Rights Act. As those who lived through the 1950s and 1960s will attest, the Civil Rights Act was backed up by the threat of coercion and would not have succeeded without it.

More broadly, Niebuhr's commitment to original sin takes us back to Kant, Pelagius, and one of the central themes of this book. Why would God create a being whose propensity to sin is ineradicable? Alternatively, why would God issue commands that no person or group of people could possibly fulfill? Although there may be ample evidence to suggest that these commands have not been fulfilled in the past, it begs the question to conclude they cannot be fulfilled in the future. We can see this in the central claim of Niebuhr's book: "Every effort to transfer a pure morality of disinterestedness to group relations has resulted in failure."[31] If things cannot be otherwise, then, as

[31] Ibid., 268.

Niebuhr himself comes to see, an uneasy balance of power "would seem to become the highest goal to which society could aspire."[32] Yet there is no reason why this must be the case. To repeat: Religion stands in defiance of history. If the record of history is all we have, and a repeat of history all we can hope for, then religion must bow to the demands of *realpolitik*. I take the lesson of the Hebrew prophets to be that society can and must aspire to something more – not just in the next life but in this one, for without such an aspiration, we run the risk that realism will become another name for defeatism, and defeatism an excuse for despair.[33]

CONCLUSION: I CAN DREAM, CAN'T I?

How will we know that redemption has occurred? In keeping with the theme of deflation, I suggest there will be no divine sign to proclaim that the messianic age has arrived. Nor will there be a sense that having done everything that can be expected of us, we can relax our efforts. But there is one lingering piece of mythology that will have to be dispensed with to know that redemption has finally arrived – that is, an answer to the question "Who is the Messiah?" There have been no shortage of pretenders. One way to approach the question is to think in Platonic terms. One of Plato's most famous observations is that mankind will never put an end to its troubles until those vested with the power to rule are those who least want it. The same sentiment lies behind the passage in Exodus 3–4, when God tells Moses that he has been chosen to lead the people out of Egyptian bondage. Instead of expressing gratitude, Moses does everything he can to decline the offer.

To carry this insight a step further, let us imagine a world in which all the lepers outside the gates of the city are attended to, a world in which nations no longer resort to war to settle their differences, in which the last vestiges of enchantment have been removed, in which justice is administered quickly and fairly, and in which arrogance and chauvinism have become rarities. Let us also imagine that in such a

---

[32] Ibid., 231–2.
[33] On Niebuhr's recognition of the need for higher aspiration despite the impossibility of achieving perfect justice, see ibid., 277.

world someone bothers to ask, "To whom should the title of *Messiah* be given?" I submit that after all of this, the question will no longer matter, so that the appropriate response will be, "Anyone who wants it." It is the job of Judaism to get the world to this point one step at a time. A tall order, but we claim to be the Chosen People.

Appendix

Cohen's Reading of Maimonides

We can begin by noting that Cohen saw Maimonides as a proponent of the Kantian notion of the primacy of practical reason. "The Good," as Cohen tells us (*CEM*, 20), "constitutes the foundation of the universe." More specifically (*CEM*, 32), "There is no greater testimony to Maimonides' stature as the most vital and genuine representative of philosophy within Judaism than the fact that his ethics constitutes the core and effective center of his metaphysics." This raises an important question. As Cohen puts it (*CEM*, 64), "How could Maimonides deny the cognition of divine attributes on the one hand, and on the other proclaim knowledge of God as the main principle of theology and his ethics?"

Cohen is certainly right to call attention to this problem. Maimonides says repeatedly in the *Guide* that knowledge of God is the primary perfection. Yet his negative theology tells us that knowledge of the essence and true reality of God is beyond our ken. How can this be? Maimonides himself takes up this question at *Guide* 1.59 by considering an objection: If knowledge of the essence and true reality of God is beyond our ken, what separates Moses or Solomon from the average student? His answer is Socratic in nature: Moses and Solomon labored for years to come to the realization that they do not know the essence and true reality of God, whereas an average student, it is assumed, either does not realize this or humors himself by thinking he grasps it right away. The chapter ends by claiming that none but God can know God, and that for human beings, we have no choice but to fall back on the wisdom of Psalm 65: "Silence is praise to Thee."

According to Cohen, however, the answer is different: Cognition of God is essentially ethical, as indicated by the fact that the only attributes revealed to Moses at Exodus 34 are ethical in nature, and that for Maimonides the only positive knowledge we can have of God concerns his governance of the world, or what Maimonides terms *attributes of action.* In keeping with Exodus 33, where Moses cannot look on the face of God and must settle for the backside, Cohen maintains that the attributes of action do not give us knowledge of the essence and true reality of God but instead provide models for the actions of human beings (*ROR*, 95). According to Cohen, this is what allows Maimonides to cite Leviticus 19:2 and the doctrine of *imitatio Dei* at *Guide* 1.54. Cohen therefore concludes (*ROR*, 94) that for Maimonides, "The place of being is taken by action." The cognition of divine attributes is the recognition of their necessity. To see what Cohen means by this, we must look in more detail at his interpretation of Maimonides' negative theology as well as his use of the concept of an attribute of action.

Cohen argues (*ROR*, 62) that Maimonides stands out among medieval Jewish and Islamic thinkers by giving negative theology a new twist: Rather than positive attributes, what are negated are privations, as in "God is not inert." For Cohen, the reason for this is that if God lacks positive attributes altogether, there would be nothing to negate. If a privation like inertness is negated, then, in Cohen's opinion (*ROR*, 63), the deeper meaning lies not in excluding inertness from God but in establishing something positive: God's activity and the fact that God serves as a principle of origin (*Ursprung*) for everything else. Cohen continues (*ROR*, 64), "God is not inert; this means he is the *originative principal of activity.* In this way Maimonides explains the original name of God, which has been understood from the very beginning as meaning *omnipotence*: 'He is sufficient to produce things beside himself.'" Simply put, "God is not inert" translates to the positive claim, "God is a creator."

Along these lines, it is noteworthy that at *Guide* 1.58, Maimonides does say something very close to what Cohen attributes to him: "We apprehend ... that the existence of this being [God] suffices not only for His being existent, but also for many other existents flowing from it." For Cohen, a similar analysis applies to knowledge, life, unity, existence, and the other negative attributes. Cohen therefore assures us that (*CEM*, 79) "Maimonides … did not conceive of the negative attributes in a purely negative way"; and (*CEM*, 91) "Maimonides proposes no *docta ignorantia*. He is not even ultimately concerned only with the unknowability of God's essence. Rather, by enlarging the realm of negations, Maimonides promotes the true, seminal, i.e. ethical knowledge of God."

Is this how Maimonides understood negative predicates? The problem is that privation is subject to various interpretations. Because "God is not inert" contains a double negative, we could follow Cohen in taking it to imply the positive claim that God is active. On this reading, what we are denying is that God admits any degree of inertness and belongs instead to the class of active things as its ground or source. Because that class is infinite in extension, Cohen links Maimonides' theory of negative attributes with the infinite judgment in Kant.

However, we could also take "God is not inert" in a different way. According to Aristotle (*Meta.* 1004a), negation and privation are distinct. Negation means nothing more than the absence of the predicate in question, whatever it might be; by contrast, privation means the absence of a quality that would normally belong to the subject. As Aristotle goes on to show (*Meta.* 1022b), there is a difference between saying that a man is deprived of sight and saying that a mole is deprived of sight, because the former is deprived of something that belongs to its nature whereas the latter is not.[1]

If Maimonides understood negative attributes as denials of privation, then Cohen would be right: He would be trying to establish something positive about God in the way that the statement "John is not blind" establishes that John can see. To return to *Guide* 1.58, Maimonides does maintain what Cohen attributes to him: that everything we can say about God is either an attribute of action or the negation of a privation. However, Maimonides goes on to qualify his position by referring to a view with which he assumes the reader is already familiar. I take this as a reference to Aristotle's distinction between negation and privation.

---

[1] Actually moles do have tiny eyes, but that need not concern us here.

In Maimonides' words, "One sometimes denies with reference to a thing something that cannot fittingly exist in it. Thus we say of a wall that it is not endowed with sight." To say that a man cannot see is to speak of privation; to say that a wall cannot see is to make a category mistake. To underscore his point, Maimonides cites the example of the heavenly spheres, whose motion we can measure but whose essence is beyond our comprehension. He continues, "For this reason we are unable to predicate of it any attributes except in terms whose meaning is not completely understood, but not by means of affirmations that are completely understood. Accordingly we say that the heavens are neither light nor heavy nor acted upon … that they have no taste and no smell; and we make other negations of this kind." When it comes to God, about whom all we can know is *that* He is, not *what* He is, our ignorance is even more pronounced. Maimonides then sums up his analysis of negative predicates by saying, "Glory then to Him who is such that when the intellects contemplate His essence, their apprehension turns into incapacity."

In view of these remarks and others like them, such as his reference to Psalm 65, there is little question that Maimonides did propose a *docta ignorantia*. In saying that God is not inert, he is therefore making two claims: (1) that God does not have a privation, *and* (2) that God does not possess the corresponding perfection (activity) in a manner known to us. It follows that to attribute *either* inertness *or* activity to God in a way that we can understand is to commit a category mistake analogous to saying that a wall can see or a heavenly sphere has weight. Thus *Guide* 1.59: *Any* affirmation we make with respect to God takes us further away from God – exactly the insight that Moses came to understand but the average student cannot.

For Cohen (*CEM*, 80), on the other hand, Maimonides' basic stance toward knowing God is through not negation but only apparent negation, directing the mind away from defects and toward perfection. Yet surely the issue here is not ethical but metaphysical: God resists any attempt at determination, even if such determination were to ascribe to God superlatives. As Maimonides indicates, the advantage that negative attributes have over positive ones has to do with particularity. We know from *Guide* 1.52 that if we tried to define God, we would be subsuming God under a larger category and thus positing a cause anterior to God. By the same token, if we specify a part of God's essence or try to identify an accident of God, we take something that is radically simple and try to break it into parts. Thus negative attributes are superior to positive because they provide less particularity, which is to say less knowledge of the essence of the thing in question.

Note, however, that for all his remarks on the advantages of negative predication, Maimonides stops short of a complete endorsement. Although negative attributes do not tell us anything about God's essence, according to Maimonides (*Guide* 1.58), they still introduce some degree of particularity, "even if the particularization due to them only exists in the exclusion of what has been negated." Strictly speaking, negative attributes are still attributes and for that reason are objectionable. In the end, the best that they can do is "conduct the mind toward the utmost reach that man may attain in the apprehension of Him."

This takes us to attributes of action. According to Maimonides, these are not really attributes of God but of the natural world, considered as the consequence or effect of God's activity. Cohen glosses this by saying (*CEM*, 68), "God's attributes are 'His ways' and His ways are the vectors of His actions. His attributes are therefore 'attributes of action.' They are not essential attributes. The divine actions are only attributes insofar as they serve as paradigms for human conduct." Cohen is right to say that the attributes of action are not attributes of essence and that Maimonides conceives of them as paradigms for humans to emulate.

However, we must add an important qualification. Although Maimonides allows us to make God the subject of an attribute of action and speaks of "His ways," we are barred from thinking of God as a moral agent in the normal sense of the term. Thus the analogy is not between God and us, but between the consequences of our activity and the consequences of God's. This prevents us from allowing attributes of action to imply anthropomorphism.

Even something as basic as the ascription of free will to God is presumptive, because it follows from our inability to explain the reason or purpose behind phenomena we observe in nature. Recall that Maimonides' primary argument in defense of divine volition – the argument from particularity – maintains that because there are heavenly phenomena for which we have no explanation, and no real hope of finding one, the most reasonable conclusion is that they are the product of volition rather than necessity. As Maimonides saw (*GP* 1.24), this argument is open to the objection that at a future date, someone could find an explanation for what now seems perplexing. That is why creation cannot be demonstrated and why the ascription of free will to God is only a best inference given the evidence at our disposal. Without divine free will, the whole idea of God as a paradigm for human behavior collapses.

As one who thinks that Maimonides is committed to creation, I submit that he does believe in divine volition. Nonetheless, he insists at *Guide* 2.18 that *will* is a homonym when applied to God and us, again rejecting any suggestion of anthropomorphism. So although we have ethical qualities that can be inferred from the natural order, we do not have unqualified support for Cohen's God of ethics. At most, we have the admission that the only *positive* attribute we can predicate of God is a moral one, with all the hesitations and limitations inherent in that claim. The ultimate insight Maimonides takes us to is the realization that strictly speaking we cannot attribute anything to God at all.

At the beginning of *Guide* 1.58, Maimonides says, "Know that the description of God ... by means of negations is the correct description." I take this to mean that for all their utility, attributes of action are not the highest form of divine description. Their purpose is to allow us to make sense of Exodus 33 and the doctrine of *imitatio Dei*. Yet Maimonides never says that they conduct the mind to "the utmost reach that man may attain in the apprehension of Him." That is reserved for negative attributes, which imply that God neither is deprived of perfection nor possesses it in a manner comparable to us. In the end, even negative attributes must give way to silence and a confession of learned ignorance.

By contrast, Cohen's discussion of attributes of action leads directly to the idea of divine/human correlation. According to Cohen (*RR*, 96),

"Ye shall be holy; for I the Eternal your God am holy." This word "holy" has a double meaning: it relates holiness to God and to man. And one is to assume that only through this unified relation to God, as well as to man, can holiness be thought of as possible with regard to God himself; as on the other hand one might say that only through the coming to be of holiness in God does its relation to man simultaneously become possible. The correlation becomes effectual and with it mythology and polytheism cease to be.

Maimonides' position can be seen in a clearer light if we view the *Guide* not as a simple statement of doctrine, but as a process of bringing the reader to an ever more enlightened grasp of the complexities of the material. We begin with biblical passages that imply anthropomorphism and interpret them in such a way that God is no longer viewed as material. Then we reject normal forms of attribution and settle on attributes of action. Then we introduce the idea that words that apply to both God and us are equivocal. From there, we go to negative attributes and from there to a studied ignorance that culminates in silence. Each step brings us closer to the realization that God is beyond our comprehension, so that although we may be able to say with certainty that God is not material or contingent, when it comes to what God is, our words and categories fail us.

The difference between Maimonides and Cohen is that the former began to question the Aristotelianism prevalent in his day, whereas the latter wanted mainly to extend or modify the Kantianism prevalent in his. With regard to the primacy of ethics, there is the obvious fact that Maimonides claims (*GP* 3.54) that the acquisition of the rational virtues, namely, the conception of the intelligibles, is the true and the highest human perfection. He is clear that this is a higher perfection than moral virtue, in part because it belongs to us alone and does not involve us with other people. Moreover, we saw that according to *Guide* 1.2, judgments of good and bad presuppose a social setting and therefore rest on social conventions. In no sense are they valid a priori. As a necessary being who does not exist in a social setting, God is beyond the reach of judgments of good and bad.

At *Guide* 3.51, Maimonides suggests that the closest we can get to imitating God is in moments of solitude and isolation, when no ethical issues are involved. Such moments are short-lived and still presuppose the limits of the human conditions. To sum up, our imitation of God is both imperfect and indirect. That such moments can *lead* one to acts of justice and loving-kindness is beyond dispute. That we can find traces of justice and loving-kindness in the natural order is also beyond dispute. But any supposed similarity stops there. Strictly speaking, God is not just or kind but above and beyond all such descriptions.

Why was Cohen misled? The immediate answer has to do with negative versus positive attributes. Although it is true that the only positive knowledge of God available to us involves divine governance of the world, it is also true that for Maimonides, negative knowledge constitutes a significant achievement – in fact, a more significant achievement than positive. If the highest level of perfection we can reach is a studied silence in the face of God, then ultimately positive knowledge of God's governance of the world is a stepping-stone to something greater.

Beyond that, there is the question of metaphysics. For Maimonides, metaphysics is the foremost of the sciences. It is capable of establishing the existence and unity of God to a degree that no reasonable person can doubt them. In doing so, it offers a conception of God vastly superior to anything afforded by the imagination. It is therefore impossible to reach a state of perfection without some degree of metaphysical knowledge.

Unfortunately, metaphysics runs into difficulty for two reasons. First, the material world acts as a dark veil (*GP* 3.9) that prevents us from understanding the metaphysical realm as it truly is. Second, although metaphysics can establish the existence and unity of God, it cannot tell us what God is. Even though metaphysics must give way to a studied silence, Maimonides never suggests that it be jettisoned entirely. As we learn in the introduction to the *Guide*, some individuals are able to get glimpses or flashes of the metaphysical realm, that, though fleeting and not always systematic, are nonetheless valuable. One of the reasons Maimonides wrote the *Guide* was to piece them together in a way that makes rational sense.

For Kant, the picture is quite different. Metaphysics rests on a transcendental illusion: the tendency to confuse the subjective necessity of our ideas with an objective necessity descriptive of things in themselves. So far from being a prerequisite for human perfection, metaphysics gets in the way. As Kant puts it (*1CR* Bxxx), "The dogmatism of metaphysics, that is, the preconception that it is possible to make headway in metaphysics without a previous criticism of pure reason, is the source of all that unbelief, always very dogmatic, which wars against morality." This passage is important because it indicates that for Kant, human perfection is not based on the acceptance of doctrine but on proper behavior. Even if metaphysics could establish its conclusions with certainty, from Kant's standpoint, it would still not give us what we are seeking: a morally pure will. For Maimonides, it is the opposite. Human perfection means coming to know everything that is within our capacity to know (*Guide* 3.27). The performance of moral actions is secondary.

Although both Maimonides and Kant stress the limits of human knowledge and express doubts about the claim of metaphysics to be a science, their motivations are different. From the standpoint of a Neo-Kantian philosopher trying to show that Judaism had taken a practical turn long before Kant, downplaying the importance of proper belief and emphasizing the importance of proper behavior, it is easy to see Maimonides as a precursor to Kant. Cohen was right about Judaism as a whole: It does downplay proper belief and emphasize proper behavior. However, he did not see the extent to which Maimonides does not fit the normal picture and tried to introduce a conceptual component to Judaism that puts him at odds with much of the Kantian tradition. Cohen, then, presented an idiosyncratic view of Maimonides just as Maimonides himself often presented idiosyncratic views of Plato and Aristotle. Although much can be learned by studying these views, we should never forget that they are designed for polemical purposes and sometimes depart from historical fact.

Bibliography

Adams, Marilyn McCord. *Horrendous Evils and the Goodness of God*. Ithaca: Cornell University Press, 1999.

Allison, Henry E. *Kant's Theory of Freedom*. Cambridge: Cambridge University Press, 1990.

Arendt, Hannah. *The Origins of Totalitarianism*. 1950; reprint: New York: Harcourt Brace & Co, 1979.

"Organized Guilt," in *The Jew as Pariah*. New York: Grove Press, 1978.

Auerbach, Erich. *Mimesis*. Translated by W. Trask. Princeton: Princeton University Press, 1953.

Avinieri, Shlomo. *Hegel's Theory of the Modern State*. Cambridge: Cambridge University Press, 1972.

The Making of Modern Zionism. New York: Basic Books, 1981.

Barth, Karl. *Protestant Thought from Rousseau to Ritschl*. New York: Harper & Brothers, 1959.

Bauer, Yehuda. *Rethinking the Holocaust*. New Haven: Yale University Press, 2001.

Beck, Nicholas White. *A Commentary on Kant's Critique of Practical Reason*. Chicago: University of Chicago Press, 1960.

Berger, David. *The Rebbe, the Messiah, and the Scandal of Orthodox Indifference*. London: Littman Library, 2001.

"Some Ironic Consequences of Maimonides' Rationalist Approach to the Messianic Age," in *The Legacy of Maimonides: Religion, Reason and Community*. Edited by Yamin Levy and Shalom Carmy. Brooklyn: Yashar Books, 2006.

Bienenstock, Myriam. "Recalling the Past in Rosenzweig's *Star of Redemption*," *Modern Judaism* 23 (2003): 226–39.

Beiser, Frederick. "Hegel's Historicism," in *The Cambridge Companion to Hegel*. Edited by Frederick Beiser. Cambridge: Cambridge University Press, 1993.

"Moral Faith and the Highest Good," in *The Cambridge Companion to Kant and Modern Philosophy*. Edited by Paul Guyer. New York: Cambridge University Press, 2006.

Benjamin, Walter. "On the Concept of History," in *Selected Writings*, Vol. 4. Translated by Edmund Jephcott and Others. Cambridge: Harvard University Press, 2004.

Blanchot, Maurice. *The Step Not Beyond*. Translated by Lycette Nelson. Albany: SUNY Press, 1992.

Bloch, Ernst. *The Spirit of Utopia*. Translated by Anthony A. Nassar. Stanford: Stanford University Press, 2000.

X Bouretz, Pierre. "Messianism and Modern Jewish Philosophy," in *The Cambridge Companion to Modern Jewish Philosophy*. Edited by Michael L. Morgan and Peter Eli Gordon. New York: Cambridge University Press, 2007.

XX *Witnesses for the Future*. Translated by Michael B. Smith. Baltimore: The Johns Hopkins University Press, 2010.

Browning, Christopher. *Ordinary Men*. New York: Harper Collins, 1992.

Buford, Bill. *Among the Thugs*. New York: Random House, 1990.

Butler, Bishop John. *Fifteen Sermons Preached at Rolls Chapel*, 1725; reprint. London: Bells and Sons, 1967.

Caputo, John D. *The Prayers and Tears of Jacques Derrida*. Bloomington: Indiana University Press, 1997.

Card, Claudia. *The Atrocity Paradigm*. New York: Oxford University Press, 2002.

Cohen, Arthur A. *The Tremendom*. New York: Crossroad, 1981.

Cohen, Hermann. *Kants Begründung der Ethik*. Berlin: Cassirer, 1910.

  Jüdische Schriften. Vol. 2. Edited by Bruno Strauss. Berlin: C. A. Schwtschke & Sohn, 1924.

  Religion der Vernunft aus den Quellen des Judentums. 2nd Edition. Cologne: Joseph Melzer, 1928.

  Reason and Hope. Translated by Eva Jospe. New York: W. W. Norton, 1971.

  Religion of Reason out of the Sources of Judaism. Translated by Simon Kaplan. New York: Ungar, 1972.

  Ethics of Maimonides. Translated by A. Bruckstein. Madison: University of Wisconsin Press, 2004.

Cohen, Richard A. *Elevations: The Height of the Good in Rosenzweig and Levinas*. Chicago: University of Chicago Press, 1994.

Cohn, Norman. *The Pursuit of the Millennium*. London: Pimlico, 1957; reprint: 2004.

Derrida, Jacques. *Specters of Marx*. Translated by Peggy Kamuf. New York and London: Routledge, 1993.

Diamond, James. "Maimonides On Kingship: The Ethics of Imperial Humility," *Journal of Religious Ethics* 34:1 (2006): 113–14.

Dostoevsky, Fyodor. *The Brothers Karamazov*. Translated by Constance Garnett. New York: Random House, 1950.

Fackenheim, Emil. *The Religious Dimension in Hegel's Thought.* Bloomington: Indiana University Press, 1968.

"Hermann Cohen – After Fifty Years," *Leo Baeck Memorial Lecture* 12 (1969): 3–17.

Encounters between Judaism and Modern Philosophy. New York: Basic Books, 1973.

The Jewish Return into History. New York: Schocken Books, 1978.

To Mend the World. New York: Schocken Books, 1982.

"Hegel and the Jewish Problem," in *The Philosopher as Witness.* Edited by Michael Morgan and Benjamin Pollock. Albany: SUNY Press, 2008.

Firestone, Chris, and Jacobs, Nathan. *In Defense of Kant's Religion.* Bloomington: Indiana University Press, 2008.

Franks, Paul. "Jewish Philosophy after Kant: The Legacy of Salomon Maimon," in *The Cambridge Companion to Modern Jewish Philosophy.* Edited by Michael L. Morgan and Peter Eli Gordon. New York: Cambridge University Press, 2007.

Friedländer, Saul. *Nazi Germany and the Jews.* New York: Harper and Collins, 1997.

Fukuyama, Francis. "The End of History?" *The National Interest* 16 (Summer 1989): 3–18.

The End of History and the Last Man, 1992; reprint: New York: The Free Press, 2006.

Funkenstein, Amos. "Maimonides' Political Theory and Realistic Messianism," *Miscellanea Mediaevalia* 11 (1977): 92–3.

"Theological Interpretations of the Holocaust: A Balance," in *A Holocaust Reader.* Edited by Michael Morgan. New York: Oxford University Press, 2001.

Gibbs, Robert. *Correlations in Rosenzweig and Levinas.* Princeton: Princeton University Press, 1992.

Goldhagen, Daniel. *Hitler's Willing Executioners.* New York: Random House, 1997.

Goodman, Lenn. *On Justice.* New Haven: Yale University Press, 1991.

Gordon, Peter Eli. "Franz Rosenzweig and The Philosophy of Jewish Existence," in *The Cambridge Companion to Modern Jewish Philosophy.* Edited by Michael L. Morgan and Peter Eli Gordon. New York: Cambridge University Press, 2007.

Graetz, Solomon. "The Stages in the Evolution of the Messianic Belief," in *The Structure of Jewish History and Other Essays.* Translated by Ismar Schorsch. New York: Jewish Theological Seminary, 1975.

Halevi, Judah. *Kuzari.* Translated by I. Heinemann. Oxford: East and West Library, 1947.

Hartman, David. *Crisis and Leadership: Epistles of Maimonides.* Philadelphia, New York, Jerusalem: Jewish Publication Society of America, 1985.

Israelis and the Jewish Tradition. New Haven: Yale University Press, 2000.

Hartmann, Klaus. "Hegel: A Non-metaphysical View," in *Hegel: A Collection of Critical Essays*. Edited by Alasdair McIntyre. Garden City: Doubleday, 1972.

Hegel, G. W. F. *Philosophy of Right*. Translated by T. M. Knox. Oxford: Oxford University Press, 1952.

  Reason in History. Translated by David S. Hartman. Upper Saddle River: Prentice-Hall, 1997.

Hertzberg, Arthur. *The Zionist Idea*. Garden City: Doubleday, 1969.

Hilberg, Raul. *The Destruction of the European Jews*. New York: New Viewpoints, 1973.

Hume, David. *An Enquiry Concerning Human Understanding*. 2nd Edition. Edited by L. A. Selby-Bigge. Oxford: Oxford University Press, 1902.

Idel, Moshe. "Maimonides and the Kabbalah," in *Studies in Maimonides*. Edited by Isadore Twersky. Cambridge: Harvard University Press, 1990.

  "Maimonides' *Guide of the Perplexed* and the Kabbalah," *Jewish History* 18 (2004): 197–226.

Inbari, Motti. *Jewish Fundamentalism and the Temple Mount*. Translated by Shaul Vardi. Albany: SUNY Press, 2009.

Josephus, Flavius. *The Jewish War*. Translated by G. A. Williamson. Middlesex: Penguin, 1959.

Kant, Immanuel. *The Conflict of the Faculties*. Translated by Mary J. Gregor. Lincoln: University of Nebraska Press, 1979.

  Perpetual Peace and Other Essays. Translated by T. Humphrey. Indianapolis: Hackett, 1983.

  The Metaphysics of Morals. Translated by Mary Gregor. Cambridge: Cambridge University Press, 1991.

  Critique of Practical Reason. Translated by Mary Gregor and Andrews Reath. Cambridge: Cambridge University Press, 1997.

  Religion within the Boundaries of Mere Reason. Translated by Allen Wood and George Di Giovanni. Cambridge: Cambridge University Press, 1998.

  Groundwork of the Metaphysics of Morals. Translated by Mary Gregor. Cambridge: Cambridge University Press, 1998.

  Critique of the Power of Judgment. Translated by Paul Guyer and Eric Matthews. Cambridge: Cambridge University Press, 2000.

Katz, Steven T. "The Unique Intentionality of the Holocaust," in *Post Holocaust Dialogues*. New York: New York University Press, 1983.

  "Technology and Genocide: Technology as a 'Form of Life,'" in *Echoes from the Holocaust*. Edited by Alan Rosenberg and Gerald E. Myers. Philadelphia: Temple University Press, 1988.

  The Holocaust and Mass Death before the Modern Age, Vol. I of *The Holocaust in Historical Context*. New York: Oxford University Press, 1994.

  Historicism, the Holocaust, and Zionism: Critical Studies in Modern Jewish Thought and History. New York: New York University Press, 1992.

Kavka, Martin. *Jewish Messianism and the History of Philosophy*. New York: Cambridge University Press, 2004.

Kaplan, Lawrence. "Maimonides and Soloveitchik on the Knowledge and Imitation of God," in *Moses Maimonides 1138–1204: His Religious, Scientific, and Philosophical Wirkungsgeschichte in Different Cultural Contexts*. Edited by Gorg Hasselhoff and Otfried Fraise. Würzburg: Ergon Verlag, 2004.

Kellner, Menachem. *Maimonides on Human Perfection*. Atlanta: Brown Judaic Studies. 1990.

Maimonides on Judaism and the Jewish People. Albany: SUNY Press, 1991.

"Messianic Postures in Israel Today," in *Essential Papers on Messianic Movements and Personalities in Jewish History*. Edited by Marc Saperstein. New York: New York University Press, 1992.

Maimonides on the "Decline of the Generations" and the Nature of Rabbinic Authority. Albany: SUNY Press, 1996.

Maimonides' Confrontation with Mysticism. Oxford: Littman Library, 2006.

Science in the Bet Midrash. Brighton: Academic Studies Press, 2009.

Kershaw, I. *The Hitler Myth: Image and Reality in the Third Reich*. New York: Oxford University Press, 1997.

Hitler, the Germans and the Final Solution. New Haven: Yale University Press, 2008.

Klausner, Joseph. *The Messianic Idea in Israel*. Translated by W. F. Stinespring. New York: Macmillan, 1955.

Kook, Abraham Isaac. *The Lights of Penitence, The Moral Principles, Lights of Holiness, Essays, Letters, and Poems*. Translated by Ben Zion Bokser. New York: Paulist Press, 1978.

Korn, Eugene. "Gentiles, the World to Come, and Judaism: The Odyssey of a Rabbinic Text," *Modern Judaism* 14 (1994): 265–87.

Korsgaard, Christine. *The Sources of Normativity*. New York: Cambridge University Press, 1996.

Kraemer, Joel. "Maimonides' Messianic Posture," in *Studies in Medieval Jewish History and Literature*, Vol. 2. Edited by Isadore Twersky. Cambridge, MA: Harvard University Press, 1984.

Kreisel, Haim. *Maimonides' Political Thought*. Albany: SUNY Press, 1995.

"Maimonides on Divine Religion," in *Maimonides after 800 Years: Essays on Maimonides and His Influence*. Edited by J. Harris. Cambridge: Harvard University Press, 2007.

Lang, Berel. *Act and Idea in the Nazi Genocide*. Chicago: University of Chicago Press, 1990.

"The Humanities," in *The Oxford Handbook of Holocaust Studies*. Edited by Peter Hayes and John K. Roth. Oxford: Oxford University Press, 2011.

Le Bon, Gustave. *The Crowd*. West Valley City: Waking Lion Press, 2006.

Levinas, Emmanuel. *Face to Face with Levinas.* Edited by Richard A. Cohen. Albany: SUNY Press, 1986.

  The Levinas Reader. Edited by Seán Hand. Oxford: Basil Blackwell, 1989.

  Difficult Freedom: Essays in Judaism. Translated by Seán Hand. Baltimore: Johns Hopkins University Press, 1990.

  Collected Philosophical Papers. Translated by Alphonso Lingis. Pittsburgh: Duquesne University Press, 1998.

Liver, J. "The Doctrine of the Two Messiahs," *Harvard Theological Review* 52 (1959): 149–85.

Löwith, Karl. *Meaning in History.* Chicago: University of Chicago Press, 1949.

  From Hegel to Nietzsche. Translated by David E. Green. Garden City: 1964.

Luther, Martin. *The Bondage of the Will.* Translated by Henry Cole. Watchmaker Publishing, 2010.

Maimonides, Moses. *Dalalat al-Haririn (Guide of the Perplexed).* Arabic text. Edited by I. Joel. Jerusalem: Junovitch, 1929.

  Guide of the Perplexed. Translated by Shlomo Pines. Chicago: University of Chicago Press, 1963.

  Mishneh Torah (Code of Jewish Law). Hebrew Text. Edited by S. T. Rubenstein et al. Jerusalem: Mossad Harav Kook: 1967–73.

  Moreh Nevukhim (Guide of the Perplexed). Arabic text and Hebrew translation by Joseph Kafih. Jerusalem: Mossad Harav Kook, 1972.

  Le Guide Des Egares. Translated by Salomon Munk. Paris: G.-P. Maisonneuve and Larose, 1981.

  Crisis and Leadership: Epistles of Maimonides. Translated by A. Halkin; discussions by D. Hartman. Philadelphia: Jewish Publication Society of America, 1985.

  Mishneh Torah. Translated by E. Touger. New York and Jerusalem: Moznaim Publishing, 1989.

Marina, Jacqueline. "Kant on Grace: A Reply to His Critics," *Religious Studies* 33 (1997): 379–400.

McRobert, Laurie. "Emil L. Fackenheim and Radical Evil," *Journal of the American Academy of Religion* 57 (1989): 325–40.

Mendelssohn, Moses. *Jerusalem.* Translated by Alan Arkush. Hanover: University Press of New England, 1983.

Michalson, Gordon. *Fallen Freedom: Kant on Radical Evil and Moral Regeneration.* (Cambridge: Cambridge University Press, 1990.

Mittleman, Alan. *Hope in a Democratic Age.* New York: Oxford University Press, 2009.

Moltmann, Jürgen. *The Coming of God.* Translated by Margaret Kohl. Minneapolis: Fortress Press, 1996.

Morgan, Michael. *Beyond Auschwitz.* New York: Oxford University Press, 2001.

  Discovering Levinas. New York: Cambridge University Press, 2007.

Mosès, Stéphane. *System and Revelation*. Translated by Catherine Tihanyi. Detroit: Wayne State University Press, 1992.

The Angel of History. Translated by Barbara Harshav. Stanford: Stanford University Press, 2009.

Myers, David N. "Hermann Cohen and the Quest for Protestant Judaism," *Leo Baeck Institute Year Book* 46 (2001): 195–214.

Resisting History. Princeton: Princeton University Press, 2003.

Nachmanides. *Commentary on the Torah*. Translated by Charles B. Chavel. New York: Shilo, 1971–76.

Niebuhr, Reinhold. *Moral Man and Immoral Society*. Louisville: Westminster John Knox Press, 1932; reprint: 2001.

Neusner, Jacob. "Messianic Themes in Formative Judaism," *Journal of the American Academy of Religion* 52 (1984): 357–74.

Messiah in Context: Israel's History and Destiny in Formative Judaism. Philadelphia: Fortress Press, 1984.

Ostertag, Heinrich. "Luther and Kant," *Neue Kirchliche Zeitschrift* 36 (1925): 765–807.

Overy, Richard. *Russia's War*. New York: Penguin Books, 1997.

Pelagius. *The Letters of Pelagius and His Followers*. Edited by B. R. Rees Woodrbridge: The Boydell Press, 1991.

Patterson, David. "Though the Messiah May Tarry: A Reflection on Redemption," *May Smith Lecture on Post-Holocaust Christian Jewish Dialogue*. Florida Atlantic University, January 26, 2009.

Pippin, Robert. *Hegel's Idealism: The Satisfactions of Self-consciousness*. New York: Cambridge University Press, 1989.

Pines, Shlomo. "The Limitations of Human Knowledge According to Al-Farabi, ibn Bajja, and Maimonides," in *Studies in Medieval Jewish History and Literature*, Vol. 1. Edited by Isadore Twersky. Cambridge: Harvard University Press, 1979.

Pinkard, Terry. *Hegel's Phenomenology*. Cambridge: Cambridge University Press, 1996.

Pollock, Benjamin. "Thought Going to School with Life? Fackenheim's Last Philosophical Testament," *AJS Review* 31:1 (2007): 145–6.

Postone, Moishe. "The Holocaust and the Trajectory of the Twentieth Century," in *Catastrophe and Meaning*. Edited by Moishe Postone and Eric Santer. Chicago: University of Chicago Press, 2001.

Putnam, Hilary. *The Many Faces of Realism*. LaSalle: Open Court, 1987.

Quinn, Philip L. "Original Sin, Radical Evil and Moral Identity," *Faith and Philosophy* 7 (1984): 36.

Rabinbach, Anson. "Between Enlightenment and Apocalypse: Benjamin, Bloch and Modern German Jewish Messianism," *New German Critique* 34 (1985): 81

Rashi. *Chumash with Rashi's Commentary: Exodus*. Translated by A. M. Silbermann. Jerusalem: The Silbermann Family, 1934.

Ravitzky, Aviezer. "'To the Utmost Human Capacity': Maimonides on the Days of the Messiah," in *Perspectives on Maimonides*. Edited by Joel L. Kraemer. Oxford: Oxford University Press, 1991.

Messianism, Zionism, and Jewish Religious Radicalism. Translated by Michael Swirsky and Jonathan Chipman. Chicago: University of Chicago Press, 1993.

Rosenberg, Alan, and Marcus, Paul. "The Holocaust as a Test of Philosophy," in *Echoes from the Holocaust*. Edited by Alan Rosenberg and Gerald E. Myers. Philadelphia: Temple University Press, 1988.

Rosenzweig, Franz. *Briefe und Tagebücher* Vol. 2. The Hague: Martinus Nijhoff, 1979.

The Star of Redemption. Translated by William W. Hallo. Notre Dame: University of Notre Dame Press, 1970.

Philosophical and Theological Writings. Edited by Paul W. Franks and Michael L. Morgan. Indianapolis: Hackett, 2000.

Roth, John K. "On Losing Trust in the World," in *Echoes from the Holocaust*. Edited by Alan Rosenberg and Gerald E. Myers. Philadelphia: Temple University Press, 1988.

Rubenstein, Richard. *The Cunning of History*. New York: Harper and Row, 1975.

Saadia Gaon. *The Book of Beliefs and Opinions*. Translated by Samuel Rosenblatt. New Haven: Yale University Press, 1948.

Savage, Denis. "Kant's Rejection of Divine Revelation and His Theory of Radical Evil," in *Kant's Philosophy of Religion Reconsidered*. Edited by Philip J. Rossi and Michael Wren. Bloomington: Indiana University Press, 1991.

Schnall, David J. *Beyond the Green Line: Israeli Settlements West of the Jordan*. New York: Praeger, 1984.

Scholem, Gershom. *The Messianic Idea in Judaism*. New York: Schocken Books, 1971.

Schwarzschild, Stephen S. "The Democratic Socialism of Hermann Cohen," *Hebrew Union College Annual* 37 (1956): 417–38.

The Pursuit of the Ideal. Edited by Menachem Kellner. Albany: SUNY Press, 1990.

Seeskin, Kenneth. *Jewish Philosophy in a Secular Age*. Albany: SUNY Press, 1990.

Autonomy in Jewish Philosophy. New York: Cambridge University Press, 2001.

Maimonides on the Origin of the World. New York: Cambridge University Press, 2005.

Silber, John. "Kant's Conception of the Highest Good as Immanent and Transcendent," *Philosophical Review* 68 (1959): 469–92.

Smoler, L., and Aberbach, M. "The Golden Calf Episode in Postbiblical Literature," *Hebrew Union College Annual* 39 (1968): 91–116.

Spinoza, Baruch. *Theological-Political Treatise*. 2nd Edition. Translated by Samuel Shirley. Indianapolis: Hackett, 1998.

Stroumsa, Sarah. *Maimonides in His World*. Princeton: Princeton University Press, 2009.

Taylor, Charles. *Hegel*. Cambridge: Cambridge University Press, 1975.

Thucydides. *The Peloponnesian War*. Edited by John H. Finley. New York: Random House, 1951.

Urbach, Ephraim. *The Sages*. Translated by Israel Abrahams. Jerusalem: Magnes Press, 1979.

Walzer, Michael. *Exodus and Revolution*. New York: Basic Books, 1985.

Wand, Bernard. "Religious Concepts and Moral Theory: Luther and Kant," *Journal of the History of Philosophy* 9 (1971): 329–48.

Wiesel, Elie. *Legends of Our Time*. 1968; reprint: New York: Schocken Books, 1882.

White, Hayden. *Tropics of Discourse: Essays in Cultural Criticism*. Baltimore: Johns Hopkins University Press, 2006.

Wimpfheimer, Barry. *Narrating the Law*. Philadelphia: University of Pennsylvania Press, 2011.

Wolfson, Elliot R. *Open Secret*. New York: Columbia University Press, 2009.

Wolterstorff, Nicholas. "Conundrums in Kant's Philosophy of Religion," in *Kant's Philosophy of Religion Reconsidered*. Edited by Philip J. Rossi and Michael Wren. Bloomington: Indiana University Press, 1991.

Wood, Allen W. *Kant's Moral Religion*. Ithaca and New York: Cornell University Press, 1970.

Kant's Ethical Thought. Cambridge: Cambridge University Press, 1999.

"Kant and the Intelligibility of Evil," unpublished manuscript.

Wyschogrod, Edith. *Emmanuel Levinas: The Problem of Ethical Metaphysics*. New York: Fordham University Press, 2000.

Yerushalmi, Yosef. *Zakhor, Jewish History and Jewish Memory*. Seattle: University of Washington Press, 1982.

Yovel, Yirmiyahu. *Kant and the Philosophy of History*. Princeton: Princeton University Press, 1980.

Index